Sweet Charlotte

SWEET CHARLOTTE

Disclaimer

In compiling the recipes for this cookbook, I have no reason to doubt that the ingredients, instructions and directions given to me will work successfully. However, I have not tested these recipes and you should not hesitate to test and question procedures and directions before preparation.

These recipes have been collected from various sources and neither I, nor the contributor, publisher, printer or seller of this book is responsible for errors or omissions.

These recipes were given freely and without restriction as to their authenticity and/or origin.

WIMMER
COOKBOOKS
ConsolidatedGraphics
800.548.2537
www.wimmerco.com

Table of Contents

Sassy Sippin'
5

Taste Temptations
33

Sweets for the Sweet
87

Notions 'n Potions
239

Dedication

This book is dedicated to
the sweets in my life,
John Wolfe, Mark, Pam, Anna Page
and *John Mark Wolfe,*
and of course *Russ Wolfe,*
1970-1990.

~ Charlotte ~

Sassy Sippin'

The Art of Champagne 7
Christmas Brew for the Senses 7
Afternoon Delight 8
Bride's Pink Punch................................. 8
Banana Punch 9
Brunch Juice 9
Cool Splash 9
Coffee Punch 10
Christmas Eve Punch 10
Dreamcicle Orange Punch 11
Four Fruit Cooler 11
Frosty Fruit Cooler 11
Grand Pete's Summer Tea 12
Holiday Cocoa 12
Homemade Amaretto 12
Homemade Kahlúa 13
Hot Spiced Tea 13
Instant Russian Tea 13
Key Lime Shake 14
Make-Ahead Lemonade Mix 14
Mock Champagne 14
Mama Rock's Boiled Custard 15
Tropical Tea 15
Party Lemonade 16
Party Punch 16
Southern Lemonade 16
Slush Punch 17
Spicy Apple Cider 17
Wassail 18
Wassail 18
White Sangría 18
Beach Bubble....................................... 19
Brave Bull 19
Bucking Bronco 19
Bulldog 19
Canadian Slipper 20
Caribbean Chiller 20

Carpet Tax 20
Dew Drop 20
Charlotte's Bloody Marys 21
Dizzy Blond 21
Frozen Margaritas 21
Fantastic T 22
Frozen Russian 22
Holly's Here 22
Hot Buttered Rum 23
Hot Buttered Rum Mix 23
Island Bubbly....................................... 23
Irish Cream Liqueur 24
Monkey Wrench 24
Peaches and Cream 24
Pink Pussycat 25
P K's Sting 25
Dwanna Pusser 25
Ruby Martini 26
Silver Monkey...................................... 26
Snow Bunny 26
Suffering Bastard 27
Luscious Lips 27
Stacey's Cosmopolitans 27
Wicked Woo Woo 28
Bavarian Mint Coffee Mix 28
Cappuccino Mix 28
Coffee Nog 29
Tipsy Coffee 29
Flirtini 29
Vanilla Coffee 30
Southern Breeze 30
Watermelon Margaritas 31
The Infamous Chocolate Martini 31
Sea Breeze Cocktail 31
Happy Undertaker 32
Martimmy 32
Raspberrytini 32

The Art of Champagne

1 bottle Champagne	2 strawberries
2 champagne flutes	

Gently chill the champagne for 1 hour in the refrigerator with the temperature set at 43°, or place bottle in a silver ice bucket half filled with ice and water for 20 minutes or so. Remove from ice and dry with a bar towel. Cut off the foil surrounding the cork. Untwist and remove the wire muzzle. Place the bottle on a table or flat surface. Grasp the bottle firmly in one hand and hold the cork with the other. Gently, ease the cork out of the bottle by turning the bottle. As soon as the cork begins to release, it is essential to tilt the bottle at an angle with the palm of one hand acting as a brake to prevent the cork from shooting out. Never allow the cork to fly out of the bottle. A soft subdued pop is desired. Slowly pour into glasses, about ¾ full. Add 1 strawberry to each glass and enjoy.

Helio Brasil
Modesto, CA

Christmas Brew for the Senses

1 tablespoon pickle spice, remove pepper	1 tablespoon whole cloves
2 teaspoons lemon peel	1 tablespoon ginger
2 teaspoons orange peel	1 bay leaf
2 cinnamon sticks	1 tablespoon allspice
1 drop cinnamon oil	4 cups boiling water

Put ingredients in a crockpot and simmer. Your house will smell wonderful. When the scent begins to fade, add more cinnamon oil. Add water as needed. May be kept in refrigerator in a jar when not in use.

Charlotte Wolfe
Fort Lauderdale, FL

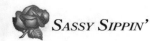

Afternoon Delight

1 (46-ounce) can pineapple juice
1 (12-ounce) can frozen orange juice, undiluted
1 (12-ounce) can frozen lemonade, undiluted
1 (12-ounce) can frozen limeade, undiluted
5 cups cold water

4 cups chilled club soda or lemon-lime carbonated beverage
½ pint vodka
½ pint rum
½ pint gin.
½ pint bourbon
½ pint scotch

Combine pineapple juice, orange juice, lemonade, limeade and water in a large container. Mix well. Just before serving add club soda or lemon-lime carbonated beverage and all the liquors. Serve over ice.

Careful, this is a very strong drink and will make your afternoon a delight.

Charlotte Wolfe
Fort Lauderdale, FL

Bride's Pink Punch

1 (3-ounce) package strawberry gelatin
1 cup boiling water
1 package strawberry drink mix
2 quarts cold water
2¼ cups sugar

1 (46-ounce) can pineapple juice
1 (10-ounce) bottle lemon-lime carbonated beverage
2 pints pineapple sherbet

Dissolve gelatin in boiling water. Combine drink mix and cold water. Mix in sugar and stir well. Add pineapple juice and gelatin mixture. Refrigerate. Just before serving add lemon-lime carbonated beverage and sherbet.

Yield 35 servings.

Robaya Wolfe Ellis
Savannah, TN

Banana Punch

1½	quarts water	1	(46-ounce) can pineapple-grapefruit
3	cups sugar		juice drink
1	(12-ounce) can frozen juice, thawed	4	bananas, mashed
		1½	quarts club soda

Mix water and sugar. Add orange juice, pineapple-grapefruit drink and bananas. Pour into container and freeze. To serve add club soda to punch mix and stir.

Yield 1¼ gallons.

Linda Neill
Savannah, TN

Brunch Juice

1	(6-ounce) can orange juice concentrate	1	cup cranberry juice
4	tablespoons sugar	1	pint club soda

Mix orange juice, sugar and cranberry juice and freeze until slushy. Remove from freezer and add club soda.

Yield 6 to 8 (4-ounce) servings.

Barbara Williams
Savannah, TN

Cool Splash

This is so easy and simply delicious.

1	(6-ounce) can frozen orange juice	1	(12-ounce) lemon-lime carbonated
1	cup water		beverage
1	lemon, juiced		

Mix orange juice, water and lemon juice together. To serve add carbonated beverage.

Jane Riddell
Savannah, TN

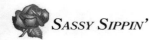

Coffee Punch
Outrageously delicious.

1 quart heavy cream
5 teaspoons vanilla
5 tablespoons sugar
2 quarts vanilla ice cream
1 gallon strong coffee, chilled

1 (750-milliliter) bottle Jamaican coffee
   flavored liqueur
1 cup Mexican coffee flavored liqueur
1 cup brandy

Whip cream and gradually add vanilla and sugar. Set in refrigerator. Place large, scooped balls of vanilla ice cream in bottom of large punch bowl. Add whipped cream to punch bowl. Blend coffee and liqueurs. Gently pour coffee mixture over the ice cream and whipped cream.

Yield 50 servings.

Florida State Senator, Debby Sanderson
Coral Springs, FL

Christmas Eve Punch

1 (32-ounce) bottle cranberry juice
   cocktail
1 (46-ounce) can unsweetened
   pineapple juice
2 cups orange juice

⅔ cup lemon juice
½ cup sugar
2 teaspoons almond extract
1 (33.8-ounce) bottle ginger ale

Combine all ingredients except ginger ale. Chill. To serve add ginger ale and stir well.

Yield 4½ cups.

Sharon Bain
Humboldt, TN

Dreamcicle Orange Punch

3 cans frozen orange juice concentrate, thawed

1 large can pineapple juice

1 gallon orange sherbet, thawed

1 small can cream of coconut

Mix all ingredients together.

Robaya Wolfe Ellis
Savannah, TN

Four Fruit Cooler

4 cups water

1½ cups sugar

3 cups pineapple juice

1 (6-ounce) can frozen orange juice concentrate, thawed, undiluted

2 tablespoons fresh lemon juice

3 ripe bananas, mashed

1 quart lemon-lime carbonated beverage, chilled

Combine water and sugar and bring to boiling point. Boil 3 minutes. Cool to room temperature. Add pineapple juice, orange juice concentrate, lemon juice and mashed bananas. Freeze. To serve thaw slightly and add lemon lime carbonated beverage.

Shelby Gallien
Savannah, TN

Frosty Fruit Cooler

4 cups apricot nectar, chilled

2 cups pineapple juice, chilled

2 cups orange juice, chilled

1 quart lemon-lime carbonated beverage, chilled

½ gallon orange sherbet

In a 1 quart non-metal container, combine apricot nectar, pineapple juice and orange juice. Chill. Just before serving, add lemon lime carbonated beverage. Put scoops of sherbet on top. Serve immediately.

Yield 24 servings.

Linda Neill
Savannah, TN

Grand Pete's Summer Tea

2 cups sugar
4 cups hot water
½ cup lemon juice

2 cups white grape juice
9 heaping teaspoons instant tea
6 mint sprigs

Mix sugar, water, lemon juice, grape juice and tea in a gallon container. Finish filling with water to make a gallon. Garnish with mint leaves.

Robaya Wolfe Ellis
Savannah, TN

Holiday Cocoa

*A pair of mugs filled with this along
with the instructions make a nice holiday gift.*

6 cups unsweetened cocoa powder
3 cups malted milk powder
7 cups granulated sugar

2 tablespoons cinnamon
1 vanilla bean, cut in half lengthwise
6 ounces milk for each serving

Blend dry ingredients and let sit for 3 days. Mix ¼ cup of mix into a 6-ounce mug of hot milk.

Charlotte Wolfe
Fort Lauderdale, FL

Homemade Amaretto

4 cups sugar
3 cups water
2½ cups vodka

1½ ounces almond flavoring
1 empty liquor bottle or glass jar

Combine sugar and water in saucepan. Stir over high heat until sugar dissolves and reaches boiling point. Reduce heat and simmer for 1 hour. Remove from heat and stir in vodka and flavoring. Cool and bottle. Shake bottle each day for 3 weeks.

Charlotte Wolfe
Fort Lauderdale, FL

Homemade Kahlúa

4 cups sugar	1 vanilla bean, crushed
4 cups water	1 (750-milliliter) bottle vodka
¾ cup instant coffee	1 empty liquor bottle or glass jar

Combine sugar and water and boil for 10 minutes. Cool. Add coffee, vanilla bean and vodka. Pour into bottle. Let stand 3 weeks, being sure to shake each day.

Charlotte Wolfe
Fort Lauderdale, FL

Hot Spiced Tea

3 quarts water	1 large can pineapple juice
2 sticks cinnamon	Juice of 5 oranges
30 whole cloves	Juice of 4 lemons
3 family size tea bags	Sugar or sweetener to taste

Combine water, cinnamon, and cloves and boil for 10 minutes. Remove from heat and add tea bags and steep for 5 minutes. Remove spices and tea bags. Add juices and sweetener to taste.

Laverne Calvert
Savannah, TN

Instant Russian Tea

½ cup instant tea	2 packages lemonade mix
2½ cups sugar	2 teaspoons cinnamon
2 cups orange flavored drink mix	1 teaspoon powdered cloves

Mix ingredients in a mixing bowl. To serve, put 2 heaping teaspoons of mix into a cup of boiling water.

Charlotte Wolfe
Fort Lauderdale, FL

Key Lime Shake

1 cup milk
½ cup frozen undiluted lemonade
  concentrate
4 scoops vanilla ice cream

2 scoops lime sherbet
2 tablespoons whipped heavy cream
½ teaspoon grated lime peel

Blend milk, lemonade concentrate and vanilla ice cream. Add lime sherbet and blend until smooth. Pour into 2 tall glasses and top with whipped cream. Add grated lime.

Beth Pippin
Savannah, TN

Make-Ahead Lemonade Mix

2½ cups water
1½ cups sugar

½ teaspoon finely shredded lemon peel
1¼ cups lemon juice

In a medium saucepan, heat and stir water and sugar over medium heat until sugar is dissolved. Remove from heat and cool for 20 minutes. Add lemon peel and lemon juice to sugar syrup. Pour into a jar, cover and chill. To serve, mix ½ cup of the base and ½ cup cold water and pour over ice.

This may be used instead of sour mix.

Carole Appleby
Fort Lauderdale, FL

Mock Champagne

This is a very refreshing beverage and a great beverage for showers.

1 quart ginger ale

1 quart white grape juice

Chill beverages. To serve mix equal parts of each. One beverage or both mixed can be frozen with fruit in a ring or in ice trays for decorative use.

Pam Wolfe
Savannah, TN

SASSY SIPPIN'

Mama Rock's Boiled Custard

Roxie Linam's recipe. She was my mother and Charlotte's grandmother.

6 eggs, separated and beaten	½ gallon whole milk
3 tablespoons plus 1 heaping teaspoon flour	2 cups orange juice
1½ cups sugar	Vanilla

Separate eggs and beat. Set aside. Mix flour and sugar and pour into milk. Stir to dissolve. Pour beaten egg yolks into mixture and stir. Cook over simmering water, stirring constantly until thickens. Fold in beaten egg whites. Refrigerate. When ready to serve add orange juice or vanilla to taste.

My sister and Charlotte's mother, Jo Ann Johnson, really liked this custard. But I think along with the orange juice she spiked it.

Nancy White
Adamsville, TN

Tropical Tea

¼ cup Make-Ahead Lemonade Mix	6 ounces lemon-lime carbonated beverage
¼ cup orange juice	
2 teaspoons instant tea powder	Orange or lemon wedge
Ice	

In a tall glass combine Make-Ahead lemonade mix, orange juice and tea powder. Add some ice and the carbonated beverage. Garnish with orange or lemon wedge.

Yield 1 serving.

Carole Appleby
Fort Lauderdale, FL

15

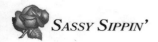

Party Lemonade

This is great for children's parties.

1 (10-ounce) bottle maraschino cherries
1 (12-ounce) can pink frozen lemonade, thawed
1 liter, sugar-free, lemon-lime carbonated beverage

Put cherries in each section of ice cube tray. Fill with water and freeze. Mix lemonade as directed on can. To serve, add lemon-lime carbonated beverage and cherry ice cubes. Enjoy.

Neeley Bennett Harwood
Corinth, MS

Party Punch

1 box cherry flavored gelatin
2 cups boiling water
1½ cups sugar
½ cup lemon juice
1 (46-ounce) can pineapple juice
1½ quarts cold water

Mix gelatin and water together until dissolved. Add sugar, lemon juice, pineapple juice and water and stir. This may also be frozen and used as a slush.

Demetrice Winters Hart
Savannah, TN

Southern Lemonade

5 lemons
5 oranges
5 limes
3 quarts water
1½-2 cups sugar

Squeeze the juice of 4 of the lemons oranges and limes. Pour into a gallon pitcher. Slice remaining fruits thin and set aside for garnish. Add water and sugar to juice mixture and chill in refrigerator. Serve on ice with fruit slices.

Linda Neill
Savannah, TN

Slush Punch

4 cups water
4 cups sugar
2 cups lemon juice
1 (6-ounce) can frozen orange juice
1 (46-ounce) can pineapple juice

1 (1½-ounce) bottle almond extract
4 cups water
3 quarts lemon-lime carbonated
    beverage or ginger ale

Mix water and sugar and boil until sugar dissolves. Cool to room temperature. When mixture is cool, add lemon juice, orange juice, pineapple juice, almond extract and water. Stir until well mixed. Divide into 3 equal portions and freeze. Set out 1 hour before serving. Add 1 quart carbonated beverage or ginger ale to each container. This makes a slushy punch type beverage.

This is good for showers and wedding receptions.

Yield 30 servings.

Vivian Epps
Adamsville, TN

Spicy Apple Cider

1 gallon apple cider

1 (8 to 10-ounce) package cinnamon
    candies

Heat apple cider and cinnamon candies over medium heat, stirring until candies are melted. Serve in a mug. This may also be done in a crockpot.

Suzanne Morel
Morel European Spa
Fort Lauderdale, FL

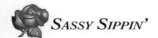

Wassail

2 quarts apple cider
½ cup brown sugar
½ teaspoon whole cloves

Dash nutmeg
¼ teaspoon salt
1 medium orange, sliced

Put cider, brown sugar, cloves, nutmeg and salt in large sauce pan. Heat over medium heat until warm and sugar is dissolved. Strain. Serve in a mug with slice of orange.

Mackie Nell Linam
Savannah, TN

Wassail

1 cup sugar
2 cinnamon sticks
1 tablespoons whole cloves
3 cups water

2 lemons, juiced
2 oranges, juiced
2 gallons apple cider

Put sugar and spices in water. Bring to a boil. Add other ingredients and heat. Serve hot.

Nettye Beck
Savannah, TN

White Sangria

Jon and I served this at our summer wedding reception.

1 (750-milliliter) bottle white Zinfandel wine
2 cups lemon-lime carbonated beverage, chilled
1 orange, sliced

1 lemon, sliced
8 fresh strawberries
¼ cup fresh blackberries
¼ cup fresh raspberries
1 unpeeled kiwi, sliced

In large pitcher mix together wine and carbonated lemon-lime beverage. Add fruits and stir.

Beth Pippin
Savannah, TN

Beach Bubble

1 ounce coconut rum
1 ounce peach schnapps

3 ounces pineapple juice
3 ounces orange juice

Mix together and pour over ice.

Kathleen Oros
Fort Lauderdale, FL

Brave Bull

2 ounces white tequila

1 ounce Mexican coffee flavored liqueur

Pour over ice and gentle swirl.

Sandra Moss
Fort Lauderdale, FL

Bucking Bronco

1 ounce orange liqueur
2 ounces club soda

5 ounces champagne
1 orange slice

Pour orange liqueur, club soda, champagne over ice. Garnish with orange slice.

P K Johns
Nogal, NM

Bulldog

Juice of ½ orange
2 ounces gin

Ginger ale

Pour juice and gin over ice cubes. Fill with ginger ale.

Lana Joy Fish
Coral Springs, FL

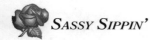

Canadian Slipper

½ cup ice
1 ounce Canadian Whiskey
½ ounce cinnamon schnapps

3 ounces apple cider
¼ ripe red apple

Put ingredients into blender and blend until smooth.

David Comanic
Fort Lauderdale, FL

Caribbean Chiller

1 ounce light rum
1 ounce banana liqueur

4 ounces champagne
Banana and cherry for garnish

Mix rum, liqueur and champagne together and pour over ice. Garnish with banana slice and cherry.

Alison Phillips
Fort Lauderdale, FL

Carpet Tax

2 ounces Drambuie

5 ounces grapefruit juice

Pour over ice.

Stacey George
Fort Lauderdale, FL

Dew Drop

1½ ounces melon liqueur
2 ounces sour mix

½ teaspoon sugar
4 ounces champagne

Mix together melon liqueur with sour mix and sugar. Stir until sugar dissolves. Pour over ice and add champagne.

Tricia Rutsis
Fort Lauderdale, FL

Charlotte's Bloody Marys

2 (46-ounce) cans spicy vegetable-
   tomato juice
1 (5-ounce) bottle Lea and Perrins
   Worcestershire sauce, no substitutes
3 ounces lemon juice

Salt and pepper to taste
Hot sauce
Celery sticks
Vodka

Mix juice, Worcestershire sauce, lemon juice, salt and pepper, hot sauce to taste. To serve pour 1½-ounces vodka in glass with ice. Fill with mixture and stir with celery stick.

Yield 3 quarts.

Charlotte Wolfe
Fort Lauderdale, FL

Dizzy Blond

1 ounce spiced rum
1 ounce orange liqueur

1 ounce milk or cream

Shake in shaker and pour over ice.

John Wolfe
Fort Lauderdale, FL

Frozen Margaritas

1 (6-ounce) can frozen limeade
   concentrate
¾ cup tequila

¼ cup orange flavored liqueur
Margarita salt
Lime slices

Place frozen limeade in blender. Add tequila and orange flavored liqueur. Add ice to fill blender. Blend well. Serve in stemmed glasses with slated rims. Garnish with lime slices.

Bobbie Davis
Savannah, TN

21

Fantastic T

½ ounce vodka
½ ounce gin
½ ounce rum
½ ounce tequila
½ ounce blue curaçao

1 ounce liquid sour mix
1 ounce orange juice
1 ounce pineapple juice
1 cola-flavored carbonated beverage
1 slice lemon

Mix all ingredients except cola and lemon. Pour over tall glass of ice. Pour cola to fill glass and garnish with lemon.

Ina Dale Runnels
Fort Lauderdale, FL

Frozen Russian

½ cup ice
1½ ounces vodka
1 ounce coffee flavored liqueur

1 scoop chocolate ice cream
1 tablespoon chocolate sprinkles

Put ice, vodka, coffee flavored liqueur and ice cream in blender. Blend until smooth. Pour into chilled glass and garnish with chocolate sprinkles.

If too thick add a little milk. If too thin add more ice cream.

Donna Tant
Nashville. TN

Holly's Here

1 ounce raspberry flavored liqueur

5 ounces champagne

Mix together and serve in champagne flute.

Holly Norvich-Carmel
Fort Lauderdale, FL

Hot Buttered Rum

1½ quarts vanilla ice cream, softened
1 pound butter, softened
1 pound brown sugar
1 pound box confectioners' sugar

2 teaspoons cinnamon
2 teaspoons nutmeg
Rum

Mix all ingredients except rum and freeze. To serve, stir 1 to 2 tablespoons of mix with 6-ounces boiling water. Add rum. Do not allow mixture to completely thaw. It will refreeze.

Glenda Alexander
Savannah, TN

Hot Buttered Rum Mix

1 (16-ounce) box brown sugar
½ cup butter
½ teaspoon cinnamon
½ teaspoon nutmeg
½ teaspoon cloves

Dash salt
1 ounce rum, per serving
1 cinnamon stick, per serving
1 lemon wedge, per serving

Combine brown sugar, butter, cinnamon, nutmeg, cloves and salt. To serve, put 1 tablespoon of mixture into cup, add rum and fill cup with hot water. Garnish with cinnamon stick and lemon wedge.

Charlotte Wolfe
Fort Lauderdale, FL

Island Bubbly

3 ounces champagne
3 ounces pineapple juice

½ ounces grenadine

Mix together and pour over ice.

Charlotte Wolfe
Fort Lauderdale, FL

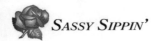

Irish Cream Liqueur

1½ cups Irish whiskey
1   teaspoon pure vanilla extract
1   tablespoon instant coffee

1   cup heavy cream
1   can sweetened condensed milk
6   eggs

Combine whiskey, vanilla and coffee and blend in blender. Add cream and sweetened condensed milk and blend for 1 minute. Add eggs and pulse stir (use lowest speed on blender and turn on-off about 8 times) just until smooth and not thick. Store in refrigerator.

Yield 4 cups.

Charlotte Wolfe
Fort Lauderdale, FL

Monkey Wrench

1½ ounces light rum   Grapefruit juice

Pour rum into an ice-filled glass. Fill with grapefruit juice and stir.

Charlotte Wolfe
Fort Lauderdale, FL

Peaches and Cream

1   ounce rum
1   ounce peach schnapps
¼   ounce cinnamon schnapps

4   ounces apple cider
Whipped cream

Put liquors into mug and fill with hot apple cider. Garnish with whipped cream.

Charlotte Wolfe
Fort Lauderdale, FL

Pink Pussycat

1½ ounces vodka	1 dash grenadine
6 ounces pineapple or grapefruit juice	

Pour vodka into an ice-filled glass. Fill with juice and add grenadine.

Charlotte Wolfe
Fort Lauderdale, FL

P K's Sting

1½ ounces Banana Liqueur	1½ ounces half-and-half
¾ ounce Rum	½ banana
3 ounces strawberries	1 heaping tablespoon vanilla ice cream

Mix in blender and serve. Very rich and delicious.

P K Johns
Nogal, NM

Dwanna Pusser

4 ounces pineapple juice	2 ounces Bahamian spiced rum
1 ounce cream of coconut	Dash cinnamon and nutmeg
1 ounce orange juice	

Without ice, blend, shake or stir pineapple juice, cream of coconut, orange juice and rum. Pour over ice and top with a touch of cinnamon and nutmeg.

Dwanna Pusser-Garrison
Adamsville, TN

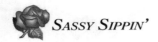

Ruby Martini

3 ounces fresh grapefruit juice   3 ounces vodka

Chill ingredients. Combine in shaker with ice cubes. Strain into martini glass.

Jo Ann Rogers
Memphis, TN

Silver Monkey

1 ounce vodka   1 ounce banana liqueur
4 ounces orange juice

Mix vodka and orange juice. Pour over ice filled glass. Pour banana liqueur on top.

John Wolfe
Fort Lauderdale, FL

Snow Bunny

½ ounce orange liqueur   1 cinnamon stick
1 cup hot chocolate

In a heavy mug, pour chocolate over orange liqueur. Garnish with cinnamon stick.

Carol Harrison
Fort Lauderdale, FL

Suffering Bastard

1½ ounces dark rum
1½ ounces light rum
1 tablespoon curaçao
½ teaspoon sugar

1 lime, juiced
1 cucumber peel
1 slice lime

Fill cocktail shaker with ice, add all ingredients except cucumber peel and lime slice. Strain into old-fashioned glass. Garnish with cucumber peel and lime slice.

Charlotte Wolfe
Fort Lauderdale, FL

Luscious Lips

1½ ounces vodka
½ ounce blackberry liqueur
½ ounce sour mix

½ ounce cranberry juice
4 ounces champagne

Pour vodka, liqueur, sour mix and cranberry juice into shaker. Shake well. Add champagne and strain into chilled glass.

Stacey George
Fort Lauderdale, FL

Stacey's Cosmopolitans

3 ounces orange flavored vodka
½ ounce lime juice
Dash cranberry juice

1 ounce lemon-lime carbonated beverage
1 lime twist

Stir vodka, lime juice, cranberry juice and carbonated beverage together. Strain into a chilled martini glass and garnish with lime twist.

Stacey George
Fort Lauderdale, FL

Wicked Woo Woo

1 ounce vodka
1 ounce peach schnapps
3 ounces sour mix

Splash lemon-lime carbonated
beverage

Mix together and pour over tall glass of ice.

Charlotte Wolfe
Fort Lauderdale, FL

Bavarian Mint Coffee Mix

⅓ cup nondairy creamer
⅓ cup sugar
⅓ cup instant coffee granules

2 tablespoons cocoa powder
5 pieces hard peppermint candies, finely
  crushed

Combine all ingredients together. Store in airtight container. To serve put 2 heaping teaspoons mix into a cup boiling water.

Charlotte Wolfe
Fort Lauderdale, FL

Cappuccino Mix

*This makes a great happy or hostess gift presented in
a pretty coffee cup with the directions tied with a pretty bow.*

6 tablespoons plus 2 teaspoons instant
  espresso coffee powder
½ cup plus 2 teaspoons sugar

3 tablespoons unsweetened cocoa
  powder
1 tablespoon vanilla extract powder
1¼ cups fat free coffee creamer

Stir ingredients together and store tightly covered in a medium container. To serve, put 4 tablespoons mix into coffee mug and stir in 6 ounces boiling water.

Charlotte Wolfe
Fort Lauderdale, FL

Coffee Nog

1 cup very strongly brewed coffee	3 cups skim milk
½ cup frozen egg substitute, thawed	1½ cups vanilla non-fat frozen yogurt
¼ cup sugar	¼ teaspoon ground cinnamon

Combine coffee, egg substitute and sugar in a large saucepan, stir well. Gradually add milk, stirring well. Cook over low heat until thoroughly heated, stirring constantly. Do not boil. Pour ¾ cup coffee mixture into each of 6 mugs. Top with ½ cup frozen yogurt and sprinkle evenly with ground cinnamon. Serve immediately.

Charlotte Wolfe
Fort Lauderdale, FL

Tipsy Coffee

¼ ounce Irish cream liqueur	5 ounces hot coffee
¼ ounce hazel nut flavored liqueur	1 ounce heavy cream, whipped
¼ ounce Mexican coffee flavored liqueur	Chocolate shavings
¼ ounce orange flavored liqueur	Ground nutmeg

Preheat coffee mug with hot water. Combine liqueurs and put in cup followed by hot coffee. Stir, garnish with dollop of whipped heavy cream and chocolate shavings.

Charlotte Wolfe
Fort Lauderdale, FL

Flirtini

3 ounces dry Champagne or sparkling wine	1 ounce orange flavored vodka
	1½ ounces pineapple juice

Pour the Champagne or sparkling wine into a chilled cocktail glass. Gently pour the orange vodka and pineapple juice on top. Carefully stir.

Jo Ann Rogers
Memphis, TN

Vanilla Coffee

1½ cups dry coffee creamer	1½ cups sugar
1 cup dry hot chocolate mix	½ cup instant coffee crystals
½ teaspoon nutmeg	2 tablespoons vanilla powder
1 teaspoon cinnamon	

Mix all ingredients together and place in airtight container. Use 2 to 4 tablespoons in a mug of boiling water.

You may use sugar substitute instead of sugar by omitting sugar and add sugar substitute to taste in mug.

Charlotte Wolfe
Fort Lauderdale, FL

Southern Breeze

This drink is basically your Southern lemonade.
No real Southern belle would be caught dead outside,
glistening without her glass of lemonade and blue ice cubes!

1 cup sugar	1 (6-ounce) can frozen lemonade concentrate, thawed
1 (22-ounce) envelope unsweetened blue raspberry lemonade mix	1 (46-ounce) can unsweetened pineapple juice, chilled
7 cups water	1 (2-liter) bottle ginger ale, chilled

Stir together the first 4 ingredients in a 2-quart pitcher; pour evenly into 5 ice cube trays and freeze at least 8 hours. Combine pineapple juice and ginger ale and serve over raspberry ice cubes.

Vicki Bennett
Memphis, TN

Watermelon Margaritas

Lime juice
Sugar
1/3 cup tequila
2 cups crushed ice
2 cups seeded, chopped watermelon

1/4 cup sugar
1/4 cup lime juice (about 1½ limes)
1 tablespoon Vodka
1 tablespoon orange liqueur

Coat rims of cocktail glasses with lime juice, dip in sugar. Process remaining ingredients in a blender until slushy. Pour into prepared glasses.

Vicki Bennett
Memphis, TN

The Infamous Chocolate Martini

2½ ounces vodka
2½ chocolate liqueur

Cocoa powder

Shake vodka and liqueur in cracked ice. Strain into a chilled martini glass rimmed with cocoa powder.

Jo Ann Rogers
Memphis, TN

Sea Breeze Cocktail

2 ounces tequila
3 ounces cranberry juice

3 ounces pineapple juice
1 lime wedge

Fill tall glass with ice. Pour tequila and juices over ice. Garnish with lime wedge.

Kathy Toriello
Midlothia, VA

Happy Undertaker

3 cups vodka
1 cup cherry brandy

4 cups orange juice

Shake all ingredients together with ice. Strain into martini glasses.

For punch double recipe and serve over ice cubes.

Charlotte Wolfe
Fort Lauderdale, FL

Martimmy

3 (12-ounce) cans of lemonade, thawed/diluted
1 bottle of ginger ale

1 cup frozen orange juice concentrate, thawed/diluted
1 quart cranberry juice cocktail
Vodka

Combine lemonade, ginger ale, orange juice and cranberry juice and mix well. Pour 1-ounce vodka into a martini glass and add juice mixture to fill glass.

Charlotte Wolfe
Fort Lauderdale, FL

Raspberrytini

½ ounce raspberry liqueur
1 ounce vodka

2 ounces pineapple juice

Mix together and pour into chilled martini glass.

Charlotte Wolfe
Fort Lauderdale, FL

Taste Temptations

Adrienne's Delight	36	Pepper Cheese Ball	53
Almond Ham Rollups	36	Rumaki	53
Alligator Eyes	37	Sausage Balls	53
Ann's Tomato Tart	37	Pizza Burgers	54
Anniversary Chicken Salad	38	Smoky Barbecue Chicken Pizza	54
Asparagus Rolls	38	Sausage Crescents	55
Bacon Filled Cherry Tomatoes	39	Shrimp Dip	55
Bacon Wrapped Water Chestnuts	39	Snappetizer	55
Black Bean Dip	39	Spinach Balls	56
Carrot Sandwiches	40	Spinach Artichoke Dip	56
Caviar Pie	40	Stuffed Mushrooms	57
Brenda's Cucumber Salad	41	Scalloped Sweet Potatoes
Cheese Ball	41	and Apples	57
Linda's Cheese Ball	42	Texas Caviar	57
Hawaiian Cheese Ball	42	Surprise Spread	58
Cheese Ham Log	42	Taco Appetizer Platter	58
Cheese Wafers	43	Tortilla Rollups	59
Country Caviar	43	Tropical Salsa	59
College Carrots	43	Vegetable Pizza	60
Cranberry-Horseradish Sauce		Warm Welcome Appetizer	60
and Cream Cheese	44	Beer Rolls	60
Cucumber Sandwiches	44	Baked French Toast	61
Date Cheese Ball	44	French Toast	61
Cream Cheese Pastry Cups	45	Banana Nut Bread	62
Encrusted Brie	45	Broccoli Cornbread	62
Drunken Wieners	46	Marshmallow Rolls	62
Four Cheese Pâté	46	Festive Bruschetta
Grilled Salmon Summer Rolls		with a Three Tomato Salsa	63
with Spicy Citrus Dipping Sauce	47	Monkey Bread	63
Ham Ball	48	Italian Flat Bread	64
Ham-Pickle Rollup	48	Monkey Bread	64
Ham Rollups	48	Jalapeño Cheese Bread	65
Hanky Panky Party Pizzas	49	Mexican Corn Bread Salad	65
Mahogany Chicken Wings	49	Onion Walnut Muffins	66
Miniature Quiches	50	Rolls	66
Mushroom Turnovers	50	Sally Lunn	67
Olive Cheese Ball	51	Barbecued Chicken Dip	67
Olive Cheese Balls	51	Bacon and Cheddar Dip	67
Onion Soufflé	51	Apple Brickle Dip	68
Party Pizzas	52	BLT Dip	68
Pepper Cheesecake	52	Brenda's Vegetable Dip	68

Bumpy Road Dip 69
Buried Treasures 69
Chili Cheese Dip 70
Chili Dip 70
Crab Dip..70
Chutney Shrimp Dip 71
Crab Dip with Crackers 71
Dilly Vegetable Dip 72
Dream Fruit Dip 72
Fruit Dip 72
Fruit Dip 73
El-Brenda's Dunk 73
Fresh Vegetable Mexican Dip 73
Fruit Kabobs
    with Margarita Dip 74
Hawaiian Grab Bag...............................74
Hawaiian Fruit Dip...............................75
Jiffy Fruit Dip 75
Layered Mexican Dip 75
French Bread Spread 76
Hot Dip 76
Mediterranean Dip 76
Layered Tamale Dip 77

Mexican Dip 77
Another Mexican Dip 78
Onion Dip 78
Pacesetter Picante Dip 78
Ranch Dipping Sauce 79
Russian Dip 79
Shrimp Dip 79
Spinach and Artichoke Dip 80
Spinach Dip 80
Shrimp Dip 81
Shrimp Spread 81
Smoked Salmon Spread 82
Southwestern Shrimp Dip 82
Sunset Dip 82
Taco Dip...83
Tamale Dip 83
Tangy Grecian Spread 83
Veggie Dip 84
Vegetable Dip...84
Veggie Veggie Dip..................................84
White Cheese Dip 85
Party Mix 85
Cocktail Pecans 85

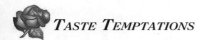

Adrienne's Delight

12 ounces cream cheese	¼ cup cold water
1 stick butter	½ cup white raisins
½ cup sour cream	1 cup slivered almonds, toasted
½ cup sugar	2 lemons, zest only
1 envelope plain gelatin	1 box saltine crackers

Let cream cheese, butter and sour cream come to room temperature. Cream well and add sugar. Soften gelatin in cold water. Dissolve over hot water. Add to cream cheese mixture. Then add raisins, slivered almonds and lemon zest. Put in a 1-quart mold and refrigerate. When firm, unmold and serve with crackers.

Do not substitute for saltine crackers.

Charlotte Wolfe
Fort Lauderdale, FL

Almond Ham Rollups

Very tasty

1 (8-ounce) package cream cheese	⅛ teaspoon pepper
2 tablespoons mayonnaise	⅛ teaspoon hot sauce
1 teaspoon instant minced onion	1 tablespoon chopped almonds
1 teaspoon Worcestershire sauce	1 (12-ounce) package thinly sliced lean
¼ teaspoon powdered mustard	ham
¼ teaspoon paprika	

Combine all ingredients except ham, stirring until well blended. Spread 1 tablespoon or more mixture on each ham slice. Roll up jelly roll style. Wrap in plastic wrap. Before serving, cut each roll into ¾-inch slices.

Fran Muller
Fort Lauderdale, FL

Alligator Eyes

Great as a dip or sauce for tacos.

1 can black olives, drained and sliced
1 (4 or 5-ounce) can green olives, drained and sliced
1 can chopped tomatoes with chiles

2 green onions, sliced
½ cup oil
¼ cup vinegar
2 teaspoons garlic salt

Mix all ingredients and chill in refrigerator before serving.

Patricia Roe
Savannah, TN

Ann's Tomato Tart

1 package frozen puff pastry, thawed for 20 to 30 minutes
3 large tomatoes or 6 romas
2 tablespoons pesto sauce
Salt and pepper to taste

1 teaspoon olive oil
1 egg yolk mixed with 2 teaspoons water
½ cup grated Parmesan cheese
1 tablespoon basil

Preheat oven to 425°. Line a cookie sheet with parchment paper and place 1 pastry sheet on it. Roll to ⅛-inch thickness; prick with a fork. Refrigerate until firm. From remaining pastry sheet, cut 4 (½-inch wide) strips. Brush with cold water and attach to edges of rolled out pastry, corners overlapping. Refrigerate until ready to bake. Cut tomatoes in half and remove seeds and juice. Cut into slices and place on paper towels to dry. Brush pesto sauce over pastry but not edges. Arrange tomato slices on top. Season lightly with salt and pepper and brush with olive oil. Paint raised edges with egg glaze. Sprinkle surface and edges with grated cheese. Bake for 15 minutes. Garnish with basil and serve hot or cold.

Sherry Decker
Shammamish, WA

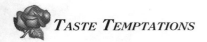
Anniversary Chicken Salad

This is a crowd pleaser every time it is served.

1   chicken, cooked and deboned
½   cup chopped nuts
½   cup finely chopped green onions
½   cup seasoned breadcrumbs
½   cup finely chopped celery
1   can chopped ripe olives

1   cup mayonnaise (do not use salad
      dressing)
¼   teaspoon salt
4   dashes garlic salt
1   dash pepper

Combine all ingredients.

This was served at the bed and breakfast where Pat and I spent our first wedding anniversary in Galveston, TX.

Vivian Epps
Adamsville, TN

Asparagus Rolls

Betcha can't eat just one. These will melt in your mouth.

1   loaf thin sliced white bread
1   (8-ounce) package cream cheese,
      softened
1   (3-ounce) package blue cheese,
      softened

1   large egg
1   (12-ounce) can whole asparagus
      spears, drained
1   stick butter, melted

Remove crusts from bread and flatten slices with rolling pin. Combine cheeses and egg with an electric mixer. Spread mixture evenly over bread slices. Place an asparagus spear on each slice and roll up. Brush outside of bread in melted butter. Place on cookie sheet and cut each roll into 3 even slices. Bake for 15 minutes or until lightly browned in 400° oven. Serve immediately.

Nancy Virgin
Coconut Creek, FL

Bacon Filled Cherry Tomatoes

Make these when you are alone, because your
family will eat them faster than you can put them together.

1 pound bacon, fried crisp and crumbled
¼ cup finely chopped green onions
2 tablespoons chopped parsley
½ cup mayonnaise
24 cherry tomatoes

Combine all ingredients except tomatoes. Cut a thin slice off the top of each tomato. With a small spoon or melon baller, hollow out tomato. Fill tomatoes with bacon mixture. Refrigerate 1 hour before serving.

Jo Ann Rogers
Memphis, TN

Bacon Wrapped Water Chestnuts

1 can whole water chestnuts
½ cup soy sauce or teriyaki sauce
1 tablespoon sugar
Bacon slices, cut into thirds

Drain chestnuts. Mix soy sauce (or teriyaki sauce) and sugar together and pour over chestnuts. Let marinate for at least 1 hour. Drain. Wrap chestnuts in bacon. Secure with toothpick. Bake at 425° until bacon is crisp, approximately 20 to 25 minutes.

Johnna Shaw
Savannah, TN

Black Bean Dip

2 (16-ounce) cans black beans, rinsed
  and drained
2 (10-ounce) cans tomatoes with chiles
1 bunch green onions, green parts only,
  chopped
1 teaspoon cumin
1 teaspoon chili powder
1 teaspoon salt
½ teaspoon garlic powder
1 cup fresh cilantro, chopped
1 teaspoon lemon juice
1 bag tortilla chips

Combine all ingredients except chips in a bowl. Cover and refrigerate overnight. Serve with tortilla chips.

Stacey George
Fort Lauderdale, FL

Carrot Sandwiches

1 (8-ounce) package cream cheese,
   softened
2 large carrots
1 (8-ounce) can water chestnuts, chopped

1 tablespoon onion, grated with juice
2 tablespoons mayonnaise
1 loaf cocktail bread slices

Place cream cheese in mixer and lightly beat until creamy. Grate carrots on fine side of grater or use a food processor. Add carrots, water chestnuts, onion and mayonnaise. Mix until well blended. Spread on bread and serve open-faced.

Bobbie Lou Peck
Florence, AL

Caviar Pie

¾ cup minced sweet onions
1 pat of butter
6 hard-boiled eggs
3 tablespoons mayonnaise

1 (8-ounce) package cream cheese
⅔ cup sour cream
1 (4-ounce) jar caviar
3 tablespoons minced onions

Spread minced onions on paper towel and drain for 30 minutes. Lightly butter sides and bottom of an 8-inch springform pan. Chop eggs and mix with mayonnaise. Spread on bottom of prepared pan. Sprinkle with minced onions. Beat cream cheese and sour cream together until smooth. Carefully drop onto onion layer, gently spreading to edges. Cover and chill overnight. Just before serving, gently rinse caviar with cold water. Drain in strainer and then on paper towel. Spoon onto cheese layer in a decorative pattern. Garnish with onions. Gently remove sides of springform pan and serve.

Charlotte Wolfe
Fort Lauderdale, FL

Brenda's Cucumber Salad

3 cucumbers (6 to 8-inches long)
1 tablespoon salt
½ cup sour cream

½ cup mayonnaise
1 teaspoon sugar
½ teaspoon pepper

Peel cucumbers and slice very, very thin. Sprinkle salt on cucumbers and let stand for 30 minutes. Rinse lightly and let drain for 10 minutes. Combine sour cream, mayonnaise, sugar and pepper. Mix in cucumbers. Refrigerate for at least 1 hour before serving.

Brenda Morenc
Kenner, LA

Cheese Ball

2 (8-ounce) packages cream cheese
1 (8-ounce) can crushed pineapple,
     drained

¼ cup chopped onions
1 tablespoon seasoned salt
2 cups chopped nuts, divided

Set aside 1 cup of chopped nuts. Mix remaining ingredients and form into a ball. Roll in remaining nuts.

Pam Wolfe
Savannah, TN

Cheese Ball

This is so easy and everyone loves it.

2 (8-ounce) packages cream cheese
1½ cups extra sharp cheese, grated

1 package ranch dressing mix
½ cup chopped nuts

Mix all ingredients together except nuts. Form into a ball and roll in nuts. Chill for 2 hours.

Ruth Hughes
Alta Loma, CA

Linda's Cheese Ball

1 jar dried beef
2 green onions, including blades, chopped
2 (8-ounce) packages cream cheese, softened

1 teaspoon Worcestershire sauce
1 cup chopped nuts

Chop beef and onions. Mix with cream cheese and add Worcestershire sauce. Roll in nuts.

Linda Callins
Savannah, TN

Hawaiian Cheese Ball

2 (8-ounce) packages cream cheese, softened
1 (8-ounce) can crushed pineapple, drained

2 cups chopped pecans, divided
¼ cup finely chopped bell pepper
3 tablespoons finely chopped onions
1 tablespoon seasoned salt

Mix cream cheese with pineapple, 1 cup of the pecans, bell pepper, onion and salt. Shape into a ball and chill for 1 hour, then roll in remaining pecans.

Laverne Calvert
Savannah, TN

Cheese Ham Log

2 (8-ounce) packages cream cheese, softened
8 ounces sharp Cheddar cheese, grated
1 small can deviled ham
2 teaspoons minced onion
½ teaspoon seasoned salt
¼ teaspoon salt

2 teaspoons Worcestershire sauce
2 teaspoons parsley flakes
1 teaspoon powdered mustard
1 teaspoon lemon juice
½ teaspoon paprika
1 cup chopped pecans

Mix all ingredients together except pecans. Form into ball and roll in pecans.

Sharon Bain
Humboldt, TN

Cheese Wafers

½ cup margarine
2 cups grated Cheddar cheese
1 cup flour

1 teaspoon salt
¼ teaspoon cayenne pepper
¾ cup chopped nuts

Cream margarine and Cheddar cheese. Add flour, salt, cayenne pepper and nuts. Form into a log. Wrap in waxed paper and chill in refrigerator overnight. Slice and place on greased cookie sheet. Bake at 350° for 10 to 15 minutes.

Janice Hooper
Whitwell, TN

Country Caviar

2 (14-ounce) cans black-eyed peas
1 (15-ounce) can white hominy
2 medium tomatoes, chopped
4 green onions, chopped

1 medium bell pepper, chopped
1 (8-ounce) bottle zesty Italian dressing
Assorted crackers

Combine all ingredients except crackers and mix well. Cover and refrigerate overnight. Drain and serve with assorted crackers.

Charlotte Wolfe
Fort Lauderdale, FL

College Carrots

2-3 pounds carrots
1 small bell pepper, cut into strips
1 medium onion, sliced very thin
1 can tomato soup
¼ cup salad oil

1 cup sugar
¾ cup cider vinegar
1 teaspoon mustard
1 teaspoon Worcestershire sauce

Cut carrots into ¼-inch slices. Cook carrots in water until tender. Drain and cool. Mix remaining ingredients together and pour over cooked carrots. Mix well and refrigerate for 24 hours.

Lyla Alexander
Pompano Beach, FL

Cranberry-Horseradish Sauce and Cream Cheese

1 (16-ounce) can whole-berry cranberry
    sauce
½ cup sugar
⅓ cup minced onions

2 tablespoons prepared horseradish
    sauce
½ teaspoon salt
1 (8-ounce) package cream cheese

Stir the first 5 ingredients together in a medium saucepan. Bring to a boil, stirring often. Remove from heat. Cover and chill for 1 hour or up to 3 days. Spoon sauce over cream cheese to serve.

Rita Rasbach
Savannah, TN

Cucumber Sandwiches

1 (8-ounce) package cream cheese
¼ cup cucumber, grated and drained
½ teaspoon Worcestershire sauce
1 tablespoon mayonnaise type salad
    dressing

Dash garlic salt
Grated onion to taste
Bread

Mix all ingredients except bread. Serve on bread open-faced.

Sharon Bain
Humboldt, TN

Date Cheese Ball

1 (8-ounce) package cream cheese
1 (8-ounce) package chopped dates
1 tablespoon mayonnaise

1 cup chopped pecans
Assorted crackers

Mix cheese, dates and mayonnaise and roll into a ball. Then roll in pecans to cover ball. Refrigerate until ready to serve. Serve with crackers.

Mary Gordon Kerr
Charleston, SC

Cream Cheese Pastry Cups

These are great filled with chicken salad.

½ cup sweet butter, softened
½ cup margarine, softened
1 (8-ounce) package cream cheese,
    softened

¼ cup sugar
2½ cups all-purpose flour

Combine butter, margarine, cream cheese and sugar. Mix until well blended. Add flour, 1 cup at a time. Blend well. Form into a roll and refrigerate. When cold slice and pat into small muffin tins. Bake at 350° for 10 minutes or until golden brown.

Charlotte Wolfe
Fort Lauderdale, FL

Encrusted Brie

1 round of Brie with rind
1 refrigerated pie crust
¼ cup strawberry or blackberry jam
1 teaspoon cinnamon

1 teaspoon sugar
   Berries, sliced apples, crackers and
   French bread

Flatten the pie crust and spread with jam. Place the wheel of Brie in the center. Fold the edges of the pie crust up around the cheese. Flip it over onto a cookie sheet. Sprinkle with cinnamon and sugar. Bake for 20 minutes in a 250° oven or until golden brown. Serve on platter with berries, sliced apples, crackers and French bread.

Charlotte Wolfe
Fort Lauderdale, FL

Drunken Wieners

1 cup bourbon
1 cup confectioners' sugar, sifted
2 cups catsup

1 tablespoon Worcestershire sauce
2 pounds cocktail wieners

Mix together bourbon, sugar, catsup, Worcestershire sauce and put in large saucepan. Add wieners and simmer for 40 minutes. Serve in chafing dish.

May be prepared ahead of time.

Charlotte Wolfe
Fort Lauderdale, FL

Four Cheese Pâté

1 (8-ounce) package cream cheese, softened
2 tablespoons milk
2 tablespoons sour cream
¾ cup chopped pecans
2 (8-ounce) packages cream cheese, softened

1 (4½-ounce) package Camembert cheese, softened
1 (4-ounce) package blue cheese
1 cup shredded Swiss cheese, softened
2 apples, 1 red and 1 green, cut into wedges
Pecan halves

Line a 9-inch pie plate with plastic wrap; set aside. Combine the first 3 ingredients in a small mixing bowl; beat at medium speed on mixer until smooth. Spread into pie plate and sprinkle with chopped pecans. Combine remaining cream cheese, Camembert cheese, including rind, blue cheese and Swiss cheese in mixing bowl; beat at medium speed on mixer until smooth. Spoon into pie plate and spread to edge. Cover with plastic wrap and chill up to 1 week. To serve, invert onto serving plate. Carefully peel away plastic wrap. Garnish with pecans. Arrange apple wedges around cheese. Put out about an hour prior to serving to soften.

Fran Muller
Fort Lauderdale, FL

Grilled Salmon Summer Rolls with Spicy Citrus Dipping Sauce

1 (8-ounce) salmon fillet, fresh,
  boneless, skinless
1 tablespoon olive oil
  Salt and pepper to taste
2 cups shredded cabbage
1 cup shredded red cabbage
½ cup grated carrots
  Fresh mint leaves to taste
½ cup fresh orange juice

½ cup low sodium soy sauce
¼ cup seasoned rice vinegar
2 tablespoons garlic chili sauce
  (Chinese product)
½ cup honey
  Zest from 1 fresh orange
8 (6-ounces) Vietnamese rice paper
  wrappers

Preheat char-broiler to medium high heat. Rub salmon fillet with olive oil to coat well. Season with salt and pepper to taste. Grill on each side 3 to 4 minutes or until salmon is fully cooked. Remove from grill and chill. Flake salmon into medium size pieces and reserve to place inside summer rolls. In a medium size bowl combine cabbages with carrots and mint leaves. Keep well chilled. In a small bowl combine orange juice, soy sauce, rice vinegar, chili sauce, honey and orange zest. Whisk well to combine and keep well chilled. To assemble rolls, dip each rice paper wrapper in a water bath for 3 to 4 minutes to soften. Remove wrapper from water and place on a clean damp towel. In the center of the wrapper place 2 tablespoons of the cabbage mixture and a portion of the salmon. Roll the wrapper up as in the formation of a cylinder, tucking in the sides, holding the filling. Continue to wrap the roll to seal and crate a seam. Rolling it as tight as possible without tearing the delicate wrapper. Place the finished rolls on a chilled plate to rest. Slice tolls in half at a diagonal. Serve with the prepared dipping sauce.

Chef Jill K. Bosich
ACF Culinary Team 2000

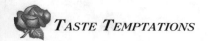

Ham Ball

1 (8-ounce) package cream cheese
1 can deviled ham
3 green onions, finely chopped

Dash Worcestershire sauce
1 cup chopped pecans

Mix cream cheese, ham, onions and Worcestershire sauce. Shape into a ball and rolled in chopped pecans. Chill overnight.

This is very good served with wheat thin crackers.

Johnna Shaw
Savannah, TN

Ham-Pickle Rollup

1 (8-ounce) package cream cheese,
     softened
1 teaspoon garlic powder

12 ham slices
12 dill pickle spears

Mix cream cheese and garlic powder. Spread on ham slices. Place pickle on edge of ham and roll up. Chill overnight. Slice into rounds before serving.

Johnna Shaw
Savannah, TN

Ham Rollups

1 (8-ounce) package cream cheese
½ teaspoon angostura bitters
½ tablespoon finely chopped onions

¾ cup pecans, finely chopped
¾ pound thinly sliced ham

Combine first 4 ingredients. Spread on ham slices. Roll up and refrigerate. Cut into slices.

Charlotte Wolfe
Fort Lauderdale, FL

Hanky Panky Party Pizzas

I always double this recipe. It's great for parties or snacks.

1   pound ground beef
1   pound spicy sausage
1   pound processed cheese loaf
½ teaspoon oregano

½ teaspoon garlic salt
2   teaspoons Worcestershire sauce
1½ packages party rye bread

Brown meats separately and drain. Melt cheese in the same skillet used to brown meats. Add seasons, stirring constantly over low heat. Return meat to skillet. Stir until mixture is well blended. Spoon onto party rye slices. To serve, broil several minutes until cheese bubbles. Watch carefully. To freeze, place pizzas on a cookie sheet. When frozen, place in a plastic bag. They will not stick together. Removed desired amount from bag and place under broiler. They thaw and cook very fast.

George Ann Ingram
Fort Myers, FL

Mahogany Chicken Wings

15 chicken wings
½ cup soy sauce
½ cup honey
¼ cup molasses

2   tablespoons chili sauce
1   teaspoon ground ginger
2   cloves garlic, finely chopped

Cut each chicken wing at joints to make 3 pieces. Cut off excess skin and discard. Mix remaining ingredients and pour over chicken. Cover and refrigerate 1 hour, turning occasionally. Heat oven to 375°. Line broiler pan with aluminum foil. Remove chicken from marinade; reserve marinade. Place chicken in single layer on rack in foil lined broiler pan. Brush chicken with reserved marinade. Bake 30 minutes; turn and bake 20 minutes longer brushing occasionally with marinade until deep brown. Chicken should not be pink when centers of thickest pieces are cut.

Brenda Thrasher
Savannah, TN

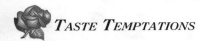

Miniature Quiches

2 (8-ounce) packages refrigerated crescent rolls
1 small can shrimp, washed and well drained
1 egg, beaten
½ cup half-and-half cream
1 tablespoon brandy
½ teaspoon salt
Dash of pepper
1½ ounces Swiss cheese

Grease miniature muffin tins. Separate rolls and divide each one in half. Press into muffin tins to make a shell. Place 1 or 2 shrimp in each shell. Combine egg, cream, brandy, salt and pepper. Divide evenly among the shells. Place a small slice of Swiss cheese atop each quiche. Bake at 375° for 10 minutes. Serve hot.

Quiches may be baked, wrapped in foil and frozen. Reheat for 10 to 12 minutes.

Beth Pippin
Savannah, TN

Mushroom Turnovers

1 (8-ounce) package cream cheese, softened to room temperature
1 stick butter, softened to room temperature
1½ cups flour
1 large onion, minced
½ pound mushrooms, minced
3 tablespoons butter
1 teaspoon salt
¼ teaspoon thyme
2 tablespoons flour
¼ cup sour cream
Egg wash of 1 egg yolk and 1 teaspoon water

Cream together cream cheese, butter and flour. Chill for 2 hours. Sauté onion and mushrooms in utter. Add salt, thyme and flour. Cook until thickened. Remove from heat, add sour cream. Whisk together egg yolk and water. Set aside. Roll dough out thinly on a lightly floured surface approximately ⅛-inch thick. Cut out circles with a big glass. Put 1 teaspoonful of filling on each circle. Seal together forming a half moon. Brush top of each with egg wash. Bake at 450° for 12 to 15 minutes. Watch carefully.

Vivian Epps
Adamsville, TN

Olive Cheese Ball

10 ounces sharp Cheddar cheese, grated
2 (8-ounce) packages cream cheese
¼ cup sliced olives
2 tablespoons minced onion

2 tablespoons minced bell pepper
2 teaspoons Worcestershire sauce
1 teaspoon lemon juice
1 cup chopped pecans

Mix all ingredients except pecans together and form into a ball. Roll in pecans.

Sharon Bain
Humboldt, TN

Olive Cheese Balls

2 cups shredded sharp Cheddar cheese
1¼ cups all-purpose flour

½ cup margarine, melted
36 small pimento stuffed olives, drained

Mix cheese and flour, add margarine. From the dough mixture, mold 1 teaspoonful around each olive. Shape into a ball. Place on ungreased cookie sheet and refrigerate at least 1 hour. Bake 15 to 20 minutes at 400°.

Kay Alexander
Savannah, TN

Onion Soufflé

1 (10-ounce) package frozen chopped onions
3 (8-ounce) packages cream cheese

2 cups Parmesan cheese
½ cup mayonnaise
Chips

Thaw and drain onions on paper towel to dry. Mix all ingredients except chips and pour into a 2-quart soufflé dish. Bake at 425° for 15 minutes. Serve with chips.

Pam Wolfe
Savannah, TN

51

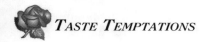

Party Pizzas

1	pound sausage	1	teaspoon oregano
1	pound ground chuck	¼	teaspoon garlic powder
1	pound processed cheese loaf	½	teaspoon parsley
1	teaspoon basil	1	package party rye bread slices

Brown meats and drain grease. Add cheese and spices and stir until melted. Spread on bread slices. Bake at 350° until hot and bubbly.

These freeze well on a cookie sheet and then store in a zip-top plastic bag.

Diane Hardin
Savannah, TN

Pepper Cheesecake

2	(8-ounce) packages cream cheese	½	cup diced sweet red pepper
2	cups shredded sharp Cheddar cheese	½	cup hot salsa
1	(1¼-ounce) package taco seasoning	2	(8-ounce) containers frozen
3	eggs		guacamole, thawed
1	(16-ounce) carton sour cream, divided		Chopped tomatoes, olives and
1	(4-ounce) can chopped green chiles, drained		shredded cheese

Combine cream cheese, Cheddar cheese and taco seasoning; beat well on high speed of mixer. Add eggs, one at a time, beating well after each addition. Stir in half of sour cream. Fold in chiles and red pepper. Pour mixture into a greased 10-inch springform pan. Bake at 350° for 35 minutes or until set. Combine remaining sour cream and salsa. Spread mixture evenly over cheesecake. Bake an additional 5 minutes. Let cool in pan on wire rack. Cover and chill at least 8 hours. To serve, carefully remove sides of springform pan. Spread with guacamole and garnish with tomatoes, olives and shredded cheese.

Charlotte Wolfe
Fort Lauderdale, Fl

Pepper Cheese Ball

1 (8-ounce) package cream cheese
1 package ranch dressing mix

½ cup coarse ground black pepper
Crackers

Mix cream cheese and dressing mix until smooth. Roll into a ball or log. Sprinkle with pepper to cover. Serve with crackers.

Pam Wolfe
Savannah, TN

Rumaki

1½ tablespoons honey
1 tablespoon soy sauce
2 tablespoons oil
½ clove garlic, crushed

½ pound chicken livers, cut in half
1 (7-ounce) can water chestnuts
18 slices bacon, cut in half

Mix honey, soy sauce, oil and garlic. Pour over livers and marinate for 30 minutes. Remove from marinade and wrap bacon slice around 1 liver and 1 water chestnut, secure with toothpick. Bake at 350° until bacon is crisp. Cover with foil to keep warm.

Yield 36 pieces.

George Ann Ingram
Fort Myers, FL

Sausage Balls

3 cups biscuit baking mix
1 pound spicy pork sausage

10 ounces sharp Cheddar cheese, grated
4 dashes hot sauce

Mix ingredients and form into balls the size of a walnut. Bake at 350° for 20 minutes.

Charlotte Wolfe
Fort Lauderdale, FL

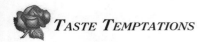

Pizza Burgers

In honor of Annie Gail Johnson.

1 pound ground beef, browned and drained	½ teaspoon oregano
	⅛ teaspoon sage
6 ounces bologna, grated	¼ teaspoon salt
⅔ cup spaghetti sauce	1 package buns
1 teaspoon chopped parsley	6 ounces shredded Cheddar cheese

Combine ground beef, bologna, spaghetti sauce, parsley, oregano, sage and salt. Spread on bun halves. Top each with Cheddar cheese. Bake at 300° until cheese melts.

Kids love this. The mix may be prepared ahead and frozen. It's ready when the grandchildren visit.

Sharon Bain
Humboldt, TN

Smoky Barbecue Chicken Pizza

1 can refrigerated pizza dough	1 cup barbecue sauce
2 cups Colby-Jack cheese, shredded	1 small onion, chopped
2 cups cooked chicken, cubed	1 small bell pepper, chopped

Roll out pizza dough with rolling pin onto a rectangular pan. Sprinkle 1 cup of cheese on the dough. Mix chicken and barbecue sauce together until evenly coated. With hands spread mixture onto pizza dough. Top with onion and pepper. Sprinkle remaining cheese on top. Place on top rack of 425° oven for 15 to 20 minutes.

Sharon Bain
Humboldt, TN

Sausage Crescents

1 pound hot sausage
1 (8-ounce) package cream cheese

2 cans crescent dinner rolls

Brown sausage in skillet. Drain. Mix sausage with cream cheese in a bowl until well blended. Unroll crescent rolls. Dip 1 spoonful of mixture in each crescent roll and roll up. Bake at 350° for 11 to 13 minutes or golden brown. Let cool and cut if desired.

Yield 16 whole or 32 cut rolls.

Sharon Bain
Humboldt, TN

Shrimp Dip

1 (8-ounce) carton sour cream
1 (8-ounce) package cream cheese
1 package Italian salad dressing mix

1 (4¼-ounce) can shrimp, drained and finely chopped
Assorted crackers

Mix all ingredients except crackers and chill. Serve with crackers.

Kay Alexander
Savannah, TN

Snappetizer

1 (8-ounce) package cream cheese
1 can crabmeat, drained

1 bottle cocktail sauce
Assorted crackers and chips

Place the cream cheese on a party plate. Pour the drained crabmeat on the cream cheese. Pour the cocktail sauce over the crab meat. Arrange crackers and chips around the edge of the plate.

Robaya Wolfe Ellis
Savannah, TN

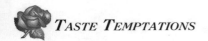

Spinach Balls

2 (10-ounce) packages frozen chopped spinach
1 tablespoon minced dried onions
2 cups herb seasoned stuffing croutons
1 cup grated Parmesan cheese
2 eggs, beaten
3 tablespoons butter or margarine, melted

In a saucepan cook the spinach and dried onions according to spinach package directions. Drain well. In a mixing bowl, combine the spinach mixture, croutons and Parmesan cheese. Stir in beaten eggs and melted butter. Shape into 1-inch balls. Place on a shallow pan. (They may be frozen at this point.) Bake at 375° for 15 to 20 minutes or until thoroughly heated.

Nancy Virgin
Coconut Grove, FL

Spinach Artichoke Dip

1 can artichoke hearts
1 (8-ounce) package cream cheese
2 tablespoons Parmesan cheese
¼ cup milk
1 tablespoon butter
1 (9-ounce) package frozen spinach, cooked and dried
1 teaspoon seasoned salt
4½ tablespoons fresh shredded Parmesan cheese
1 cup sour cream
Tortilla chips

Drain and chop artichokes. Melt cream cheese, Parmesan cheese, milk and butter in microwave. Add spinach, artichokes and seasoning. Top with fresh Parmesan cheese. Bake in 350° oven for 15 minutes. Serve with sour cream and tortilla chips.

Tracy Love Linam
Savannah, TN

Stuffed Mushrooms

1 pound sausage
1 (12-ounce) box processed cheese loaf

3 boxes mushrooms

Brown, drain and crumble sausage. Add cheese to sausage and melt. Clean and stem mushrooms. Stuff mushrooms with mixture and bake 20 to 30 minutes at 350°.

Barbara Prather
Iuka, MS

Scalloped Sweet Potatoes and Apples

A family favorite I learned from my grandmother, Gladys Martin.

8 medium sweet potatoes, cooked
4 medium apples, cored and sliced
½ cup brown sugar

½ cup pecans, chopped
1 teaspoon salt
2 tablespoons butter

Peel cooked and cooled sweet potatoes and cut into ½-inch slices. Arrange layers of potatoes, apples, brown sugar, and pecans in a seasoned, 2-quart casserole dish. Sprinkle with salt and butter. Cover and bake in 350° oven for 50 minutes.

Suzanne Thomas
Savannah, TN

Texas Caviar

1 (14-ounce) can black-eyed peas, drained
1 (15½-ounce) can white hominy, drained
2 medium tomatoes, seeded and chopped

4 green onions, thinly sliced
2 garlic cloves, minced
1 medium bell pepper, finely chopped
½ cup chopped onions
⅓ cup chopped, fresh cilantro or parsley
1 cup picante sauce

Combine all ingredients and mix lightly. Cover and chill at least 2 hours or up to 24 hours, stirring occasionally. Drain.

Yield 7 cups.

Pam Wolfe
Savannah, TN

57

Surprise Spread

You will be tempted to eat this no-bake spread by the spoonful.

1 (8-ounce) package cream cheese, softened
½ cup sour cream
¼ cup mayonnaise
1 small can shrimp, rinsed and drained
1 cup seafood cocktail sauce

2 cups shredded mozzarella cheese
1 bell pepper, chopped
3 green onions, chopped
1 medium tomato, chopped
Assorted crackers

Combine cream cheese, sour cream and mayonnaise. Spread over a 12-inch pizza pan. Scatter shrimp over cheese mixture. Add layers of seafood sauce, cheese, green pepper, onions and tomato. Cover and chill until ready to serve.

Yield 10 to 12 servings.

Jane Riddell
Savannah, TN

Taco Appetizer Platter

1½ pounds ground beef
½ cup water
1   package taco seasoning
2   (8-ounce) packages cream cheese, softened
¼   cup milk
1   (4-ounce) can chopped green chiles, drained

2   medium tomatoes, seeded and chopped
1   cup chopped green onions
1½ cups chopped lettuce
¾   cup honey barbecue sauce
1½ cups shredded Cheddar cheese
Corn chips

In a skillet, cook beef over medium heat until no longer pink. Add water and taco seasoning; simmer for 5 minutes. In a bowl, combine the cream cheese and milk; spread on a 14-inch serving platter or pizza pan. Top with meat mixture. Sprinkle with chiles, tomatoes, onions and lettuce. Drizzle with barbecue sauce. Sprinkle with Cheddar cheese. Serve with corn chips.

Yield 8 to 10 servings.

Becky Kerr
Savannah, TN

Tortilla Rollups

3 (8-ounce) packages cream cheese
1 (8-ounce) carton sour cream
5 small green onions, finely chopped
4 jalapeños, remove seeds and chop finely
1 tablespoons picante sauce
2 tablespoons lime juice
1 package large flour tortillas

Cream together cream cheese and sour cream. Add onions, jalapeños, picante sauce and lime juice. Spread mixture on flour tortillas. Roll each tortilla up. Using a serrated knife, slice each rolled up tortilla into approximately 6 to 8 slices.

Vivian Epps
Adamsville, TN

Tropical Salsa

This is great with tortilla chips, grilled shrimp or black beans and rice.

1 (20-ounce) can pineapple tidbits
1 cup chopped mango
¼ cup honey roasted peanuts, chopped
¾ cup flaked coconut, toasted
¼ cup coconut milk
½ teaspoon lime zest
2 tablespoons fresh lime juice
1 teaspoon sugar
¼ teaspoon salt
¼ teaspoon ground ginger
¼ teaspoon cayenne

Drain pineapple, reserving juice. Stir together pineapple, mango, peanuts and coconut. Stir together reserved pineapple juice, coconut milk and next 6 ingredients; add to pineapple mixture, toss to coat. Chill 30 minutes.

Yield 3 cups.

Rita Rasbach
Savannah, TN

59

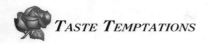

Vegetable Pizza

2 packages crescent dinner rolls
1 (8-ounce) package cream cheese
1 cup mayonnaise

1 package ranch dressing mix
Vegetables, finely chopped (carrots, broccoli, red pepper, cauliflower, etc.)

Spray pizza pan with cooking spray. Spread dinner rolls out onto the pizza pan covering the bottom. Bake at 350° for 10 minutes. Mix cream cheese, mayonnaise and dressing mix. Spread mixture onto baked crust. Sprinkle vegetables over rolls. Refrigerate at least 2 hours before serving.

Yield 36 servings.

Beth Pippin
Pam Wolfe
Savannah, TN

Warm Welcome Appetizer

Serve this with plenty of drink and be prepared to give everyone the recipe.

1 cup sliced jalapeño peppers
16 ounces grated Cheddar cheese

6 eggs, beaten

Place the sliced peppers in a 12 x 12 x 2-inch greased casserole dish. Scatter grated cheese over peppers and drizzle beaten eggs over cheese. Bake for 30 minutes in 350° oven. Cool slightly and cut into 1-inch squares.

Tracy Love Linam
Savannah, TN

Beer Rolls

3 cups all-purpose baking mix
1 cup beer

½ cup sugar

Mix together and drop by spoonfuls into greased muffin tins. Bake at 400° for 15 minutes. Serve immediately.

Charlotte Wolfe
Fort Lauderdale, FL

Baked French Toast

½ cup butter
½ cup maple syrup
½ cup brown sugar
1 loaf day old bread

12 large eggs, beaten
1 cup half-and-half
Salt to taste

Melt the butter, syrup and brown sugar in a skillet. Pour into a 9 x 13 x 2-inch casserole dish. Place 2 layers of bread over the melted mixture. Mix together the beaten eggs, milk and salt over the bread. Soak overnight in the refrigerator. Bake at 375° for 35 to 45 minutes or until browned.

You can vary this by putting cream cheese and/or jam and/or fresh peaches and berries between the layers.

Lois Eyre
Lake Havasu City, AZ

French Toast

8 (⅜-inch thick) slices firm white bread
3 ounces commercial almond paste
3 ounces cream cheese
4 large eggs

½ cup milk
½ teaspoon pure vanilla
3 tablespoons butter
1 tablespoon vegetable oil

Trim the crusts from the bread. In a food processor with the metal blade, process the crust until very fine. Set aside in a shallow dish. Process the almond paste and cream cheese with the metal blade until smooth. Set aside. Put the eggs, milk and vanilla in the work bowl and process just until well mixed. Pour into a shallow dish. Make 4 sandwiches using the almond mixture as a filling. Slice each to form 2 triangles. Dip each in the egg mixture, both sides, then in the crumbs, then in the egg mixture again. Heat the butter and oil in a large skillet over medium high heat. Cook the triangles about 3 minutes per side, or until golden brown.

Yield 4 large servings or 8 brunch servings.

Charlotte Wolfe
Fort Lauderdale, FL

Banana Nut Bread

⅓ cup oil
3 ripe bananas, mashed
½ teaspoon vanilla
3 eggs

2⅓ cups all-purpose baking mix
1 cup sugar
½ cup chopped nuts

Heat oven to 350°. Spray loaf pan with cooking spray. Mix all ingredients until moist. Bake 30 to 40 minutes. Cool before slicing.

Pam Wolfe
Savannah, TN

Broccoli Cornbread

2 sticks butter
4 whole eggs, blended
1 medium onion, diced

1 (10-ounce) package chopped frozen broccoli, thawed and well drained
5 cups cornbread mix

Mix 1½ sticks of butter, eggs, onion broccoli and cornbread mix together. Meanwhile melt the remaining ½ stick of butter in a 13 x 9 x 2-inch glass casserole dish in the oven. Immediately pour batter (it will be thick) into pan and spread evenly. Bake in 350° oven for 30 to 45 minutes.

Janet Hickok
Forest Grove, OR

Marshmallow Rolls

3 cans refrigerated crescent rolls
24 large marshmallows
4 teaspoons cinnamon
1 cup sugar

½ cup butter or margarine, melted
½ cup powdered sugar
2 tablespoons milk
½ teaspoon vanilla

Unroll and separate crescent dough into triangles. Place 1 marshmallow in center of each triangle and roll up, pinching seams to seal. Combine cinnamon and sugar. Dip each roll into melted butter and roll in cinnamon sugar. Place in greased muffin tins and bake at 375° for 10 to 12 minutes. Remove rolls to wire rack to cool. Combine remaining ingredients and drizzle over warm rolls.

A cookie sheet may be placed under muffin tins to catch any drippings.

Robaya Wolfe Ellis
Savannah, TN

Festive Bruschetta with a Three Tomato Salsa

1 cup roma tomatoes, diced
1 cup yellow tomatoes, diced
1 cup tomatillos, diced
½ cup red onion, finely diced
½ teaspoon garlic, minced
½ cup fresh lime juice
¼ cup fresh cilantro, chopped
1 small jalapeño, roasted, de-seeded, minced
2 tablespoons fresh basil leaves, finely shredded
¼ cup extra virgin olive oil
Salt to taste
¼ cup olive oil
1 teaspoon garlic
1 loaf French bread, sliced 1-inch thick, on an angle

In a medium bowl combine the 3 tomatoes, onion, garlic, lime juice, cilantro, jalapeño, basil and ¼ cup extra virgin olive oil. Toss well. Season to taste with salt. Refrigerate salsa for 2 hours. Combine olive oil and garlic in a small bowl; brush on French bread, both sides. Place on cookie sheet and toast under broiler until golden brown. Remove from oven and arrange neatly on a serving platter. Top with generous amounts of the salsa. Serve immediately.

Chef Jill K. Bosich, CEC, CCE
Dean of Culinary Education
Culinard, The Culinary Institute of Virginia College

Monkey Bread

Easy and delicious

4 (10-count) cans buttermilk biscuits
1 stick margarine, melted
¾ cup sugar
¾ brown sugar
3 teaspoons cinnamon
1 cup chopped nuts

Cut each biscuit into fourths and dip in melted margarine. Combine sugars, cinnamon and nuts and roll each piece of biscuit to coat. Put in seasoned Bundt pan or tube pan and bake at 350° for 40 to 50 minutes.

Ruth Hughes
Alta Loma, CA

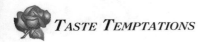 TASTE TEMPTATIONS

Italian Flat Bread

Basic Starter

1 cup bread flour
2 tablespoons dry yeast (not quick rise)

1 cup lukewarm water

Place the starter in a glass bowl and mix well. Cover with plastic wrap and bundle in a large towel. Place in a warm spot until proofed (2 hours to 2½ hours)

Bread

2 cups starter
2 cups water at room temperature
2 tablespoons olive oil

7 cups bread flour
2 tablespoons onion powder

Place starter and water in a large mixing bowl. In another bowl combine the rest of the ingredients. Gradually add the flour mixture to the starter. Work with the dough until it forms a ball. Transfer to a floured working space and knead until smooth and elastic, approximately 7 to 10 minutes. Place dough in a well oiled bowl. Cover with plastic wrap and a towel. Place in a warm place and let dough rise until doubled. Remove from bowl and separate down into 3 equal amounts. Pat dough onto 12-inch greased pizza pans. With fingers poke dough to make indentations. Bake at 400° for 20 to 30 minutes.

Anita Ewoldt
Savannah Cooks
Savannah, TN

Monkey Bread

2 (10-count) cans biscuits
½ teaspoon cinnamon
½ cup granulated sugar
½ cup butter, sliced

¾ cup brown sugar
1 (8-ounce) package cream cheese
½ (7-ounce) jar marshmallow cream
Splash orange juice

Cut biscuits in fourths. Roll in mixture of cinnamon and sugar. Drop pieces in Bundt pan and cover with butter and sprinkle with brown sugar. Bake at 400° for 30 to 40 minutes. Stir together cream cheese, marshmallow cream and orange juice. Serve as dip for pieces of monkey bread.

Charlotte Wolfe
Fort Lauderdale, FL

Jalapeño Cheese Bread

1	cup shortening	2	packages yeast, dissolved in 1 cup warm water
¾	cup sugar		
1½	teaspoons salt	¾	cup honey flavored wheat germ
1	cup boiling water	6	cups whole wheat flour
2	eggs, well beaten	1	cup sliced jalapeño peppers
		1	cup shredded Cheddar cheese

Cream shortening, sugar and salt. Add boiling water; stir until dissolved. Set aside until lukewarm. When the first mixture is lukewarm add beaten eggs and yeast mixture. Sift wheat germ and flour together. Gradually add flour mixture to liquid mixture. Put in a warm area to proof. After first rising, turn onto floured board and knead. Divide dough in half. Roll out into triangle about ¾-inch thick. Spread half of jalapeño peppers on dough and sprinkle half of cheese on top of peppers. Carefully roll dough as in jelly roll fashion. Seal edges and put into greased loaf pan. Let rise again until doubled in size. Bake for 45 minutes at 400°.

Yield 2 loaves.

Charlotte Wolfe
Fort Lauderdale, FL

Mexican Corn Bread Salad

1	package ranch dressing mix	2	(15¼-ounce) cans whole kernel corn, drained
1	cup sour cream		
1	cup mayonnaise	3	large tomatoes, chopped
6	cornbread muffins	10	slices bacon, cooked and crumbled
2	(16-ounce) cans pinto beans, rinsed and drained	2	(8-ounce) packages shredded Mexican cheese blend
1	medium bell pepper, chopped	6	green onions, sliced

In a small bowl, combine the dressing mix, sour cream and mayonnaise. Set aside. Crumble half of the corn muffins into a large glass bowl or trifle dish. In the following order, add layers of half of the beans, bell pepper, sour cream mixture, corn tomatoes, bacon, cheese and onions. Repeat the layers once more with the remaining half of each ingredient. Cover and chill for at least 2 hours. Just before serving, toss the salad until well combined.

Jane Linam
Savannah, TN

Onion Walnut Muffins

4 medium onions, peeled and quartered	1½ teaspoons salt
2 sticks butter, melted and cooled	1 tablespoon baking powder
¾ cup sugar	3 cups walnuts, coarsely chopped
4 eggs, lightly beaten	3 cups all-purpose flour

Preheat oven to 425°. Spray 2 (12-cup) muffin tins with nonstick spray. In a food processor, pulse the onions until pureed. Transfer 2 cups of the onion to a bowl and stir in butter, sugar and eggs. One at a time stir in salt, baking powder, walnuts and flour. Mix thoroughly. Spoon the batter into the prepared tins and bake for 20 minutes, or until the muffins are brown and toothpick inserted in the center comes our clean. Cool muffins in the pan for 10 minutes, then unmold on a wire rack and continue to cool.

The muffins can be frozen for up to 1 week. Thaw completely and rewarm before serving.

Anita Ewoldt
Savannah Cooks
Savannah, TN

Rolls

2 cups milk	2 cups flour, un-sifted
½ cup sugar	¾ teaspoon soda
½ cup solid vegetable shortening	1 teaspoon baking powder
1 package dry yeast	1½ teaspoons salt
3 cups flour, sifted	

Scald milk. Pour milk over sugar and solid shortening. Let cool until lukewarm. Dissolve yeast into milk mixture. Add 3 cups sifted flour and let this rise in bowl for 30 minutes. Sift 2 cups flour, soda, baking powder and salt together and add to mixture. Put in bowl and cover. Refrigerate overnight. Cut out rolls and spread with butter on both sides, fold over and let rise for 2 hours. Bake in 350° oven until golden brown.

Yield 30 to 40 rolls.

Chaney Graham Winters
Savannah, TN

Sally Lunn

4½ cups all-purpose flour
⅓ cup sugar
1 teaspoon salt
2 packages dry yeast

1¼ cups milk
½ cup butter
3 eggs, beaten

Mix 2 cups flour, sugar, salt and yeast in electric mixer. Heat milk and butter until very warm, approximately 120 to 130°. Gradually add to dry ingredients and beat at low speed 2 minutes. Add eggs plus ½ cup flour. Beat 2 minutes. Stir in remaining flour to make soft dough. Cover and let rise 1 hour. Bake a 400° for 35 to 45 minutes. Turn out and cool on rack. Serve warm with butter.

Charlotte Wolfe
Fort Lauderdale, FL

Barbecued Chicken Dip

1 (8-ounce) package cream cheese
2 tablespoons barbecue sauce
½ cup cooked chicken

2 tablespoons green onions, finely chopped
1 box wheat crackers

Spread the cream cheese on a shallow plate to make a 6-inch circle. Spread with barbecue sauce. Sprinkle with chopped chicken and green onions. Serve with crackers.

Robaya Wolfe Ellis
Savannah, TN

Bacon and Cheddar Dip

1 package ranch dip mix
1 pint sour cream

¼ cup bacon bits
1 cup shredded Cheddar cheese

Mix together and serve.

Robaya Wolfe Ellis
Savannah, TN

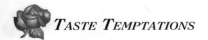

Apple Brickle Dip

1 (8-ounce) package cream cheese, softened
½ cup brown sugar, packed
¼ cup confectioners' sugar
1 teaspoon vanilla

1 (7½-ounce) package almond Brickle chips or 10 ounces English toffee bits
3 medium tart apples, sliced

Mix cream cheese, brown sugar, sugar until smooth. Add vanilla and chips or bits. Serve with sliced apples.

Chris Roberts
Savannah, TN

BLT Dip

1 cup mayonnaise
1 cup sour cream
1 (3-ounce) jar real bacon bits

1 tomato, chopped
Crackers

Mix mayonnaise, sour cream and bacon bits together. Just before serving add 1 chopped tomato. Spread on crackers.

Tastes just like a bacon, lettuce and tomato sandwich

Diane Hardin
Savannah, TN

Brenda's Vegetable Dip

1 (8-ounce) container sour cream
1 (8-ounce) cup mayonnaise
3 tablespoons dried onion flakes or onion powder

3 tablespoons dill weed
Vegetables for dipping

Combine sour cream, mayonnaise, onion flakes or powder and dill weed and mix well. Refrigerate at least 30 minutes to allow flavors to blend (overnight is better.) Serve with chilled vegetables.

Brenda Morenc
Kenner, LA

Bumpy Road Dip

2 pounds lean ground beef
1 package onion soup mix
1 pound American cheese, cubed
1 package light Swiss cheese slices
1 can tomatoes with chiles

1 small can diced jalapeño peppers, drained
1 cup sour cream
   Tortilla chips

Brown ground beef and drain. Place over medium heat in a saucepan. Add onion soup mix and both cheeses and stir until melted, being careful not to scorch. Add tomatoes with chiles and jalapeño peppers. Stir until well blended. Gradually add sour cream, stirring to blend. Continue heating until all ingredients are warm. Do not allow to boil. Serve with tortilla chips.

Charlotte Wolfe
Savannah, TN

Buried Treasures

2 cups mayonnaise
½ cup horseradish, well drained
½ teaspoon MSG, optional
2 teaspoons dry mustard
2 teaspoons lemon juice
½ teaspoon salt
1 pound boiled shrimp

1 pint basket small cherry tomatoes
1 (6-ounce) can pitted black olives, drained
1 (8-ounce) can water chestnuts, drained
½ pound whole mushrooms
½ head cauliflower, broken into bite-size florets

Combine mayonnaise with the seasonings. Add shrimp, tomatoes, olives, water chestnuts and mushrooms. Refrigerate overnight. Just before serving add cauliflower.

Charlotte Wolfe
Fort Lauderdale, FL

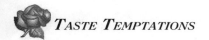

Chili Cheese Dip

1 can tomatoes with chiles
1 can chili with beans
1 can chili without beans
1 (16-ounce) package processed cheese
   loaf

½ pound hot sausage, browned and
   drained
½ pound ground beef, browned and
   drained
1 teaspoon cayenne, more if desired
1 tablespoon garlic powder

Put all ingredients into crockpot and heat until warm.

Sharon Bain
Humboldt, TN

Chili Dip

1 (8-ounce) package cream cheese
¼ cup diced onions, optional

1 (13-ounce) can chili
8 ounces shredded mild Cheddar cheese

Spread cream cheese on the bottom of an 8-inch microwave safe casserole dish. Sprinkle with onions. Pour chili on top. Cover with cheese. Bake at 350° for 10 minutes or microwave on high for 2 minutes. Allow to stand up to 10 minutes before serving.

Robaya Wolfe Ellis
Savannah, TN

Crab Dip

1 (8-ounce) package cream cheese
½ cup sour cream
¼ cup mayonnaise
1 (4 to 6-ounce) can crabmeat
1 cup cocktail sauce

2 cups mozzarella cheese
1 green pepper, chopped
3 green onions, chopped
1 tomato, chopped

Combine cream cheese, sour cream and mayonnaise and spread in the bottom of a 9 x 13-inch dish. Layer remaining ingredients over cheese mixture in order given.

Diane Hardin
Savannah, TN

Chutney Shrimp Dip

6   ounces small shrimp, fresh or frozen, cooked and peeled
3   tablespoons sliced almonds
3   tablespoons coarsely shredded coconut
1   (8-ounce) package cream cheese, softened

3   tablespoons sour cream
1½ teaspoons curry powder
½   cup sliced green onions
½   cup golden raisins, coarsely chopped
1   (8½-ounce) jar prepared chutney

Thaw shrimp, if frozen. Preheat oven to 350°. Spread almonds and coconut in baking pan. Bake for 5 to 10 minutes or until light golden brown, stirring once. In medium bowl, stir together cream cheese, sour cream and curry powder until smooth. Stir in onions and raisins. Gently fold in shrimp. Shape into ball and place on a serving plate. Pour chutney over top and sprinkle with additional almonds and coconut if desired.

Yield 4 cups.

Hilda Crane
Fulton, MS

Crab Dip with Crackers

1   pound crabmeat, flaked
2   (8-ounce) packages cream cheese, softened
1   (8-ounce) carton sour cream
1   tablespoons powdered mustard
¼   cup mayonnaise
    Juice of ½ lemon

Dash of Worcestershire sauce
3   shakes of garlic salt
1½ cups shredded medium Cheddar cheese, divided
Paprika to taste
Crackers

Combine the crabmeat in a large bowl with cream cheese, sour cream, mustard, mayonnaise, lemon juice, Worcestershire sauce, garlic salt and 1 cup of the cheese. Spoon the mixture into a 2-quart casserole dish. Sprinkle with the remaining cheese and paprika. Bake at 325° for 40 minutes. Serve hot or warm with crackers.

Brenda Thrasher
Savannah, TN

Dilly Vegetable Dip

1 (8-ounce) package cream cheese
½ cup finely chopped onion
½ teaspoon minced garlic
1 cup mayonnaise

½ cup fresh parsley, finely chopped, if
    dried, use less
1 boiled egg

Mix cream cheese, onion, garlic, mayonnaise and parsley. Chop the white of the boiled egg and add. Chop yolk and reserve. Refrigerate mixture overnight. Garnish with reserved chopped egg yolk.

George Ann Ingram
Fort Myers, FL

Dream Fruit Dip

My friends love this dip. It is great for parties.

4 (3-ounce) packages cream cheese,
    softened
1 cup confectioners' sugar, un-sifted
1 cup sour cream
1 (7-ounce) jar marshmallow cream

2 teaspoons vanilla extract
1 teaspoon almond extract
2 teaspoons cinnamon
2 tablespoons cognac, optional
    Assorted fruits

In a small bowl of electric mixer, cram the cheese until soft and smooth. Add confectioners' sugar and beat until well blended, add the sour cream and the rest of the ingredients. Blend just until well combined. Place in a pretty bowl. Cover and chill several hours before serving.

Jo Ann Rogers
Memphis, TN

Fruit Dip

1 (8-ounce) package cream cheese
1 cup marshmallow cream

1 (8-ounce) container piña colada
    flavored yogurt
    Assorted fruit

Whip together and serve with assorted fruit.

Vivian Epps
Adamsville, TN

Fruit Dip

1 (8-ounce) can crushed pineapple, undrained
1 (3-ounce) package instant coconut pudding and pie filling
¾ cup milk
½ cup sour cream
Assorted fruit

Combine pineapple, pudding mix, milk and sour cream in blender. Refrigerate several hours before serving with assorted fruit.

May be served in a cantaloupe or pineapple cut in half.

Charlotte Wolfe
Fort Lauderdale, FL

El-Brenda's Dunk

1 (8-ounce) package cream cheese
1 (8-ounce) carton sour cream
1 teaspoon beau monde seasoning
1 teaspoon Worcestershire sauce
1 jar dried beef
2 whole loaves bread

Mix first 5 ingredients together and refrigerate overnight. When ready to serve, cut center from bread leaving a small portion in the bottom. Pour dip in scooped out cavity of bread. Cut the scooped out bread and the second loaf into cubes to use for dipping.

Brenda Dillard
Tupelo, MS

Fresh Vegetable Mexican Dip

3 ripe avocados
3 ripe and firm tomatoes
1 bunch green onions
¾ cup mayonnaise
¾ cup sour cream
2 packages taco seasoning mix
1 can pitted black olives, sliced
Grated Cheddar cheese
Grated Monterey Jack cheese

Peel and mash avocados and spread on bottom of 13 x 9-inch dish. Chop tomatoes and onions and layer on top of avocados. Mix mayonnaise, sour cream and seasoning mix. Spread on top of first mixture. Top with black olives and cheese.

Shelby Gallien
Savannah, TN

73

Fruit Kabobs with Margarita Dip

½ cup sour cream
1 (3-ounce) package cream cheese, cut up and softened
¼ cup sifted confectioners' sugar
1 tablespoon tequila

1 tablespoon orange juice concentrate
1 tablespoon lime juice
½ cup heavy cream
   Angel food or pound cake cubes
   Assorted fresh fruit

For dip, place sour cream, cream cheese, confectioners' sugar, tequila, orange juice concentrate and lime juice in a blender container or food processor bowl. Cover, blend or process until combined. Add heavy cream. Cover, blend or process until fluffy and mixture mounds. Serve immediately or cover and chill up to 24 hours. Serve with small skewers of cake and fruit on serving platter.

Yield 1¾ cups.

Rita Rasbach
Savannah, TN

Hawaiian Grab Bag

2 cups mayonnaise
½ cup sour cream
2 tablespoons horseradish, drained
2 teaspoons powdered mustard
½ teaspoon salt

1 tablespoon freshly squeezed lemon juice
   Black olives, shrimp, water chestnuts, avocado chunks, mushrooms, cherry tomatoes and bell pepper chunks

Combine mayonnaise, sour cream, horseradish, mustard, salt and lemon juice. Add any 5 of remaining ingredients.

Charlotte Wolfe
Fort Lauderdale, FL

Hawaiian Fruit Dip

½ cup sour cream
1 cup milk
1 (3-ounce) package instant vanilla
   pudding

1 (8-ounce) can crushed pineapple,
   undrained
⅓ cup shredded coconut

Combine sour cream, milk and pudding until smooth. Add pineapple and coconut. Mix to combine. Refrigerate for 30 minutes before serving.

Robaya Wolfe Ellis
Savannah, TN

Jiffy Fruit Dip

½ cup marshmallow cream
¼ cup creamy peanut butter
1 teaspoon lemon juice

2 teaspoons water
Assorted fresh fruit

Combine marshmallow cream, peanut butter, lemon juice and water. Stir with fork or whisk until blended. Cover and refrigerate 30 minutes before serving. Serve with fresh fruit.

Robaya Wolfe Ellis
Savannah. TN

Layered Mexican Dip

1 package ranch party dip mix
1 (16-ounce) container sour cream
1 (16-ounce) can refried beans
1 cup shredded Cheddar cheese

1 (2¼-ounce) can sliced ripe olives,
   drained
Chopped tomatoes
Green onions

Mix dip mix with sour cream. Set aside. Spread refried beans in a serving dish. Spread dip and sour cream mixture over beans. Top with Cheddar cheese and olives. Garnish with tomatoes and onions.

Robaya Wolfe Ellis
Savannah, TN

French Bread Spread

1 ounce cream cheese
½ cup mayonnaise
½ cup chopped green onions
   Pepper to taste

   Garlic, if desired
1 loaf French Bread
   Grated cheese

Blend cream cheese, mayonnaise, onions, pepper and garlic in food processor or mixer. Cut bread ¾ through horizontally. Spread evenly with spread tip to tip. Sprinkle with grated cheese. Place on aluminum foil and wrap around loaf. Bake in a 350° oven for 20 minutes or until warm.

Robaya Wolfe Ellis
Savannah, TN

Hot Dip

1 (16-ounce) container sour cream
1 package onion soup mix
1 can chili peppers, chopped

1 can tomatoes with chiles, extra hot
   Chopped jalapeño peppers to taste

Mix together and refrigerate 24 hours before serving.

Charlotte Wolfe
Fort Lauderdale, FL

Mediterranean Dip

1 cup crumbled feta cheese
3 tablespoons cream cheese, softened
1 tablespoon olive oil

   Chopped fresh basil
¾ cup sliced olives
¾ cup sliced tomatoes

Mound mixture of cheeses and olive oil on a plate; press chopped fresh basil around edges. Top with the chopped olives and tomatoes.

Robaya Wolfe Ellis
Savannah, TN

Layered Tamale Dip

2 cans refried beans, heated	1 pint guacamole
2 cups picante sauce	3 tomatoes, seeded and diced
1 small onion, chopped	1 pint sour cream
¼ cup sliced jalapeños	½ pound grated Monterey Jack cheese
1 dozen tamales, steamed and sliced into fourths	1 small can sliced black olives

Mix beans and picante sauce together. Add chopped onions and jalapeños, mix well. In a large clear bowl, put half of the bean mixture. Next add half of the tamales, then half of the guacamole, then half of the diced tomatoes, then half of the sour cream, then half of the grated cheese and half of the black olives. Repeat all layers gain in the same order using the remaining ingredients. May serve at once or refrigerate before serving.

This is tasty warm or cold.

Yield 4 cups.

Judy Leatherwood
Nogal, NM

Mexican Dip

1 can chili with no beans	1 can tomatoes with chiles
1 pound box processed cheese loaf	

Mix all ingredients together and heat on low until it bubbles.

Carole Coats
Savannah, TN

Mexican Dip

1 pound processed cheese loaf	1 can tomato soup
1 can tomatoes with chiles	1 cup rice
1 can whole kernel corn, drained	1 package taco seasoning

Put all ingredients into a crockpot and cook on low for 4 hours.

Lynette Linam
Savannah, TN

Another Mexican Dip

2 (15-ounce) cans turkey chili with
  beans
1 (16-ounce) container sour cream

1 (12-ounce) jar salsa
1½ cups shredded Cheddar cheese
1 (1¼-ounce) package taco seasoning

Layer the chili, sour cream, salsa, Cheddar cheese and ⅓ of the package of taco seasoning on a pie plate or casserole. Heat covered in microwave for 5 minutes or until cheese is thoroughly melted.

Charlotte Wolfe
Fort Lauderdale, FL

Onion Dip

3 (8-ounce) packages cream cheese
2 cups Parmesan cheese

1 cup frozen onions
½ cup mayonnaise

Blend together and bake for 20 minutes at 350°.

Mary Ellen Parks
Bartlett, TN

Pacesetter Picante Dip

1 pound lean ground beef
1 (16-ounce) processed cheese loaf, cut
  into 1-inch squares

1 (8-ounce) jar picante sauce, mild,
  medium or hot
2 cups sour cream

Brown ground beef over medium heat, drain. Add chopped cheese and return to low heat, stirring until cheese is melted. Remove from heat and add picante sauce and sour cream. Stir until blended.

Charlotte Wolfe
Fort Lauderdale, FL

Ranch Dipping Sauce

½ cup creamy ranch dressing
¼ cup sour cream

¼ cup chunky salsa

Mix ingredients together and stir well.

Yield 1 cup.

Robaya Wolfe Ellis
Savannah, TN

Russian Dip

1 medium onion, chopped
2 tablespoons butter
1 can black-eyed peas
1 package ranch dressing mix
1 can artichoke hearts

½ cup mayonnaise
2 tablespoons Parmesan cheese
½ cup sour cram
4 ounces mozzarella cheese
   Crackers

Sauté onion in butter. Mix peas, dressing mix, artichoke hearts, mayonnaise and Parmesan cheese and sour cream. Pour into an 8-inch baking dish. Top with mozzarella cheese. Bake at 350° for 20 minutes. Serve with crackers.

Yield 8 servings.

Bernice Bennett
Florence, AL

Shrimp Dip

1 (8-ounce) package cream cheese,
   softened
½ cup mayonnaise
½ cup chili sauce

¼ cup finely chopped onions
1 small can shrimp, rinsed and well
   drained

Combine ingredients and stir. Refrigerate 3 to 4 hours before serving.

Glenda Alexander
Savannah, TN

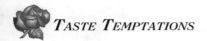

Spinach and Artichoke Dip

This is Kelly Jane's favorite.

1 (8-ounce) package cream cheese, softened
¼ cup mayonnaise
¼ cup grated Parmesan cheese
¼ cup Romano cheese, or omit and use ½ cup Parmesan cheese
 Garlic salt to taste

½ teaspoon dried basil
 Salt and pepper to taste
1 small can artichoke hearts, drained and chopped
½-1 cup frozen chopped spinach, thawed and drained
¼ cup shredded mozzarella cheese

Preheat oven to 350°. Lightly spray a small baking dish with nonstick cooking spray. In a medium bowl, mix together cream cheese, mayonnaise, Parmesan and Romano cheese, garlic salt, basil and salt and pepper. Gently stir in artichoke hearts and spinach. Transfer to baking dish. Top with mozzarella cheese and bake for 25 minutes until bubbly and lightly browned.

Diane Hardin
Savannah, TN

Spinach Dip

1 loaf Hawaiian bread
1 package frozen spinach, cooked and drained, towel dry
1 can water chestnuts, drained and chopped

1 (8-ounce) container sour cream
1 cup mayonnaise
1 package dry vegetable soup mix

Hull out the center of bread. Combine the ingredients and stir until well blended. Pour into the hulled out bread. Use hulled out pieces for dipping.

Lynette Linam
Savannah, TN

Spinach Dip

1 (10-ounce) package frozen chopped
   spinach, drained
1 cup mayonnaise
1 cup sour cream

1 medium onion, chopped
1 (8-ounce) can water chestnuts, chopped
1 (1⅝-ounce) package vegetable soup
   mix

Thaw spinach. Place on a paper towel and press until barely moist. Combine spinach, mayonnaise, sour cream, onion, water chestnuts and vegetable soup mix; stir well. Cover and chill mixture several hours.

Charlotte Wolfe
Fort Lauderdale, FL

Shrimp Dip

2 cups sour cream
2 cups real mayonnaise
1 package Italian dressing mix

1 can small shrimp
1 can water chestnuts, chopped
2 tablespoons grated onion

Mix all ingredients and chill overnight.

Brenda Cornelius
Savannah, TN

Shrimp Spread

1 (3-ounce) package cream cheese
1 cup sour cream
2 teaspoons lemon juice

1 package Italian dressing mix
1 (4¼-ounce) can shrimp, rinsed and
   drained

Blend ingredients. Let stand at least 4 hours before serving.

Charlotte Wolfe
Fort Lauderdale, FL

Smoked Salmon Spread

1 (8-ounce) package cream cheese, softened
1 (8-ounce) tub mascarpone cheese
8 ounces chopped smoked salmon

Salt and pepper to taste
2 teaspoons drained capers
2 tablespoons red onions, finely chopped

In a food processor fitted with the metal blade; use on/off pulses to combine the cream cheese, mascarpone, salmon, salt, pepper, capers and onions until very smooth. Refrigerate for 2 hours before serving.

Charlotte Wolfe
Fort Lauderdale, FL

Southwestern Shrimp Dip

1½ cups sour cream
¾ cup (4-ounces) frozen salad shrimp, thawed, divided

¼ cup prepared salsa
1¼ teaspoons Mexican seasonings
¼ teaspoon salt

In a medium bowl, combine sour cream, ½ cup shrimp, salsa, Mexican seasonings and salt. Mix well. Cover and refrigerate at least 30 minutes or up to 24 hours before serving. To serve, garnish with the remaining ¼ cup shrimp.

Yield 2 cups.

Robaya Wolfe Ellis
Savannah, TN

Sunset Dip

1 (8-ounce) package cream cheese
1 cup shredded Cheddar cheese

1 cup chunky salsa

Spread the cream cheese in a 9-inch microwave-safe pie plate. Sprinkle with Cheddar cheese. Microwave on high for 2 to 3 minutes or until cheese is melted. Top with salsa.

Robaya Wolfe Ellis
Savannah, TN

Taco Dip

2 cans bean dip	1 cup grated Cheddar cheese
1 (8-ounce) carton sour cream	1 can pitted black olives, finely chopped
1 package taco seasoning	1 cup green onions, finely chopped
1 cup mayonnaise type salad dressing	1 large tomato, chopped

Spread bean dip in bottom of glass casserole dish. Mix together sour cream, taco seasoning and salad dressing. Spread over bean dip. Layer remaining ingredients in order given. Chill.

Charlotte Wolfe
Fort Lauderdale, FL

Tamale Dip

1 large can tamales, mashed	1 can tomatoes with chiles
1 pound processed cheese loaf	2 (15-ounce) cans chili

Combine mashed tamales and cheese and heat until cheese is melted. Add tomatoes with chiles and chili. Heat and serve warm.

Charlotte Wolfe
Fort Lauderdale, FL

Tangy Grecian Spread

1 (8-ounce) package cream cheese, softened	2 tablespoons chopped oil packed sun-dried tomatoes
½ cup (2-ounces) crumbled feta cheese	1 clove garlic, minced
3 tablespoons ripe olives	

In a medium bowl, combine all ingredients. Cover and refrigerate at least 30 minutes or up to 24 hours before serving.

Yield 1½ cups.

Robaya Wolfe Ellis
Savannah, TN

Veggie Dip

1 carton frozen spinach, thawed and drained
1 small onion, chopped
1 can water chestnuts, chopped

1 package vegetable soup mix
1 cup sour cream
1 cup real mayonnaise

Mix together and chill.

Charlotte Wolfe
Fort Lauderdale, FL

Vegetable Dip

1 pint mayonnaise
½ cup buttermilk
2 packages dry Italian dressing mix

Dash garlic
Assorted vegetables for dipping

Mix mayonnaise, buttermilk, dressing mix and garlic. Chill 2 hours. Cut up vegetables in bite-sizes.

Linda Callins
Savannah, TN

Veggie Veggie Dip

½ teaspoon powdered mustard
½ teaspoon curry powder
¾ teaspoon Worcestershire sauce
¼ teaspoon grated onion

¾ teaspoon paprika
2 cups mayonnaise
8 drops hot sauce
Salt and pepper to taste

Combine ingredients in large bowl. Mix thoroughly and chill for 24 hours.

Charlotte Wolfe
Fort Lauderdale, FL

White Cheese Dip

1 pound white American cheese
Milk

Jalapeño peppers, finely chopped

Cube cheese and put in saucepan. Over medium-low heat, add just enough milk to melt the cheese to the desired consistency, stirring constantly so the cheese does not burn. Blend in jalapeño peppers to taste. Leftovers may be refrigerated and reheated on the stovetop by adding a little milk and stirred over medium-low heat.

Robaya Wolfe Ellis
Savannah, TN

Party Mix

6 tablespoons butter
4 teaspoons Worcestershire sauce
1 teaspoon seasoned salt

6 cups bite-size, crispy-rice or corn
  cereal squares
2 cups small pretzels, broken in two
1 can mixed nuts

Melt butter and add Worcestershire sauce and salt. Set aside. Combine other ingredients and add to sauce. Microwave on high for 3 minutes and stir. Microwave additional 3 minutes.

Lynn Hinton-Wagoner
Myrtle Beach, SC

Cocktail Pecans

3 tablespoons butter
½ teaspoon seasoned salt
  Dash hot sauce

1 pound pecan halves
3 tablespoons Worcestershire sauce

Put butter, salt and hot sauce in a 12 x 8 x 2-inch baking dish. Place in 300° oven until butter melts. Add pecans, stirring until coated with melted butter. Bake for 20 minutes, stirring occasionally. Sprinkle with Worcestershire sauce and stir again. Continue baking another 15 minutes or until crisp. These freeze well.

Charlotte Wolfe
Fort Lauderdale, FL

Favorite Recipes
FROM MY COOKBOOK

Recipe Name	Page Number

Sweets for the Sweet

Sweets for the Sweet

Apple Cake with Caramel Sauce 91
Apple Nut Cake 92
Apple Sour Cream Streusel Tart 93
Aunt Edith's Fruit Cake 93
Banana Nut Cake 94
Blackberry Wine Cake 94
Best Pound Cake 95
Black Walnut Cake 95
Brazil Nut Date Cake 96
Buttermilk Cake 96
Butternut Pound Cake 97
Cappuccino Cake 97
Cappuccino Chocolate Layer Cake 98
Caramel Pound Cake 99
Cherry Cheese Cake 100
Chocolate Coconut Cake 100
Chocolate Delight Cake 101
Chocolate Cake 102
Chocolate Chip Cake 102
Chocolate Kahlúa Cheesecake 103
Chocolate Sheet Cake 104
Christmas Cake 104
Chocolate Shirley 105
Cherry Berry Cake 106
Christmas Rum Cake 106
Cola Cake 107
Cream Cake 107
Cornmeal Pound Cake 108
Cream Cheese Pound Cake 108
Cream Cheese Pound Cake 109
Crunchy Upside Down Cake 109
Cream Cheese Sheet Cake 110
Cracker Cake 110
Earthquake Cake 111
Fresh Coconut Sheet Cake 111
Fig or Preserve Cake 112
German Chocolate Cake 112
14 Layer Cake 113
Frozen Strawberry Salad 113
Glazed Buttermilk Pecan Lemon Cake
    with Tangy Lemon Icing 114
Gooey Cake 114
Green Meadows
    Six-Week Bran Muffins 115
Chocolate Cake 116
Grand Mama's Banana Pudding 116
Irene's Cake 117
Just Cake 117
Joe Bailey Cake 118
Lemon Ice Box Pie 118
Just Delicious Cake 119
Linda's Surprise 119

Lemonade Cake 120
Love Cake 120
Martian Pound Cake 121
Milk Chocolate Bar Cake 122
Mini Cheesecakes 122
Mint Chocolate Chip Cake 123
Miracle Fruit Cake 123
Miss Daisy's Five Flavor
    Pound Cake with Glaze 124
Mrs. Roxie Sawyner's Pound Cake 124
Orange Slice Cake 125
Orange Pound Cake 125
Chocolate Cookie Cake 126
Original Pound Cake 126
Payday Cake 127
Pecan Cake 127
Peach and Raspberry Meringue Cake 128
Pecan Mango Coconut Cake 129
Pecan Pie Cake 129
Peanut Butter Pound Cake 130
Piña Colada Cake 130
Pineapple Cranberry
    Upside-Down Cake 131
Salad Dressing Cake 131
Poppy Seed Cake 132
Potato Cake 132
Punch Bowl Cake 133
Red Velvet Cake 134
Skillet Coffee Cake 134
Red Velvet Cake 135
Senator Fred Thompson's Mother's
    Fresh Coconut Cake 136
Shirley's Favorite Chocolate Cake 136
Shock Cake 137
Shortcake 137
Sour Cream and Peach Pound Cake 138
Sour Cream Coffee Cake 138
Sweet and Sour Cake 139
Swiss Chocolate Sheet Cake 139
Swiss Chocolate Cake 140
Triple Chocolate Mess for the Crockpot 140
Texas Sheet Cake 141
Tiger Cake 141
Three Musketeer Cake 142
Turtle Cake 142
Uncooked Fruit Cake 143
Upside Down Chocolate Cake 143
Upside Down German Chocolate Cake 144
Wet Caramel Cake 144
Vanilla Wafer Pound Cake 145
White Chocolate Layer Cake 145
Buttermilk Frosting 146

Caramel Icing 146
Chocolate Frosting 146
Yummy Cake 147
Divinity Nut Pie 147
Wonderful Carrot Cake 148
CC's Cherry Chocolate Cake 149
Apple Dumplings 149
Bananas Foster 150
Candy Bar Dessert 150
Cherry Delight 151
Easy Cherry Tart 151
Christmas Salad 151
Chocolate Mint Frozen Dessert 152
Chocolate Yums 152
Death By Chocolate 153
Easy Chocolate Mousse 153
Easy Fruit Salad 154
Homemade Vanilla Ice Cream 154
Jon's Chocolate Dessert 154
Homemade Chocolate Frosty 155
Homemade Eggless Ice Cream 155
Ice Cream Sandwich Dessert 155
Mexican Chocolate Bread Pudding 156
Piña Colada Wedges 157
Sawdust Salad 157
Peach Crisp 158
South African Milk Tart 158
Pumpkin Cream Cheese Rollup 159
Red and White Delight 160
Strawberry Soufflé 160
Strawberry Angel Food Dessert 161
Malva Pudding 161
Telephone Pudding 162
Tiramisu 162
Summer Delight 163
Caramel Sauce 163
Hot Fudge Sauce 163
Raspberry Almond Tarts 164
Caramel Walnut Tart 164
Lemon Tart 165
Apple Cobbler Pie 165
Apple Crisp 166
Aunt Dutchie's Chocolate Pie 166
Apple Turnovers 167
Apple Pie 167
Banana Split Pie 168
Bread and Butter Pudding 168
Black Walnut Pie 169
Burnt Cream 169
Buttermilk Pie 170
Buttermilk Pie 170
Chocolate Chess Pie 170

Caramel Coconut Cream Cheese Pies 171
Caramel Custard 171
Caramel Pie 172
Cape Dutch Brandy Pudding 172
Coconut Caramel Pie 173
Chocolate Pie 173
Chocolate Chess Pies 174
Easy Lemon Chess Pie 174
Easy Pecan Pie 174
Easy Custard Pie 175
Egg Custard Pie 175
Fresh Peach Pie 175
Egg Nog Pie 176
Grandmother White's Key Lime Pie 176
Key Lime Pie 176
South Florida Key Lime Pie 177
Lemon Rub Pie 177
Marie's Apple Pie 177
Hot Lemon Sauce Pudding 178
Millionaire's Pie 178
Millionaire Pie 179
Mother's Egg Custard 179
Old-Fashioned Chess Pie 179
Mother's Old-Fashioned Coconut Pie 180
Mrs. Katye's Pecan Tarts 180
Mother's Chocolate Pie 181
Old-Fashioned Chess Pie 181
Old-Fashioned Chocolate Pie 182
Peanut Butter Pie 182
Pecan Pie Tarts 182
Pecan Pie 183
Pecan Tarts 183
Perfect Pie Crust 183
Piña Colada Pie 184
Pineapple Delight Pie 184
Sooo Easy Chocolate Pie 184
Pineapple Cloud Pie 185
Cracker Pie 185
Strawberry Custard Pie 186
Sweet Potato Pie 186
Sweet Potato Pie 187
Turtle Pie 187
Two-Minute Pie 188
Applesauce Salad 188
Broccoli-Raisin Salad 188
Wolfe's Dairy Bar Coconut Pie 189
Wolfe's Dairy Bar Chocolate Pie 189
Orange Pineapple Salad 190
Frozen Fruit Cups 190
Creamsicle Salad 190
Grape Party Salad 191
Hot Spiced Fruit 191

Mucho Good Fruit Compote 191
Lemon Strawberry Salad 192
Orange Cream Fruit Salad 192
Pineapple Delight 193
Piña Colada Wedges 193
Buckeyes 193
Strawberry Nut Salad 194
Candy Bar Fudge 194
Double Chocolate Cookies 195
Chocolate Chip Cookies 195
Chow Mein Candy Clusters 196
Coconut Bonbons 196
English Toffee 196
Date Bourbon Crispies 197
Divinity 197
Chocolate Balls 198
Chocolate Candy 198
Buttermilk Fudge 199
Microwave Candy 199
Homemade Toffee Bars 199
English Toffee 200
Holiday Orange Vodka Truffles 200
Peanut Brittle 201
Microwave Peanut Brittle 201
Millionaires 201
Peanut Butter Treats 202
Peanut Butter Snowballs 202
Cheese Fudge 202
Penuche 203
Rum Balls 203
Quick Candy Bars 204
Brownies with Caramel Sauce 204
Unbaked Chocolate Oatmeal Cookies 205
Brown Sugar Pecan Cookies 205
Cracker Cookies 206
CC's White Chocolate Chunk Cookies 206
Butterscotch Muffins 207
Cake Mix Cookies 207
Chocolate Chews 207
Chewy Oatmeal Cookies 208
Chocolate Chip Cookies 208
Chocolate Coconut Bars 209
Chocolate Oatmeal Bars 209
Chocolate Oatmeal Cookies 210
Cinnamon Buttons 210
Cream Cheese Cookies 210
Creamy Cashew Brownies 211
Crystal's Cookies 211
Date Bars 212
Della's Butter Cookies 213
Double Chocolate Bars 213
Dream Bars 214

Fudge Brownies 214
Extra Good Cookies 215
Graham Cracker Bars 215
Freckles 216
Gene's Tea Cakes 216
Gingersnaps 217
LJ's Chocolate Peanut Butter
      Oatmeal Cookies 217
Hedgehogs 218
Lemon Squares 218
Lollipop Cookies 219
Mexican Wedding Cookies 219
Mackie Nell's 100 Cookies 220
Mint Sugar Cookies 220
Mother's Brownies 221
Nana Bars 221
Oatmeal Chess Bars 222
Oatmeal Cookies 222
Orange Blossoms 223
Peachy Potato Cookies 223
Overnight Cookies 224
Peanut Butter Bars 224
Peanut Butter Oat Bars 225
Pecan Pie Muffins 225
Pecan Tassies 226
Potato Chip Cookies 226
Potato Chip Cookies 227
Pumpkin Squares 228
Rocky Road Clusters 228
Russian Tea Cakes 229
Sinful Squares 229
Skinny Hermits 230
Tea Cakes 230
Sandies 231
Sour Cream Cookies 231
Toffee Bars 232
Walnut Bars 232
Vienna Bars 233
Walnut Whoppers 233
Baked Popcorn 234
Chocolate Dipped Peppermint Crunch 234
Fruit Juice Pops 235
Jigglers 235
Party Pecans 235
Nuts and Corn 236
Party Popcorn 236
Cornflake Crunch 236
Snowflake Pecans 237
Chocolate Chip Truffles 237
Sweet Nothings 238
Snack Attack 238

Apple Cake with Caramel Sauce

2 cups self-rising flour
2 cups sugar
2 eggs
¾ cup cooking oil
1 teaspoon vanilla

1 teaspoon allspice
1 teaspoon nutmeg
1 teaspoon cinnamon
3 cups apples, sliced

Stir together flour, sugar, eggs, cooking oil, vanilla, allspice, nutmeg and cinnamon. Add apples. Cook at 350° in a 13 x 9 x 2-inch greased pan for 45 minutes.

Caramel Sauce

1 cup sugar
½ cup water

¾ cup heavy cream
1 tablespoon butter

Combine sugar and water in heavy saucepan. Bring to a boil over medium-high heat. Boil, without stirring, until syrup turns amber, about 15 minutes. Do not allow it to turn dark brown or it will be bitter. Remove pan from heat and cool 2 minutes. Carefully pour in cream, stir in butter and return pan to heat. Cook, stirring until smooth, about 1 minute. Serve warm over squares of cake.

Sauce can be cooled and refrigerated up to 1 week. Reheat slowly over low heat or in microwave before serving.

Patricia Roe
Savannah, TN

Apple Nut Cake

1 cup oil	1 teaspoon cinnamon
3 whole eggs	1 teaspoon nutmeg
2 cups sugar	1 teaspoon cloves
1 teaspoon vanilla	3 cups diced apples
3 cups flour	1 cup chopped pecans
1 teaspoon soda	½ cup baking raisins

Mix oil, eggs, sugar and vanilla. Set aside. Sift together flour, soda, cinnamon, nutmeg and cloves. Mix with first mixture. Add apples, pecans and raisins. Pour mixture into greased Bundt pan or tube pan. Place in cold oven, set at 350°. Bake 1 hour and 10 minutes. Remove from pan while hot.

Cream Cheese Frosting

1 (8-ounce) package cream cheese, softened	1 teaspoon vanilla
1 (16-ounce) box confectioners' sugar	2 teaspoons cream

Combine ingredients and mix until smooth. Mixture should be on the thick side. Frost cake.

May sprinkle cake with cinnamon sugar if desired.

Fran Muller
Fort Lauderdale, FL

Apple Sour Cream Streusel Tart

1 cup flour	½ cup sugar
2 tablespoons sugar	½ teaspoon vanilla
¼ teaspoon salt	4 medium Granny Smith apples, peeled
6 tablespoons cold butter cut in small	and quartered into slices
pieces	¾ cup pecans, coarsely chopped
2 tablespoons ice water	½ cup sugar
1 cup sour cream	½ cup flour
1 large egg	⅓ cup cold butter cut into small pieces
2 tablespoons flour	½ teaspoon cinnamon

Mix together 1 cup flour 2 tablespoons sugar, salt, 6 tablespoons butter and ice water. Roll out and put in pie pan. Set aside. Beat sour cream, egg, 2 tablespoons flour, ½ cup sugar and vanilla. Set aside. Lay sliced apples on crust and pour sour cream mixture over apples. Mix together ¾ cup pecans, ½ cup flour, ⅓ cup butter and ½ teaspoon cinnamon and sprinkle over tart. Bake at 350° for 45 minutes or until brown.

Jan Repp
Broadview Heights, OH

Aunt Edith's Fruit Cake

1 (8-ounce) box raisins	1 teaspoon baking powder
1½ cups sugar	1½ teaspoons cinnamon
1½ cups water	1 teaspoon allspice
1 tablespoon flour	½ teaspoon cloves
2 eggs, beaten	½ teaspoon salt
2½ cups flour	1 cup walnuts, chopped
1 teaspoon soda	1 cup candied fruit

Combine raisins, sugar and water. Bring to a boil and cook, covered at lowest heat for 5 minutes. Add 1 tablespoon flour. Sir and then cool. When cool add 2 beaten eggs. Sift together flour, soda, baking powder, cinnamon, allspice, cloves and salt. Add to raisin mixture. Add walnuts and candied fruit. Pour into a round tube pan or angel food pan. Bake at 350° approximately 1 hour.

Lois Eyre
Lake Havasu City, AZ

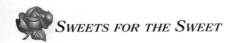

Banana Nut Cake

1½	cups vegetable oil	½	teaspoon salt
1	stick butter	3	cups all-purpose flour
2	cups sugar	1½	cups raisins
4	eggs	1½	cups chopped nuts
2	teaspoons cinnamon	6	bananas, mashed. Bananas should be
1	teaspoon cloves		very ripe
2	teaspoons soda		

Mix together oil, butter and sugar. Add eggs, cinnamon, cloves, soda and salt and cream well. Add flour, raisins, nuts and bananas. Bake in Bundt pan at 300° until cake is firm to touch.

This recipe is one my family has used for over thirty years. It was given to us by my late sister who made the best cakes in the family.

Nyoka Beer
Cordova, TN

Blackberry Wine Cake

1	box white cake mix	½	cup chopped pecans
1	package blackberry gelatin	1	stick margarine
4	eggs	½	cup confectioners' sugar
½	cup vegetable oil	½	cup blackberry wine
1	cup blackberry wine		Confectioners' sugar

Beat the first 5 ingredients in a mixer bowl at low speed just until moistened. Beat at medium speed for 2 minutes, scraping the sides of the bowl frequently. Grease and flour a tube pan. Sprinkle the pecans in the bottom of the tube pan. Add the batter. Bake at 325° for 45 to 50 minutes or until cake tests done. Melt the margarine in a saucepan over medium heat. Stir in the confectioners' sugar and ½ cup wine. Bring to a boil, stirring constantly. Remove 3 tablespoons of the glaze to a small bowl. Pour the remaining glaze over the warm cake in the tube pan. Let stand 30 minutes. Invert onto a serving plate. Let stand until cool. Stir enough additional confectioners' sugar into the reserved glaze to make of desired consistency. Spoon over cake.

Yield 16 servings

Robaya Wolfe Ellis
Savannah, TN

Best Pound Cake

2 sticks butter
½ cup shortening
3 cups sugar
5 eggs
3 cups all-purpose flour

½ teaspoon baking powder
½ teaspoon salt
1 cup milk
1 tablespoon vanilla flavoring

Cream butter, shortening and sugar. Add eggs and cream well. Add flour, baking powder, and salt alternately with milk. Add flavoring. Bake at 325° for 1½ hours.

Barbara Linam
Muscle Shoals, AL

Black Walnut Cake

1 stick butter
½ cup vegetable oil
2 cups sugar
5 egg yolks
2 cups flour
1 teaspoon soda

1 cup buttermilk
1 teaspoon vanilla
1 (3½-ounce) can flaked coconut
1 cup black walnuts, chopped
5 egg whites, stiffly beaten

Cream butter and vegetable oil. Add sugar. Beat egg yolks and add to mixture. Combine flour and soda. Add alternately with buttermilk. Stir in vanilla. Add coconut and nuts. Fold in egg whites Bake in 3 greased and floured 8-inch pans. Bake at 350° for 25 minutes. Frost

Frosting

4 (3-ounce) packages cream cheese, softened
¾ stick butter

2 teaspoons vanilla
1½ boxes confectioners' sugar
1 cup black walnuts

Cream together cream cheese and butter. Stir in remaining ingredients until smooth.

Charlotte Wolfe
Fort Lauderdale, FL

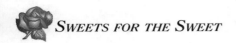

Brazil Nut Date Cake

¾ cup all-purpose flour
½ teaspoon baking powder
¾ cup sugar
½ teaspoon salt
3 cups whole Brazil nuts, about 1 pound

1 pound whole pitted dates
1 cup whole maraschino cherries, well drained
3 large eggs, well beaten
1 teaspoon pure vanilla extract

Preheat oven to 300°. Grease well a 9 x 5 x 3-inch loaf pan and line with wax paper. Set aside. In a large mixing bowl, whisk together flour, baking powder, sugar and salt. Transfer to a piece of wax paper. In same bowl, combine nuts, dates and cherries. Sprinkle dry ingredients over mixture and toss well until everything is well coated. Stir together beaten eggs and vanilla and stir into fruit mixture, mixing well. Pack into prepared pan, spreading evenly and firmly. Pan will be quite full. Bake in center of oven for 1 hour and 45 minutes. Let cool in pan on a wire rack for at least 1 hour before removing cake from the pan. Let cake cool completely, preferably overnight, before slicing.

Yield 24 servings

Mary Ann McCaleb
Fort Lauderdale, FL

Buttermilk Cake

1¾ cups butter
3⅓ cups sugar
8 eggs
4¼ cups cake flour

¼ teaspoon baking soda
½ cup buttermilk
¼ cup pure vanilla

Cream butter and sugar together until very light and fluffy. Add eggs, one at a time, beating well after each addition. Add sifted dry ingredients alternately with the buttermilk and vanilla. Bake in a buttered and floured Bundt pan at 350° for 1 hour and 15 minutes. Remove cake and immediately turn out onto cake rack, being very careful. Cool.

Mary Coats
Corinth, MS

Butternut Pound Cake

2 cups sugar
2 eggs
1 cup oil

2 tablespoons butternut flavoring
2 cups self-rising flour
1 cup milk

Combine sugar, eggs and oil. Add flavoring. Add flour alternating with milk. Pour into a well greased and floured Bundt pan and bake at 350° for 35 to 45 minutes.

This is delicious with strawberries or peaches.

Robaya Wolfe Ellis
Savannah, TN

Cappuccino Cake

1 box yellow cake mix
½ cup brown sugar
½ cup sugar

4 tablespoons baking cocoa
1 cup cold, strong, coffee

Prepare cake mix according to package directions and pour into a 13 x 9 x 2-inch baking pan. Combine sugars and cocoa and sprinkle over batter. Pour coffee over cake mixture. Bake at 350° for 40 minutes. Serve warm.

Robaya Wolfe Ellis
Savannah, TN

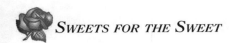

Cappuccino Chocolate Layer Cake

6	tablespoons water	2	large eggs
3	tablespoons sugar	2	teaspoons vanilla
1	tablespoon instant espresso powder	1½	sticks butter
4	ounces unsweetened chocolate, chopped	¾	cup sugar
		¾	cup half-and-half milk
2	cups flour	4	teaspoons instant coffee powder
1½	teaspoons baking powder	6	ounces unsweetened chocolate, chopped
1	teaspoon cinnamon		
¼	teaspoon salt	4	ounces semi sweet chocolate, chopped
2	teaspoons instant coffee powder		
1½	cups milk	1	teaspoon vanilla
2	cups sugar	2½	cups confectioners' sugar
1	stick butter, room temperature	4	teaspoons ground cinnamon

Combine first 3 ingredients and heat in microwave. Set aside. Preheat oven to 350°. Butter 2 (9-inch) cake pans, line with parchment paper and butter and flour. Melt chocolate in double boiler or in a plastic bag set into hot water in the microwave. Keep warm. Sift flour, baking powder, cinnamon and salt and set aside. Stir coffee into milk until dissolved and set aside. Using an electric mixer, beat sugar and butter in large bowl until well blended. Beat in eggs one at a time. Mix in melted chocolate and vanilla. Add dry ingredients alternately with milk mixture in three additions. Divide batter between pans and bake until tester comes out clean, about 35 minutes. Cool in pans for 10 minutes, turn out onto racks and cool completely. Peel off paper. Combine butter, sugar, cream and coffee and heat until all is dissolved and mix simmers. Remove from heat. Add both chocolates, whisk until smooth. Add vanilla. Sift in powdered sugar and whisk until all is incorporated and frosting is smooth. Press plastic to surface and chill until just firm enough to spread, about 1½ hours. Cut each cake in half horizontally and brush each layer with the coffee syrup and ¾ cup of the frosting. Repeat layering. Spread remaining frosting over top and sides of cake.

Janet Hickok
Forest Green, OR

Caramel Pound Cake

1 cup firmly packed dark brown sugar
1 cup firmly packed light brown sugar
1 cup sugar
1 cup butter, softened
½ cup vegetable oil
5 large eggs

3 cups all-purpose flour
½ teaspoon baking powder
½ teaspoon salt
1 cup milk
½ teaspoon vanilla extract

Beat sugars and butter at medium speed with an electric mixer until blended. Add oil, beat until blended. Add eggs, one at a time, beating just until yellow disappears. Combine flour, baking powder and salt; add to butter mixture, alternating with milk, beginning and ending with flour mixture. Beat at low speed just until blended after each addition. Stir in vanilla extract. Pour batter into a greased and floured 10-inch tube or Bundt pan. Bake at 325° for 1 hour and 20 minutes or until a wooden tooth pick inserted in center comes out clean. Cool in pan on wire rack for 10 minutes. Remove from pan and cool on wire rack. Drizzle with Caramel Frosting.

Caramel Frosting

1 (16-ounce) package light brown sugar
½ cup butter or margarine
1 (5-ounce) can evaporated milk

Dash of salt
½ teaspoon baking powder
½ teaspoon vanilla extract

Bring first 4 ingredients to a boil in a medium saucepan, stirring constantly for 3 minutes. Remove from heat; add baking powder and vanilla. Beat at medium speed with electric mixer 5 to 7 minutes or until thickened. Quickly drizzle over cake.

Barbara Linam
Muscle Shoals, AL

Cherry Cheese Cake

My whole family loves this cake. We make it quite often
for special occasions, usually around Christmas or Valentines.

1 box white cake mix	4 cups confectioners' sugar
2 (8-ounce) packages cream cheese, softened	1 pint heavy cream, whipped
	2 (21-ounce) cans cherry pie filling

Prepare cake mix according to package directions. Pour into 2 greased and floured 13 x 9 x 2-inch pans. Bake at 350° for 20 minutes. Cool. In a mixing bowl beat the cream cheese and sugar until fluffy. Fold in the whipped cream. Spread over each cake. Top with pie filling. Chill 4 hours or overnight.

Yield 24 to 30 servings

Sheryl Wolfe
Savannah, TN

Chocolate Coconut Cake

1 (7-ounce) package sweetened coconut	½ teaspoon baking soda
½ cup sweetened condensed milk	½ teaspoon salt
1 large egg white	1½ sticks butter, softened
3 ounces bittersweet or semisweet chocolate	1 cup plus 2 tablespoons sugar
2 cups all-purpose flour	3 eggs
½ cup cocoa powder	2½ teaspoons pure vanilla
2 teaspoons baking powder	1½ cups plain nonfat yogurt

Preheat oven to 350°. Butter and flour a Bundt pan. Mix coconut, sweetened condensed milk and egg white together. Shape into a rope and chill in refrigerator about 20 minutes. Melt chocolate and cool. Sift together flour, cocoa powder, baking powder, baking soda and salt. Set aside. In large mixer bowl beat butter until creamy. Add sugar and beat until light and fluffy. Add eggs, one at a time, beating well after each addition. Add melted chocolate and vanilla. Beat in the dry ingredients alternating with yogurt. Pour into Bundt pan. Take the coconut rope and join ends and press down into the batter. Be sure all coconut is covered with batter. Bake for 1 hour.

If desired you may use any chocolate icing to put only on the top.

Linda Patterson
Savannah, TN

Chocolate Delight Cake

2 cups flour
2 cups sugar
2 sticks butter or margarine
4 tablespoons cocoa powder
1 cup water

½ cup milk
1 teaspoon vinegar
1 teaspoon vanilla
1 teaspoon soda
2 eggs, beaten

Mix flour and sugar in a large bowl. Into a saucepan put butter or margarine, cocoa powder and water. Bring to a boil and pour over the flour mixture and mix well. Add milk, vinegar, vanilla, soda and eggs. Mix well and pour into a 13 x 9 x 2-inch greased pan. Bake at 375° for 25 to 30 minutes. Five minutes before cake is done prepare frosting.

Frosting

1 stick butter or margarine
4 tablespoons cocoa powder
6 tablespoons milk

1 (16-ounce) box confectioners' sugar
1 cup chopped pecans
4 teaspoons vanilla

Bring butter or margarine, cocoa powder and milk to a rolling boil. Remove from heat. Add confectioners' sugar, pecans and vanilla. Stir until well blended and pour over warm cake. Spread evenly.

George Ann Ingram
Fort Myers, FL

101

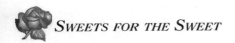

Chocolate Cake

1 stick butter	2 cups sugar
1 cup water	4 eggs
2 tablespoons cocoa powder	½ cup buttermilk
½ cup oil	1 teaspoon cinnamon
2 cups flour	1 teaspoon soda

Bring butter, water, cocoa powder and oil to boil. Pour over sifted flour and sugar. Mix well. Add eggs, mix in buttermilk, then cinnamon and soda. Bake at 400° 20 to 25 minutes. Ice while hot.

Icing

3 tablespoons cocoa powder	1 (16-ounce) box confectioners' sugar
1 tablespoon buttermilk	¾ cup chopped pecans
1 stick butter	1 teaspoon vanilla

Bring cocoa powder and buttermilk to a boil. Add butter and stir until melted. Add sugar, pecans and vanilla and stir until dissolved. Pour over cake while warm.

Hilda Riggins
Naples, FL

Chocolate Chip Cake

1 box yellow cake mix	¼ cup water
4 eggs	1 (8-ounce) carton sour cream
½ cup vegetable oil	1 cup chopped nuts
1 package instant chocolate pudding	1 (12-ounce) package chocolate chips

Mix cake mix, eggs, vegetable oil, pudding mix, water and sour cream until smooth. Add nuts and chocolate chips. Pour into greased Bundt or tube pan and bake at 350° for 55 minutes.

Icing

1 (16-ounce) box confectioners' sugar	1 stick butter
1 (8-ounce) package cream cheese, softened	1 tablespoon milk
	1 teaspoon vanilla

Combine sugar, cream cheese and butter, beating until smooth. Add milk and vanilla.

Kay Alexander
Savannah, TN

Chocolate Kahlúa Cheesecake

1½ cups chocolate wafer crumbs
¼ cup melted butter
2 tablespoons sugar
1¾ cups semi-sweet chocolate chunks, divided
1 cup heavy cream, divided
¼ cup plus 2 tablespoons Kahlúa, divided

3 (8-ounce) packages cream cheese, softened
1 cup sugar
⅓ cup cocoa powder
3 eggs
1 teaspoon vanilla extract
1 tablespoon confectioners' sugar

To prepare crust, mix chocolate wafer crumbs, butter and 2 tablespoons sugar. Press onto bottom and part way up side of a 9-inch springform pan. Freeze for 5 minutes and then bake at 350° for 10 minutes. In a microwave safe bowl, melt ¾ cup chocolate chunks on high for 1 minute or until melted, stir. Add ¼ cup heavy cream and ¼ cup Kahlúa. Stir until blended and set aside. In mixer bowl, beat cream cheese and sugar until fluffy. Add cocoa powder and blend well. Add eggs one at a time, beating well after each. Stir in vanilla and reserved chocolate mixture. Pour over crust, bake 10 minutes at 400°, then decrease to 275° and bake 45 minutes. Remove from oven to cool, loosen cake from rim of pan and remove. Melt remaining chocolate chunks in microwave on high until melted. Stir in ¼-cup heavy cream and 2 tablespoons Kahlúa and blend well. Spread over top of cake and refrigerate for 6 hours. At serving time beat remaining heavy cream and powdered sugar until stiff. Garnish cake as desired with cream. Keep refrigerated.

Pam Wolfe
Savannah, TN

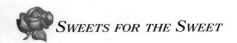

Chocolate Sheet Cake

2 cups sugar
2 cups all-purpose flour
1 teaspoon baking soda
2 sticks butter
4 tablespoons cocoa powder

1 cup water
½ cup buttermilk
2 eggs
1 tablespoon vanilla

Combine sugar, flour and soda and set aside. Over low heat, melt butter, cocoa powder and water. Bring to a boil and pour over dry ingredients. Add buttermilk, eggs and vanilla and mix well. Pour in floured 17 x 11 x ¾-inch prepared pan. Bake at 400° for 20 minutes.

Frosting
1 stick butter
4 tablespoons cocoa powder
7 tablespoons buttermilk

1 (16-ounce) box confectioners' sugar
¾ cup pecans or walnuts

Melt butter, cocoa powder and buttermilk over low heat. Remove and add confectioners' sugar and nuts. Spread over cake while frosting is hot.

Shirley Huddleston
Booneville, MS

Christmas Cake

1 box yellow cake mix
1 stick butter, melted
1 egg
1 cup pecans, chopped

1 (16-ounce) box confectioners' sugar
4 eggs
1 (8-ounce) package cream cheese

Mix first 4 ingredients together and lightly press into a 11 x 9 x 2-inch, well greased pan. Mix last 3 ingredients together until creamy. Pour on top of the cake batter and bake at 350° for 1 hour and 15 minutes.

Charlotte Wolfe
Fort Lauderdale, FL

Chocolate Shirley

1 box Devil's Food cake mix
1 small box vanilla instant pudding mix
¾ cup oil
¼ cup water
3 eggs

1 cup sour cream
⅛ teaspoon chili powder
1 tablespoon bourbon
1 cup chocolate chips
1 cup chopped nuts

Mix first 8 ingredients with mixer. Then add chocolate chips and nuts. Bake in greased Bundt pan for 45 to 50 minutes at 350°. Cool and turn out on rack and cool completely. After cake is cooled turn upside down (you may want to put it back into the pan to keep it from splitting). Dig out a trench about 1-inch deep and 1-inch wide, reserve pieces. Fill with filling and put dug out pieces of cake back onto cake covering filling. Invert onto cake plate. Top with chocolate frosting. Refrigerate.

Filling

½ cup sour cream
½ cup confectioners' sugar

1 (8-ounce) carton frozen non-dairy whipped topping, thawed

Mix sour cream and sugar together. Add whipped topping.

Chocolate Icing

2 (8-ounce) packages cream cheese, softened
1 stick butter, softened

1 (16-ounce) box confectioners' sugar
½ cup cocoa powder, more if desired

Cream cream cheese and butter until well blended. Add sugar and cocoa powder. Mix until smooth.

Charlotte Wolfe
Fort Lauderdale, FL

Cherry Berry Cake

1   box white or yellow cake mix
1   cup corn oil
½   cup whole milk
4   large eggs
1   cup coconut

1   small box cherry flavored gelatin
1   (10-ounce) package frozen
      strawberries, thawed
1½ cups chopped pecans

Mix cake mix with corn oil, whole milk, then add eggs, beating well after each egg is added. Add the remaining ingredients and blend well. Bake in 2 prepared 9-inch pans. Bake at 350° for 30 minutes or until layers test done. Cool completely and frost.

Frosting
1   stick butter
2   (8-ounce) packages cream cheese,
      softened

½   cup frozen strawberries, thawed and
      drained
1   (16-ounce) box confectioners' sugar
1   cup chopped pecans

Blend butter and cream cheese until smooth and well combined. Add remaining ingredients and mix until blended. Keep cake in refrigerator.

Charlotte Wolfe
Fort Lauderdale, FL

Christmas Rum Cake

Preparation time: Depends

Before U start, check the rum to make sure of the quantity. Select large measuring bowl, cup, etc., then check the rum again. With an electric mixer eat 1 cup of sugar in a large fluffy bowl. Check rum again.....Add 3 large eggs, 2 cups fried druit and bat until very high. If fruit sticks to beaters pry out with a drewscriber. Check rum again.....Add 3 cups of baking powder, 1 pint of rum, 1 teaspoon of toda and 1 cup of pepper. Sift in 1 pint of lemon juice and fold in chopped buttermilk and strained nuts. Check rum.....Add 1 babblespoon of scrown burger or whatever color U have. Check rum again.....Turn pan to 350°, grease oven and pour whole mess in.

What do you mean this isn't a Cerry Dristmass?????

Charlotte Wolfe
Fort Lauderdale, FL

Cola Cake

1 box yellow cake mix
4 eggs
1 (10-ounce) bottle warm cola

1 box instant chocolate pudding mix
½ cup oil
2 teaspoons vanilla flavoring

Mix above ingredients and bake according to package directions.

Icing

1 (8-ounce) package cream cheese
½ cup margarine
1 (16-ounce) package confectioners' sugar

4 tablespoons cocoa powder
2 teaspoons vanilla flavoring

Combine cream cheese and margarine and cream with mixer until well blended. Add confectioners' sugar and cocoa powder, blend well. Add vanilla.

Diane Hardin
Savannah, TN

Cream Cake

4 eggs
⅔ cup sugar
½ cup oil

1 (8-ounce) carton sour cream
1 box white or yellow cake mix
1 cup chopped pecans or black walnuts

Beat eggs, add sugar and oil. Mix well. Add sour cream and mix. Add cake mix and stir until mixture is well blended. Add nuts. Pour into prepared Bundt pan and bake at 350° for 55 minutes. This cake will crack. Check for doneness. Let cool for about 20 minutes before removing from pan.

Barbara Linam
Muscle Shoals, AL

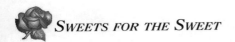

Cornmeal Pound Cake

2	sticks butter	2	cups all-purpose flour
2½	cups granulated sugar	1	cup self-rising cornmeal mix
1	teaspoon pure vanilla	1	cup buttermilk
5	eggs		

Grease and flour a 10-inch or 12-inch Bundt pan. Combine butter, sugar and vanilla in a large mixer bowl. Beat until light and fluffy. Add eggs, one at a time, beating well after each addition. Combine flour and cornmeal in a bowl and stir to mix. Add flour mixture to butter mixture alternately with buttermilk, beginning and ending with flour mixture. Mix well after each addition. Pour batter into prepared pan. Bake in preheated 350° oven for 50 to 65 minutes or until tests done. Cool upright for 30 minutes. Invert onto serving plate and cool completely.

Glaze
1	cup buttermilk	1 cup sugar

Combine buttermilk and sugar in a sauce pan and bring to a boil. Reduce heat and simmer for 5 minutes or until thick. Pour over cake.

Charlotte Wolfe
Fort Lauderdale, FL

Cream Cheese Pound Cake

1½	cups margarine, softened	6	eggs
1	(8-ounce) package cream cheese, softened	3	cups all-purpose flour
			Pinch salt
3	cups sugar	1	tablespoon vanilla

Cream margarine and cream cheese until smooth. Add sugar and blend well. Add eggs one at a time, mixing well after each addition. Gradually add flour and salt. Add vanilla. Pour into a prepared Bundt pan. Bake at 325° for 1 hour and 15 minutes or until tests done.

Yield 12 to 16 servings

Jo Anne Taylor
Dyersburg, TN

Cream Cheese Pound Cake

1 (18.5-ounce) butter recipe cake mix
1 (8-ounce) package cream cheese, at
    room temperature
4 large eggs

½ cup water
½ cup sugar
½ cup vegetable oil
1 teaspoon pure vanilla extract

Preheat oven to 350°. Lightly spray a Bundt pan with non-stick cooking spray. Set aside. Place the cake mix, cream cheese, eggs, water, sugar, oil and vanilla extract in a large mixing bowl. Blend with an electric mixer on low speed for 1 minute. Stop, scrape down sides of bowl with a rubber spatula. Increase the speed to medium and beat for 2 minutes more, scrapping down sides of bowl as needed. Pour the well blended batter into the prepared pan and place in the oven. Bake for 35 to 40 minutes until it is golden brown and springs back when lightly pressed with your finger. Remove from oven and allow to sit about 5 minutes. Invert onto a serving platter and slice the cake after it cools for about 30 minutes.

Diane Hardin
Savannah, TN

Crunchy Upside Down Cake

1 stick butter
1 cup brown sugar
1 cup flaked coconut

1 cup chocolate chips
1 cup chopped pecans
1 box chocolate cake mix

Melt the butter in a 13 x 9 x 2-inch pan. Add the next 4 ingredients in order listed by sprinkling onto the melted butter. Mix cake as directed on package and pour on top of the other mixture. Bake at 350° for about 45 minutes. Flip out of pan upside down.

Glaze

½ cup chocolate chips
¼ stick butter

1 (16-ounce) box confectioners' sugar

Melt chocolate chips and butter. Add confectioners' sugar and if needed a small amount of warm water to make consistency to spread. Drizzle over cake.

Millie Ungren
Crump, TN

Cream Cheese Sheet Cake

This tender sheet cake with its fudgy chocolate glaze
is a real crowd pleaser. It's popular at pot lucks and parties.

1 cup plus 2 tablespoons butter or
   margarine, softened
2 (3-ounce) packages cream cheese,
   softened

2¼ cups sugar
6 eggs
¾ teaspoon vanilla extract
2¼ cups cake flour

In a mixing bowl, cream butter, cheese and sugar. Add eggs, one at a time, beating well after each addition. Beat in vanilla. Add flour, mix well. Pour into a greased 15 x 10 x 1-inch baking pan. Bake at 325° for 30 to 35 minutes or until a toothpick inserted neat the center comes out clean. Cool completely.

Frosting
1 cup sugar
⅓ cup evaporated milk

½ cup butter or margarine
½ cup semi-sweet chocolate chips

Combine sugar and milk in a saucepan. Bring to a boil over medium heat. Cover and cook for 3 minutes (do not stir). Stir in butter and chocolate chips until melted. Cool slightly. Stir and spread over cake.

Robaya Wolfe Ellis
Savannah, TN

Cracker Cake

2 cups pecans, finely chopped
1½ cups saltines, finely crumbled
2 teaspoons baking powder
6 egg whites

2 cups sugar
3 (8-ounce) containers heavy cream
   Sugar to taste
1 teaspoon vanilla

Mix first 3 ingredients. Beat egg whites until stiff. Add sugar and blend until sugar is dissolved. Add nut and cracker mixture. Line 3 (8-inch) cake pans with foil. Grease and pour mixture into pans. Bake at 325° for 40 minutes until medium brown. Cool on rack. Beat heavy cream until stiff. Add sugar to taste, add vanilla. Spread small amount on plate. Place first layer on this. Spread cream between each layer. Let stand in refrigerator for 24 hours before serving.

Charlotte Wolfe
Fort Lauderdale, FL

Earthquake Cake

1½ cups chopped pecans
1 cup flaked coconut
1 box German chocolate cake mix

1 (8-ounce) package cream cheese, softened
1 stick butter, softened
2 cups confectioners' sugar

Preheat oven to 350°. Grease and flour an 13 x 9 x 2-inch baking pan. Sprinkle the nuts over the bottom of the pan. Sprinkle coconut over nuts. Prepare the cake mix according to package directions and pour over the nuts and coconut. Set aside. In medium mixing bowl beat together the cream cheese and butter on medium speed of mixer. Add confectioners' sugar, one cup at a time. Drop cream cheese mixture by tablespoonfuls over the cake mixture trying to distribute evenly. Bake 45 to 55 minutes or until done. This cake normally cracks.

Charlotte Wolfe
Fort Lauderdale, FL

Fresh Coconut Sheet Cake

1 (18-ounce) box butter flavored cake mix
1 (15-ounce) can cream of coconut
1 (14-ounce) can sweetened condensed milk

2 (6-ounce) packages frozen coconut, thawed
1 (12-ounce) carton frozen whipped topping, thawed

Prepare cake according to package directions. Pour into a 13 x 9 x 2-inch pan and bake according to package directions. When cake is done, punch holes in it with a toothpick. Mix cream of coconut and condensed milk and pour over cake. Sprinkle 6-ounces of coconut on top. Cover and refrigerate overnight. Before serving, spread with whipped topping and sprinkle remaining 6-ounces of coconut on top.

Jo Anne Taylor
Dyersburg, TN

Fig or Preserve Cake

2	cups flour	3	eggs
1	teaspoon salt	1	cup buttermilk
1	teaspoon baking soda	1	cup figs or pear preserves
1½	cups sugar	1	cup chopped pecans
1	cup margarine or oil	1	tablespoon vanilla flavoring

Sift together flour, salt, soda and sugar. Add margarine or oil and beat well. Add eggs and beat well. Gradually add buttermilk, then preserves, nuts and flavoring. Pour into greased loaf pan. Bake at 325° for 1 hour. While cake is still hot pour sauce over it.

Sauce

1	cup sugar	1	tablespoon vanilla flavoring
1	stick butter or margarine	½	cup buttermilk
1	tablespoon corn syrup	½	teaspoon salt

Mix ingredients together and boil for 3 minutes.

Shirley Huddleston
Booneville, MS

German Chocolate Cake

1	cup nuts, chopped	1	stick butter or margarine
1	cup flaked coconut	1	(8-ounce) package cream cheese
1	box German chocolate cake mix	1	(16-ounce) box confectioners' sugar

Spray a 13 x 9 x 2-inch pan with nonstick cooking spray. Sprinkle nuts and coconut in bottom of pan. Mix cake mix according to package directions and pour over nuts and coconut. Mix butter or margarine, cream cheese and powdered sugar together. Pour over batter and sink in the cake mix. Bake at 325° for 1 hour.

Janice Hooper
Whitwell, TN

14 Layer Cake

1 stick butter	2 teaspoons vanilla
½ cup vegetable shortening	3 cups self-rising flour
2 cups sugar	1 cup milk
6 eggs	

Cream butter, shortening together until smooth. Add sugar and mix well. Add eggs, one at a time beating well after each addition. Add vanilla. Add flour alternating with milk, beginning and ending with flour. This batter will be thinner than usual. Pour 4 tablespoons (¼ cup) into greased and floured cake pans. Bump pans gently with hands to spread batter over the entire pan. Bake at 350° for 5 to 7 minutes. Do not cook too long or allow layers to get brown. Partially cool before removing from pans. Continue same process until all batter is used.

Filling

2 cups sugar	Water to make a paste
1½ sticks butter	1½ cups evaporated milk
6 tablespoons cocoa powder	

Combine all ingredients in a 2 quart saucepan and bring mixture to a rolling boil. Remove from heat and beat with electric mixer for thirty seconds. Start stacking layers with filling, working quickly. Let filling run down sides of cake.

Charlotte Wolfe
Fort Lauderdale, FL

Frozen Strawberry Salad

1 (8-ounce) package cream cheese	1 (10-ounce) package frozen sliced
¾ cup sugar	strawberries, thawed and drained
1 (12-ounce) carton frozen whipped topping, thawed	1 cup pineapple tidbits, drained

Cream together cream cheese, sugar and whipped topping. Fold in drained fruits (fruit amounts can be increased if desired). Place in a 9 x 13x 2-inch glass dish and freeze. To serve, let thaw just enough to cut into squares.

Jo Anne Taylor
Dyersburg, TN

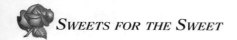

Glazed Buttermilk Pecan Lemon Cake with Tangy Lemon Icing

8 ounces sweet butter, softened
2 cups granulated sugar
3 eggs
3 cups unbleached, all-purpose flour, sifted
½ teaspoon baking soda
½ teaspoon salt
1 cup buttermilk

3 tablespoons lemon zest
2 tablespoons fresh lemon juice
1 cup toasted, chopped pecans
1 (16-ounce) box confectioners' sugar
8 tablespoons sweet butter, softened
3 tablespoons grated lemon zest
½ cup fresh lemon juice

Preheat oven to 325°. Grease a 10-inch tube pan or individual Bundt pans. Cream butter and sugar until light and fluffy. Beat in eggs, one at a time, blending well after each addition. Sift together flour, baking soda and salt. Stir dry ingredients into egg mixture alternately with buttermilk, beginning and ending with dry ingredients. Add lemon zest, juice and pecans. Pour batter into prepared tube pan. Set on the middle rack of the oven and bake for 1 hour and 15 minutes or until tests done. Cool cake in the pan and set on a rack for 10 minutes. Meanwhile, combine confectioners' sugar and butter, lemon zest and juice in medium mixing bowl and blend with a hand mixer until smooth. Set aside. When cake is slightly cooled spread icing on cake.

Chef Jill K. Bosich, CEC, CCE
Dean of Culinary Education,
Culinard, The Culinary Institute of Virginia College

Gooey Cake

1 box yellow cake mix
1 cup chopped nuts
1 stick butter, softened
1 egg

1 box confectioners' sugar
1 (8-ounce) package cream cheese
2 eggs

Combine cake mix, nuts, butter and egg and blend until forms a ball. Press into a 13 x 9 x 2-inch pan. Combine confectioners' sugar, cream cheese and eggs and beat well. Pour on top of first mixture. Bake at 300° for 30 to 40 minutes.

Kim Wolfe Nelson
Kansas City, MO

Green Meadows Six-Week Bran Muffins

This batter stays fresh for six weeks.

5 cups all-purpose flour	3 cups sugar
5 teaspoons baking soda	4 eggs
2 teaspoons salt	1 cup vegetable oil
2 teaspoons ground allspice	1 quart buttermilk
1 (15-ounce) box bran cereal with raisins	2 teaspoons vanilla

Using the largest bowl you have, combine the flour, baking soda, salt and allspice. Add the cereal and sugar and mix well. In a mixer bowl, beat the eggs. Add the oil, buttermilk and vanilla to the eggs and blend. Pour the egg mixture over the flour mixture and stir well. Transfer the batter to a large plastic container that has a tight fitting cover and store in the refrigerator until ready to use. Be sure to date the container the day you make the batter. When ready to bake, do not stir the batter when dipping out to fill the muffin pan. To bake, preheat the oven to 375°. Using about ½ cup batter for each, drop the batter into paper-lined muffin tins. Bake for 20 minutes or until the top springs back when touched with your fingers. Do not over bake.

I like to add drained pineapple pieces and extra raisins soaked in brandy for a different taste.

Lois Eyre
Lake Havasu City, AZ

115

Chocolate Cake

1 box chocolate cake mix
1 small box vanilla instant pudding
3 eggs

1 cup oil
1½ cups buttermilk

Combine all ingredients. Pour into 13 x 9 x 2-inch pan or 2 round cake pans. Bake at 350° for 25 to 30 minutes for round pans or 35 to 40 minutes in long pan. Check for doneness with toothpick.

Frosting
1 (8-ounce) package cream cheese
½ cup sugar
1 cup confectioners' sugar

1 (16-ounce) container frozen whipped topping, thawed
4 solid milk chocolate candy bars, grated

Combine all ingredients and mix well. Spread on cake and in between layers if stacking. Put grated chocolate on top and sides of cake.

You may add nuts in the batter and icing if desired.

Mary Nell Davis
Savannah, TN

Grand Mama's Banana Pudding

This is my grandson, DeWayne's, favorite and he even helps me make it.

1½ cups sugar, divided
6 tablespoons flour
   Dash salt
8 eggs

4 cups milk
1 teaspoon vanilla extract
7-8 ripe bananas
1 box vanilla wafers

Combine 1 cup sugar, flour and salt in large pan. Mix in 2 whole eggs and 6 egg yolks, reserving the whites. Stir in milk, cook on medium heat stirring constantly so it won't stick, until it thickens. Remove from heat, add vanilla and pour small amount in bottom of a large casserole dish. Cover with sliced bananas, layer of wafers and layer of custard. Repeat until all ingredients are used. Beat remaining 6 egg whites until stiff, gradually add remaining ½ cup of sugar and beat until stiff. Put on top of pudding. Place in oven and broil until brown. This will only take a minute or so. Do not burn.

Linda Callins
Savannah, TN

Irene's Cake

1 box orange flavored cake mix	½ cup vegetable oil
1 (3¾-ounce) box instant vanilla pudding	4 ounces banana flavored liqueur
4 eggs	1 ounce vodka
	4 ounces orange juice

Combine cake mix and pudding in a large bowl. Blend in eggs, oil, banana liqueur, vodka and orange juice. Mix batter until smooth and thick. Pour into a greased and floured Bundt pan. Bake at 350° for 45 minutes. Let cool in pan for 10 minutes, then remove and place on rack.

Glaze

1 cup confectioners' sugar	1 tablespoon orange juice
1 tablespoon banana flavored liqueur	1 teaspoon vodka

While cake is baking combine sugar, liqueur, orange juice and vodka. Blend until smooth. Pour over warm cake.

Irene Boyanski
Bal Harbour, FL

Just Cake

1½ cups softened butter	¼ teaspoon soda
3½ cups confectioners' sugar	¼ teaspoon salt
6 eggs	1 tablespoon pure vanilla
3½ cups sifted cake flour	1 can of ready to spread frosting

Cream butter until smooth. Gradually add sugar and beat until light and fluffy. Add eggs one at a time, beating well after each addition. Add cake flour, soda, salt and vanilla. Beat well. Spoon batter into a greased Bundt pan. Bake at 325° for 1 hour and 15 minutes. Before cake is totally cool, invert on cake stand and spoon frosting on top of cake and allow to run down the sides.

This cake is also delicious without any icing at all.

Charlotte Wolfe
Fort Lauderdale, FL

Joe Bailey Cake

2	cups sugar	1	teaspoon soda
2	sticks butter or margarine	½	cup buttermilk
3	eggs	½	cup cold coffee
2½	cups cake flour	1	teaspoon vanilla
½	cup cocoa powder		

Cream sugar and butter or margarine until fluffy. Add eggs, one at a time. Sift flour and cocoa powder. Add soda to buttermilk. Add flour and cocoa powder to sugar mixture alternately with coffee and buttermilk. Mix well. Add vanilla. Put in 2 (9-inch) cake pans, which have been greased and floured. Bake 45 minutes at 350°.

Icing

5	cups sugar	1	(12-ounce) package chocolate chips
1	(12-ounce) can evaporated milk	1	large jar marshmallow cream
2	sticks butter or margarine	1	tablespoon vanilla

Mix sugar, milk and butter or margarine in heavy saucepan. Bring to a boil and boil for 9 minutes. Remove from heat and add chocolate chips, marshmallow cream and vanilla. Beat until smooth. Spread on cake. Drop the remainder of mix on wax paper for candy.

Chaney Graham Winters
Savannah, TN

Lemon Ice Box Pie

1¼	cups graham cracker crumbs	3	eggs, separated
¼	cup sugar	1	can sweetened condensed milk
⅓	cup margarine, melted	¼	teaspoon cream of tarter
½	cup lemon juice	2	tablespoons sugar

Mix graham cracker crumbs with sugar and margarine. Press crumb mixture firmly in bottom and up side of an 8- or 9-inch pie pan. Bake at 375° for 6 minutes. Cool. Mix lemon juice, 3 egg yolks and sweetened condensed milk. Pour into crust. Beat egg whites and cream of tarter until stiff but not dry. Add sugar and spread over filling. Bake at 325° until meringue is golden brown, about 8 to 10 minutes. Refrigerate.

To make a Key Lime Pie, substitute lime juice for the lemon juice and add green food coloring.

Jo Anne Taylor
Dyersburg, TN

Just Delicious Cake

1 box yellow or white cake mix

Prepare and bake cake as directed on package.

Pineapple Filling

1 (20-ounce) can crushed pineapple
1 (3.4-ounce) box instant lemon
    pudding

1 pint heavy cream, whipped

Stir pineapple and pudding mix together. Chill for 5 minutes. Fold in whipped cream. Use to fill between cake layers.

Mocha Frosting

¼ cup butter, softened
2 tablespoons cocoa powder
2 teaspoons instant coffee
    Dash salt

3 cups confectioners' sugar
3 tablespoons milk
1½ teaspoons vanilla extract
1½ cups chopped pecans

Cream butter, cocoa powder, coffee and salt. Slowly add confectioners' sugar, one cup at a time. Add milk and vanilla extract. Beat until smooth. Put on top and sides of cake. Press chopped pecans onto sides of frosted cake.

Robaya Wolfe Ellis
Savannah, TN

Linda's Surprise

*My family calls this Linda's surprise because
they never know what kind of pie filling I will use.*

1 can cherry pie filling
1 can crushed pineapple

1 box yellow cake mix
2 sticks butter

Pour pie filling in bottom of a 12 x 9 x 2-inch pan. Then the crushed pineapple. Sprinkle cake mix evenly over whole mixture. Melt butter and pour over batter, being sure to cover all and not leave any dry spots. Bake at 350° for 45 minutes.

Linda Callins
Savannah, TN

Lemonade Cake

1 package lemon cake mix	4 eggs
1 (3.4-ounce) package lemon instant pudding	1 cup water
	¼ cup oil

Combine cake mix, pudding mix, eggs, water and oil in large mixing bowl. Blend well and then beat at medium speed of electric mixer for 4 minutes. Pour into greased and floured 13 x 9 x 2-inch pan. Bake at 350° for 45 to 50 minutes or until cake tester inserted in center comes out clean and cake begins to pull away from edges of pan. Cool in pan about 5 minutes. Thoroughly prick warm cake with utility fork completely through to the bottom of the cake. Gradually spoon glaze over the cake until completely absorbed. Cool and cut into squares.

Glaze

½ cup lemonade flavored drink mix	2 tablespoons melted butter or margarine
½ cup water	2 cups confectioners' sugar

Combine drink mix, water and butter in a bowl. Add confectioners' sugar and blend well with a fork or whisk.

You can use a 6-ounce can of frozen lemonade instead of the water and butter.

Katherine Hinton
Savannah, TN

Love Cake

1 box fudge marble cake mix	1 small package chocolate instant pudding
2 (15-ounce) containers ricotta cheese	
¾ cup sugar	1 cup milk
4 eggs	1 (8-ounce) carton frozen whipped topping, thawed
1 teaspoon vanilla	

Preheat oven to 350°. Grease and flour a 13 x 9 x 2-inch pan. Prepare cake mix as directed on package. Pour into prepared pan. Combine ricotta cheese, sugar, eggs and vanilla and mix well. Spoon over unbaked cake. Bake for 1 hour. Let cool. Mix pudding mix with milk, fold in whipped topping and spread on cake. Cover and refrigerate.

Charlotte Wolfe
Fort Lauderdale, FL

Martian Pound Cake

6 chocolate covered candy bars	2½ cups flour
1 cup sour cream	¾ teaspoon baking soda
1 stick sweet butter, softened	1 teaspoon salt
2 cups granulated sugar	1 teaspoon almond extract
4 eggs	

In top of double boiler over low heat, cook and stir candy bars and ⅓ of the sour cream until melted. Set aside. Blend butter, sugar and eggs. Add flour baking soda, salt and remaining sour cream. Mix well. Blend in almond extract and melted candy mixture. Pour into buttered and floured Bundt pan. Bake at 350° 55 minutes or until done. Let cool for 10 minutes. Remove from pan and cool completely.

Frosting

4 chocolate covered candy bars	1 teaspoon almond extract
1 stick butter	1 cup confectioners' sugar
2 tablespoons milk	

Put candy bars, butter and milk in top of double boiler. Cook over low heat, stirring until melted, about 10 minutes. Remove from heat. Immediately stir in almond extract and confectioners' sugar until smooth. Spoon frosting over top of cake so it runs down the sides a little.

Charlotte Wolfe
Fort Lauderdale, FL

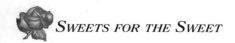

Milk Chocolate Bar Cake

My new daughter-in-law, Kristina, introduced us to this cake. We love it.

1 box Swiss chocolate cake mix	10 (1.5-ounce) milk chocolate candy bars
1 (8-ounce) package cream cheese, softened	with almonds, divided
1 cup confectioners' sugar	1 (12-ounce) container frozen whipped topping, thawed
½ cup granulated sugar	

Prepare cake according to package directions. Bake in 2 greased and floured 9-inch cake pans. Bake at 325° for 25 minutes or until a wooden toothpick inserted in center comes out clean. Cool in pans on wire racks for 10 minutes. Remove from pans and cool completely. Beat cream cheese and sugars at medium speed with an electric mixer until creamy. Chop 8 candy bars finely. Fold cream cheese mixture and chopped candy into whipped topping. Spread icing between layers and on top of cake. Chop remaining 2 candy bars. Sprinkle half of chopped candy bars over cake. Press remaining chopped candy bars along bottom edge of cake.

Diane Hardin
Savannah, TN

Mini Cheesecakes

1 roll refrigerated sugar cookies, thinly sliced	½ cup sour cream
	½ teaspoon vanilla
1 (8-ounce) package cream cheese, softened	½ teaspoon grated lemon rind
	3 tablespoons all-purpose flour
1 cup sugar	1 cup blueberries (optional)
2 eggs	

Heat oven to 325°. Line 12 muffin pan cups with foil cupcake liners. Place 1 slice of cookie dough in bottom of each liner. Beat together cream cheese and sugar on medium speed in large mixer bowl until smooth. Add eggs, beating just until blended. Beat in sour cream, vanilla and lemon rind. On low speed, beat in flour. Stir in berries. Spoon batter into cups dividing equally. Bake until cakes are set when slightly shaken. Cool on rack.

Charlotte Wolfe
Fort Lauderdale, FL

Mint Chocolate Chip Cake

1   package chocolate chip cake mix
⅔ cup water
⅔ cup mint flavored liqueur
½ cup vegetable oil
3   eggs
1   large package chocolate instant
     pudding mix

2   cups milk
⅓ cup mint flavored liqueur
1   (8-ounce) container frozen whipped
     topping, thawed
     Chocolate shavings or decors

Preheat oven to 350°. Prepare cake using water, mint flavored liqueur, oil and eggs. Bake in 2 (8-inch) prepared cake pans for 30 to 35 minutes. Cool for 10 minutes. Remove from pan and cool cake completely, approximately 30 minutes. Prepare pudding mix using 2 cups milk and mint flavored liqueur. Divide pudding and set ½ aside. Use the other half to frost between the two cake layers. Into the reserved mixture add ¾ of the whipped topping and use for top and sides of the cake. Use rest of whipped topping for decorating top of cake and sprinkle with chocolate shavings or decors. Store cake in refrigerator.

Charlotte Wolfe
Fort Lauderdale, FL

Miracle Fruit Cake

1   box spice flavored cake mix
3   cups glazed mixed fruit
1   cup dried apricots, slightly cooked and
     cubed when cool
½ cup green candied cherries
½ red candied cherries

1½ cups raisins
1   small can cubed pineapple with
     juice, if needed
4½ cups chopped pecans
1   package fluffy frosting mix, prepared
     as directed

Prepare cake mix according to directions. When baked and cooled, crumble cake into large mixing bowl and set aside. Combine mixed fruit, apricots, candied cherries, raisins, pineapple and pecans. Add fruits to crumbled cake. Mix in frosting. Knead and blend well with hands. Pack firmly in 2 foil lined and oiled bread pans. Refrigerate until firm and cold. Slice for serving.

May be garnished with additional whipped topping and a cherries.

Margaret Kerr
Savannah, TN

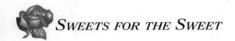

SWEETS FOR THE SWEET

Miss Daisy's Five Flavor Pound Cake with Glaze

1 cup butter, softened
½ cup vegetable shortening
3 cups sugar
5 eggs, well beaten
3 cups all-purpose flour

½ teaspoon baking powder
1 cup whole milk
1 teaspoon each, coconut, butter, lemon, rum and vanilla extracts

In large bowl, cream butter, shortening and sugar until light and fluffy. Add eggs. Combine flour and baking powder. Add to cream mixture alternately with milk. Stir in flavorings. Spoon batter into a greased 10-inch tube pan. Bake in 325° oven for 1½ hours or until cake tests done.

Glaze
1 cup sugar
½ cup water

1 teaspoon each: coconut, butter, lemon, rum and vanilla extracts

In a saucepan, combine all ingredients and gently bring to a boil. Pour over cake while in pan. Let cake sit in pan until cool.

Yield 14 to 16 slices.

Katherine Hinton
Savannah, TN

Mrs. Roxie Sawyner's Pound Cake

*Mrs. Sawyner baked many of these
cakes and donated all the money to her church.*

½ cup sugar
⅔ cup butter flavored vegetable oil
1 stick butter or margarine

4 eggs
1 box butter flavored cake mix
1 (8-ounce) carton sour cream

Beat sugar, oil and butter or margarine. Add eggs and blend well. Add cake mix gradually and sour cream. Pour into greased and floured tube pan and bake at 350° for 60 minutes.

Nancy Linam White
Adamsville, TN

Orange Slice Cake

1	pound butter	1½	ounces vanilla extract
2	cups sugar	1½	pounds orange slices (candy) cut
6	eggs, separated		into small pieces
4	cups flour	3	cups pecans

Cream butter and sugar. Add egg yolks and stir. Add flour, then vanilla. Add orange slices and pecans and mix well. Lastly fold in stiffly beaten egg whites. Bake in well greased and floured tube pan at 300° for 90 minutes. Increase heat to 350° for an additional 10 minutes. Test for doneness with toothpick.

Linda Neill
Savannah, TN

Orange Pound Cake

1	box yellow cake mix	½	cup oil
1	box orange jello	¾	cup water
4	eggs	1	teaspoon orange extract

Put all ingredients into large mixing bowl and beat for 3 minutes. Pour into a greased and floured tube pan and bake at 350° for 45 minutes. Serve plain or with glaze.

Orange Glaze
¼	cup butter or margarine	⅔ cup sugar
⅓	cup orange juice	

Heat ingredients for glaze in pan until sugar is dissolved. Pour half of the glaze evenly over cake in pan while cake is still hot. Allow cake to cool in the pan before removing. Then pour remainder of glaze over cake.

Loral Wolfe White, 1915-2001
Ft Myers, FL

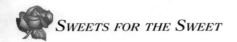

Chocolate Cookie Cake

1 box chocolate fudge cake mix
1 cup heavy cream
¼ cup water
¼ cup butter, softened
3 eggs

1 cup coarsely crushed chocolate
  sandwich cookies, about 10 cookies
1 container vanilla ready to spread
  frosting

Heat oven to 250°. Generously grease and flour 2 round pans, 9 x 1½-inch. Beat dry cake mix, heavy cream, water, butter and eggs in large bowl of mixer on low speed for 30 seconds. Beat on medium speed for 2 minutes. Reserve 2 tablespoons of crushed cookies. Fold remaining cookies into batter. Pour into pans. Bake 30 to 37 minutes or until toothpick inserted in center comes out clean. Cool 10 minutes. Remove from pans. Cool cake completely. Crush reserved cookies until they are fine. Mix into frosting. Fill layers and frost side and top of cake.

You may garnish with additional chocolate cookies cut in half.

Charlotte Wolfe
Fort Lauderdale, FL

Original Pound Cake

1 pound butter
1 pound confectioners' sugar
12 eggs, separated

1 pound flour (4½ cups, sifted)
½ cup heavy cream
1 teaspoon pure vanilla extract

Cream butter and sugar, add egg yolks, beating well after each addition. Sift flour and add alternately with the cream. Add vanilla and then the stiffly beaten egg whites. Bake in a greased and floured Bundt pan at 350° for 1 hour and 15 minutes, or until cake tests done.

Charlotte Wolfe
Fort Lauderdale, FL

Payday Cake

1 stick butter or margarine
1 box yellow cake mix
1 egg
2 cups miniature marshmallows
¼ cup butter or margarine

¾ cup light corn syrup
1 package peanut butter chips
2 cups cocktail peanuts
2 cups crispy rice cereal

Combine 1 stick of butter or margarine, cake mix and egg. Spread evenly into a 13 x 9 x 2-inch pan and bake for 15 minutes at 375°. When cake comes out of oven spread miniature marshmallows over it. Combine ¼ cup butter or margarine, corn syrup, peanut butter chips in a microwave proof bowl and microwave on high for 1½ minutes. Remove and add peanuts and crispy rice cereal. Pour over cake. Cool. You may put in refrigerator for a few minutes to set. Do not leave in refrigerator or it will get too hard.

Robaya Wolfe Ellis
Savannah, TN

Pecan Cake

Serve this rich, fruitcake-like confection sparingly.
Make at least 2 weeks ahead so flavors can mellow.

8 ounces candied red cherries, cut in quarters
8 ounces candied pineapple, coarsely chopped
8 ounces pitted dates, coarsely snipped

1 tablespoon all-purpose flour
4⅓ cups coarsely chopped pecans
4 ounces flaked coconut
1 can sweetened condensed milk

Preheat oven to 250°. Grease and flour a 10-inch tube pan with removable bottom. Set aside. Combine cherries, pineapple and dates in a very large bowl. Sprinkle with flour, toss to coat well. Add pecans and coconut, toss to mix. Add sweetened condensed milk and stir to mix well. Spoon evenly into prepared pans. Smooth top. Bake for 1½ hours. Cool in pan on rack. Remove from pan. Wrap tightly in aluminum foil. Refrigerate at least 2 weeks. Cake cuts best cold. Slice very thin with serrated knife.

Charlotte Wolfe
Fort Lauderdale, FL

Peach and Raspberry Meringue Cake

5 large eggs, separated	2 cups granulated sugar
1½ cups unbleached flour	2 teaspoons vanilla
1 teaspoon baking powder	¾ cup milk
¼ teaspoon salt	¼ teaspoon cream of tartar
½ cup sweet butter, at room temperature	¼ teaspoon almond extract
	6 tablespoons sliced almonds

Preheat oven to 350°. Butter bottom and sides of 2 (9-inch) cake pans that are 2-inches deep. Line bottom of each pan with parchment or wax paper and butter the paper. Place egg whites in large bowl and set aside. Sift together flour, baking powder and salt; set aside. In large bowl with electric mixer on medium speed, beat butter and 1½ cups granulated sugar for 2 minutes until smooth. Slowly add egg yolks and beat bout 2 minutes until creamy. Stir vanilla into the milk. Reduce speed to low and add half of the flour mixture, mixing just to incorporate it. Add milk mixture, mixing to incorporate it. Batter may look curdled. Add remaining flour mixture, mixing just until incorporated and batter is smooth. Divide batter equally between prepared pans, spreading evenly. Set aside. Beat reserved egg whites and cream of tartar until soft peaks form. Slowly beat in remaining ½ cup granulated sugar. Mix in almond extract. Spread this meringue over top of batter in each pan, spreading evenly and using half for each pan. Sprinkle sliced almonds over meringue topping. Bake about 35 minutes until meringue and almonds are lightly browned and meringue feels firm when touched lightly. Meringue will deflate as cake cools. Use small knife to loosen warm meringue and cake carefully from sides of pan. Cool layers in pan for 30 minutes. Invert layers onto wire rack and discard paper liners. Turn layers right side up about 1 hour to cool completely.

Peach and Raspberry Filling

2 cups heavy cream, chilled	2 cups fresh raspberries
⅓ cup confectioners' sugar plus extra for dusting cake	2 cups (about 1 pound) peeled, pitted and sliced peaches
1 teaspoon vanilla	

Beat cream, confectioners' sugar and vanilla in large bowl of mixer on medium speed until firm peaks form. Carefully place 1 cake layer, meringue side down on cake plate. Place raspberries evenly over cake. Spread with thin layer of whipped cream mixture over raspberries. Place peach slices evenly over cream, then spread another thin layer of whipped cream over peaches to make a level layer of filling. Top with remaining cake layer, meringue side up. Spread remaining whipped cream on side of cake. Lightly dust with confectioners' sugar. Cover and refrigerate until ready to serve.

Yield 12 servings.

Stacey George
Fort Lauderdale, FL

Pecan Mango Coconut Cake

2 cups diced, ripe mango	¼ cup vegetable oil
1 cup granulated sugar	1 teaspoon vanilla extract
1 cup all-purpose flour	1 vanilla bean, split and seeds
1 teaspoon baking powder	scraped out
1 teaspoon baking soda	½ teaspoon almond extract
½ teaspoon salt	¾ cup finely chopped pecans
1 teaspoon cinnamon	1 cup flaked coconut
2 eggs, beaten	2 ounces dark rum

Combine diced mango and sugar in a large bowl and set aside while you preheat oven to 325°. Grease 1 (9-inch) pan. Sift together dry ingredients. Stir beaten eggs, oil, vanilla extract, seeds from bean and almond extract into fruit mixture. Add dry ingredients, nuts, coconut and rum being careful not to over mix. Pour into prepared baking pan and bake for 35 to 40 minutes. May be served with ice cream or fruit compote if desired.

Glenda Fowler
Raleigh, NC

Pecan Pie Cake

1 box yellow cake mix	½ cup firmly packed brown sugar
1 stick melted butter	1 teaspoon vanilla
4 eggs	2 cups chopped pecans
1½ cups light corn syrup	

Heat oven to 325°. Place cake mix, melted butter and 1 egg in mixing bowl and beat on low speed until well combined. Measure out ⅔ cup of batter and set aside. Spread remaining batter in bottom of ungreased 13 x 9 x 2-inch baking pan. Bake for 15 minutes or until top is lightly brown and puffs up. Remove from oven and let cool for 10 minutes. Place reserved ⅔ cup of batter, corn syrup, sugar, 3 eggs and vanilla in large mixing bowl and beat on low speed until well blended. Fold in pecans. Pour mixture on top of warm cake in baking pan and smooth evenly over cake. Bake for 40 to 45 minutes or until edges are brown but middle is still soft. Cool and slice into squares.

Charlotte Wolfe
Fort Lauderdale, FL

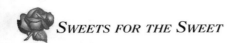

Peanut Butter Pound Cake

This cake is just as good without the icing.

1 cup butter
2 cups granulated sugar
1 cup firmly packed light brown sugar
½ cup peanut butter, smooth or crunchy
5 eggs
1 tablespoon vanilla

3 cups cake flour
½ teaspoon baking powder
½ teaspoon salt
¼ teaspoon baking soda
1 cup evaporated milk

Cream butter and granulated sugar until light and fluffy. Add brown sugar and peanut butter and continue to beat thoroughly. Add eggs, one at a time, beating well after each addition. Add vanilla and blend well. Sift together the dry ingredients and add alternately with the milk. Lightly grease a Bundt pan. Pour batter into pan and bake at 325° for 1 hour or until it tests done with a toothpick.

Frosting

½ stick butter
  Dash salt
1 ounce milk, or less
    (don't use too much)

1 (3-ounce) package cream cheese, softened
½ cup peanut butter, creamy or crunchy
1 box confectioners' sugar

Combine all ingredients and beat until smooth. Use just enough milk to make frosting of spreading consistency.

Charlotte Wolfe
Fort Lauderdale, FL

Piña Colada Cake

1 box white or yellow cake mix
1 can sweetened condensed milk
1 can cream of coconut

1 (8-ounce) container frozen whipped topping, thawed
1 can coconut

Bake cake as directed on package in a 13 x 9 x 2-inch pan. Take out of oven and while hot, punch holes in cake. Mix sweetened condensed milk and cream of coconut and pour over cake. Cool. Spread whipped topping over cake and sprinkle with coconut.

Charlotte Wolfe
Fort Lauderdale, FL

Pineapple Cranberry Upside-Down Cake

1 stick butter
¾ cup packed brown sugar
1 cup pecans

1 (20-ounce) can crushed pineapple, drained
1 cup fresh or frozen cranberries
1 box white cake mix

Melt butter in a 23 x 9 x 2-inch cake pan. Sprinkle with brown sugar. Combine nuts, pineapple and cranberries. Pour over butter and brown sugar mixture. Prepare cake mix according to package directions and pour over mixture. Bake at 350° for 45 minutes. Remove from oven and flip out upside-down.

Millie Ungren
Crump, TN

Salad Dressing Cake

¾ cup mayonnaise type salad dressing
1 box yellow cake mix
1 envelope whipped topping mix

¼ cup plus 2 tablespoons orange juice
3 eggs

Preheat oven to 350°. Combine all ingredients in mixer bowl and beat on medium speed for 2 minutes. Pour into greased and floured Bundt pan. Bake 35 to 40 minutes, testing for doneness with toothpick. Remove from oven and let stand 10 minutes, remove from pan. Cool and serve with Orange Mallow Cream.

Orange Mallow Cream

1 (8-ounce) package cream cheese, softened
1 (7-ounce) jar marshmallow cream

½ cup sour cream
2 tablespoons orange flavored liqueur

Combine cream cheese and marshmallow cream in mixer bowl. Beat at medium speed until well blended. Blend in sour cream and liqueur. Chill.

Charlotte Wolfe
Fort Lauderdale, FL

Poppy Seed Cake

1 box butter recipe yellow cake mix
1 cup sour milk (2 teaspoons vinegar in milk)
½ cup sugar
¾ cup oil
4 eggs
¼ cup poppy seeds

Mix all ingredients together and beat with mixer for 3 to 4 minutes. Bake in greased and floured tube pan at 350° for 40 to 50 minutes.

Linda Neill
Savannah, TN

Potato Cake

1 package German chocolate cake mix
1 teaspoon cinnamon
½ teaspoon nutmeg
1 cup cold, prepared instant mashed potatoes
½ cup butter or margarine, softened
½ cup water
3 eggs
½ cup chopped nuts

Heat oven to 350°. Grease and flour a Bundt pan. In large mixer bowl, combine cake mix, cinnamon, nutmeg, potatoes, butter or margarine, water and eggs at low speed until moistened. Beat for 2 minutes at high speed. Stir in nuts. Pour into prepared pan. Bake at 350° for 40 to 50 minutes or until toothpick tests done. Cool upright in pan for 25 minutes. Invert onto serving plate. Cool completely.

Glaze
½ cup chocolate chips
1 tablespoon butter or margarine
2 tablespoons milk
½ cup confectioners' sugar, sifted

In small saucepan, combine chocolate chips, butter or margarine and milk. Cook over low heat until chocolate melts, stirring constantly. Remove from heat, stir in powdered sugar until smooth. Add a few drops of milk if necessary for desired drizzling consistency. Drizzle glaze over cooled cake.

Yield 16 servings.

Charlotte Wolfe
Fort Lauderdale, FL

Punch Bowl Cake

1 box lemon cake mix
2 small boxes instant vanilla pudding
1 can cherry pie filling
1 large can crushed pineapple with juice

1 large container frozen whipped
  topping, thawed
1 can coconut

Prepare cake mix according to package directions. Cool. Prepare vanilla pudding according to package directions. Crumble half of cake in bottom of punch bowl. Next add half of each of ingredients in order listed. Repeat until all ingredients are used. Keep in refrigerator until ready to serve.

Bobbie Lou Peck
Florence, AL

Punch Bowl Cake

1 box cake mix
1 (20-ounce) can crushed pineapple,
  with juice
1½ cups sugar
3 jars strawberry glaze

3 (8-ounce) cartons frozen whipped
  topping, thawed
3 bananas
1 cup coconut
1 cup chopped pecans

Prepare and bake in a 13 x 9 x 2-inch pan as directed on package. Combine pineapple and sugar and heat over medium heat until mixture thickens. Cool completely. Half the cake and crumble one of the halves in a glass punch bowl. Spread strawberry glaze over cake. Spread 1 carton of whipped topping over the glaze. Repeat the cake, glaze, and topping. Slice the bananas and place over the topping. Add cooled crushed pineapple mixture. Spread with remainder of the topping. Sprinkle coconut and chopped pecans on top. Keep refrigerated.

Charlotte Wolfe
Fort Lauderdale, FL

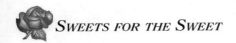

Red Velvet Cake

1½ cups cooking oil	1 teaspoon salt
1½ cups sugar	1 teaspoon vanilla
2 eggs	1 cup buttermilk
2½ cups all-purpose flour	1 (1-ounce) bottle red food coloring
1 teaspoon soda	1 teaspoon vinegar

Mix oil, sugar and eggs. Sift dry ingredients together. Add to oil mixture with vanilla, buttermilk, coloring and vinegar. Beat well with mixer. Bake in 3 layers in 325° oven until it pulls away from sides of pan, about 25 to 30 minutes. This is a thin batter.

Icing

1 stick butter, softened	1 (16-ounce) box confectioners' sugar
1 (8-ounce) package cream cheese, softened	1 cup chopped nuts

Mix butter and cheese and cream with sugar until. Add nuts and use between layers and sides and top of cake.

Charlotte Wolfe
Fort Lauderdale, FL

Skillet Coffee Cake

2 eggs	1 teaspoon vanilla flavoring
1½ cups sugar	1½ cups all-purpose flour
1½ sticks melted butter or margarine	Sugar
1 teaspoon almond flavoring	Almonds

Mix eggs, sugar, butter or margarine with flavorings. Add flour and beat well. Pour into a skillet lined with aluminum foil. Sprinkle with sugar and almonds. Bake at 350° for 40 minutes.

Angeline Gray
Savannah, TN

Red Velvet Cake

This recipe was given to me by my third grade teacher.

½ cup solid vegetable shortening	1 cup buttermilk
1½ cups sugar	1 teaspoon vanilla
2 eggs	2 (1-ounce) bottles red food coloring
2 cups all-purpose flour	1 teaspoon soda
1 tablespoon cocoa powder	1 tablespoon vinegar
½ teaspoon salt	

Cream shortening and sugar. Add eggs. Sift flour, cocoa and salt together 3 times. Add to sugar mixture alternately with buttermilk, starting and ending with dry ingredients. Add vanilla and food coloring. Beat well. Dissolve soda in vinegar and fold in. This batter will be thin, but bakes beautifully.

Frosting

1 cup milk	1 stick butter or margarine
¼ cup all-purpose flour	1 cup sugar
Dash salt	1 teaspoon vanilla
½ cup solid vegetable shortening	

Combine milk, flour and salt. Cook over low heat to a pudding stage. Set aside to cool. Cream shortening, butter or margarine, sugar and vanilla. Add to the cooled pudding mixture. Beat until smooth. Refrigerate before spreading on cake. Icing will be thin until it is refrigerated.

If desired you may add 1 cup coconut to icing.

Nyoka Beer
Cordova, TN

Senator Fred Thompson's Mother's Fresh Coconut Cake

1 fresh coconut	¼ teaspoon salt
½ cup vegetable shortening	1 cup milk
1¼ cups granulated sugar	1 teaspoon vanilla extract
2 cups sifted cake flour	3 egg whites, beaten stiff
2½ teaspoons baking soda	

Grate fresh coconut and save the milk. Set aside. Cream shortening and sugar until fluffy. Sift flour, baking soda and salt together 3 times. Then add alternately with milk, small amount at a time, beating after each time until smooth. Add vanilla extract. Stir stiffly beaten egg whites into batter. Bake in two greased and floured 9-inch cake pans at 350° for 30 minutes. Cool. Dribble coconut milk over each layer before icing.

Frosting

1⅔ cups sugar	¼ teaspoon cream of tartar
½ cup water	3 egg whites

To make syrup, combine sugar, water and cream of tartar. Stir over low heat until sugar is dissolved. Boil without stirring until syrup threads from a spoon. Beat egg whites until stiff. Add syrup gradually, beating all the time until cool enough to spread. Frost top and sides of cake. Sprinkle coconut on top and sides of cake

Robaya Wolfe Ellis
Savannah, TN

Shirley's Favorite Chocolate Cake

1 box Devil's Food cake mix	3 eggs
1 small box vanilla instant pudding mix	1 cup sour cream
¾ cup vegetable oil	1 cup chocolate chips
¼ cup water	

Mix together all ingredients except chocolate chips. Mix well and add chocolate chips. Bake in greased and floured Bundt pan for 50 minutes at 350°.

Shirley Huddleston
Booneville, MS

Shock Cake

If you are a chocolate lover, this cake is wonderful. It has a
like chocolate taste. My sister, Betty, gave me this recipe when I was a
teenager. My nieces all request it to be made when they come for a visit.

2 cups self-rising flour	1 cup water
2 cups sugar	½ cup buttermilk
1 stick butter or margarine	2 eggs, slightly beaten
¼ cup solid vegetable shortening	1 teaspoon soda
4 tablespoons cocoa powder	1 teaspoon vanilla

Sift together flour and sugar. Set aside. In a saucepan mix butter or margarine, solid shortening, cocoa powder and water. Bring this mixture to a boil. While hot, pour over flour and sugar mixture. Mix well and then add buttermilk, eggs, soda and vanilla. Mix well. Pour into a greased and floured 13 x 9 x 2-inch pan. Bake at 350° for 30 to 40 minutes.

Icing

1 stick butter or margarine	1 teaspoon vanilla
4 tablespoons cocoa powder	1 cup pecans
6 tablespoons milk	1 cup coconut (optional)
1 (16-ounce) box confectioners' sugar	

Melt butter or margarine with cocoa powder and milk. Bring to a rapid boil and remove from heat. Add confectioners' sugar, vanilla and beat well. Add pecans and coconut. Spread on cake while both are hot.

Katherine Hinton
Savannah, TN

Shortcake

2⅓ cups biscuit baking mix	3 tablespoons sugar
½ cup milk	3 tablespoons melted butter

Mix ingredients together until soft dough forms. Spread in one cake pan of individual tart pans. Bake until brown, 15 to 20 minutes at 350°. May be served with any fruit and whipped cream.

Charlotte Wolfe
Fort Lauderdale, FL

Sour Cream and Peach Pound Cake

3 cups sugar
1 cup butter
5 eggs
1 teaspoon pure vanilla
3 cups flour

¼ teaspoon soda
¼ teaspoon salt
1 (8-ounce) container sour cream
      (not fat free)
¼ cup peach flavored schnapps

Cream sugar and butter, add vanilla. Add eggs, one at a time, beating well after each addition. Add flour and soda and salt alternately with sour cream, beating well after each addition. Add peach schnapps and blend until well combined. Pour into a greased and floured Bundt pan and bake for 1 hour and 15 minutes at 325°.

Charlotte Wolfe
Fort Lauderdale, FL

Sour Cream Coffee Cake

1 cup butter or margarine
1½ cups sugar
1 cup sour cream
2 eggs, well beaten
1 teaspoon vanilla extract
2 cups all-purpose flour

1 teaspoon baking powder
¼ teaspoon salt
½ teaspoon soda
1 cup finely chopped nuts
1½ teaspoons sugar
2½ teaspoons ground cinnamon

Cream butter or margarine and sugar. Add sour cream, eggs and vanilla and beat well. Combine flour, baking powder, salt and soda and add to creamed mixture. Beat well. Thoroughly grease and flour a Bundt pan. Set aside. Combine nuts, sugar and cinnamon. Put a third of topping mixture in bottom of prepared Bundt pan. Alternate layers of batter and topping and end with topping. Bake at 350° for 45 minutes.

Fran Muller
Fort Lauderdale, FL

Sweet and Sour Cake

1 box yellow cake mix
1 cup heavy cream
1 can peach pie filling

1 (14-ounce) can crushed pineapple, no sugar added
2 cups coconut
1 cup pecans

Prepare cake mix according to box directions, except substitute 1 cup heavy cream for 1 cup of the water. Spray an 11 x 9 x 2-inch pan with nonstick spray. Pour pie filling into pan. Drain pineapple and reserve juice. Pour pineapple over pie filling. Sprinkle coconut and pecans over this. Pour cake batter evenly over this. Bake at 350° for 45 to 55 minutes or until cake tests done. Remove from oven and pour reserved pineapple juice over cake. Cool completely. Spread with frosting.

Frosting

½ cup sour cream
½ (16-ounce) box confectioners' sugar

1 (9-ounce) container frozen whipped topping, thawed

Mix sour cream with confectioners' sugar. Add whipped topping. Spread on cake.

Charlotte Wolfe
Fort Lauderdale, FL

Swiss Chocolate Sheet Cake

1 box Swiss chocolate cake mix

1 (7-ounce) jar marshmallow cream

Prepare cake mix according to package directions and bake in a 13 x 9 x 2-inch pan. As soon as cake is done remove from oven and spread marshmallow cream by spoonfuls over cake. As it melts spread it evenly over cake. Put in refrigerator and cool completely before frosting.

Frosting

1 stick butter
2 heaping tablespoons cocoa powder
¼ cup evaporated milk

1 (16-ounce) box confectioners' sugar
1 teaspoon vanilla

Heat butter, cocoa and milk until it comes to a boil stirring often. Add sugar and beat well. Add vanilla and mix until frosting is smooth. Pour over cake immediately.

Muriel Smith
Savannah, TN

139

Swiss Chocolate Cake

This is a pretty cake and a family favorite.

1 box Swiss chocolate cake mix	1½ cups buttermilk
1 (4-ounce) package vanilla instant pudding mix	3 eggs
	1 cup oil

Combine all ingredients and mix well. Pour into 3 (9-inch) round cake pans. Bake at 350° for 25 to 30 minutes. Cool completely.

Frosting

1 (8-ounce) package cream cheese, softened	1 (16-ounce) carton frozen whipped topping, thawed
1 cup confectioners' sugar	6 chocolate candy bars with almonds, grated
½ cup granulated sugar	

Beat cream cheese with sugars until well blended. Gradually add thawed whipped topping. Beat until smooth and fluffy. Gradually add candy bars, reserving enough to garnish the top of cake. Spread generous amount of frosting between cake layers and on top of cake and on sides. Garnish with reserved chocolate curls. Keep refrigerated.

Linda Colbert Hunt
Savannah, TN

Demetrice Winters Hart
Savannah, TN

Triple Chocolate Mess for the Crockpot

1 box chocolate cake mix, not pudding cake	1 (6-ounce) package chocolate chips
1 pint sour cream	¾ cup oil
1 small package instant chocolate pudding	4 eggs
	1 cup water

Spray crockpot with non-stick spray. Mix all the ingredients together and put in crockpot. Turn on low and cook for 6½ hours. Do not open lid while cooking. May be served with ice cream if desired.

Janice Hooper
Whitwell, TN

Texas Sheet Cake

1 cup water
2 sticks butter or margarine
4 tablespoons cocoa powder
2 cups sugar
2 cups self-rising flour

½ teaspoon salt
2 eggs
½ cup sour cream
1 teaspoon soda

Bring water, butter or margarine and cocoa powder to a boil. Mix together sugar, flour and salt. Pour boiling mixture over sugar mixture and beat. Add eggs, sour cream and soda. Beat well. Pour into well greased 13 x 9 x 2-inch pan. Bake 20 minutes at 350°. Ice cake while hot.

Icing

1 stick butter or margarine
4 tablespoons cocoa powder
5 tablespoons milk

1 (16-ounce) box confectioners' sugar
4 teaspoons vanilla
1 cup chopped nuts

Combine butter or margarine, cocoa powder and milk and bring to a boil. Add confectioners' sugar, vanilla and nuts. Spread on cake.

Demetrice Winters Hart
Lynette Linam
Savannah, TN

Tiger Cake

1 box yellow cake mix
4 eggs
1 cup water

¾ cup oil
½ cup chopped pecans
1 can coconut pecan prepared frosting

Combine all ingredients in mixer and beat until well blended. Pour into a greased and floured tube or Bundt pan. Bake for 50 minutes at 350°. Cool in pan for 10 minutes. Turn out onto plate an drizzle glaze over cake while it is hot.

Glaze

1 cup confectioners' sugar
2 tablespoons water

1 teaspoon vanilla flavoring.

While cake is baking combine ingredients in mixer. When smooth, drizzle on hot cake.

Becky Kerr
Savannah, TN

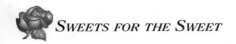

Three Musketeer Cake

This cake is delicious served with or without the icing.

8 Three Musketeer candy bars	2½ cups all-purpose flour
2 sticks butter	½ teaspoon soda
2 cups sugar	1¼ cups buttermilk
4 eggs	1 cup chopped pecans

Melt candy bars and 1 stick of butter, set aside. Cream sugar and 1 stick of butter. Add eggs and beat well. Add alternately flour, soda with buttermilk. Add melted candy and butter mixture. Add pecans. Bake in Bundt pan at 325° for 1 hour and 10 minutes.

Icing

2½ cups sugar	1 cup marshmallow cream
1 cup evaporated milk	1 stick butter
1 (6-ounce) package semi-sweet chocolate chips	

Cook sugar and milk to soft ball stage. Add chocolate chips, marshmallow cream and butter. Stir until smooth and of spreading consistency to ice cake.

Charlotte Wolfe
Fort Lauderdale, FL

Turtle Cake

1 box German chocolate cake mix	½ stick butter
½ cup milk	1 (6-ounce) package chocolate chips
1 (14-ounce) package caramel candy squares	1 cup pecans

Mix cake as directed on box. Pour half of the batter into a greased and floured 13 x 9 x 2-inch pan. Bake 15 minutes. Mix together milk, caramel candy squares and butter and melt over low heat. Pour over cake. On top of this mixture sprinkle chocolate chips and pecans. Pour remaining batter on cake. Bake at 250° for 20 minutes and then at 350° for 10 minutes. Cool and cut into squares.

May be served with whipped cream or you may pour ½ can of prepared chocolate icing that has been heated in microwave on top of cake.

Charlotte Wolfe
Fort Lauderdale, FL

Uncooked Fruit Cake

1 cup evaporated milk	1 cup seedless white raisins
40 miniature marshmallows	1 cup dark raisins
6 tablespoons orange juice	1 cup dates, finely chopped
8 cups crushed graham crackers	1½ cups walnuts, chopped
½ teaspoon cinnamon	1½ cups pecans, chopped
½ teaspoon nutmeg	1½ cups mixed candied fruit
½ teaspoon ground cloves	

Combine all ingredients in a large mixing bowl using a large spoon. Press into 3 loaf pans or roll into logs on wax paper. Cover and store in refrigerator for 24 hours before using.

You may add candied cherries or coconut if desired.

Mabel Callens
Bartlett, TN

Upside Down Chocolate Cake

1 box German chocolate cake mix	1 can coconut
2 cups chopped pecans	

Prepare cake as directed on box. Heavily grease a 13 x 9 x 2-inch pan. Sprinkle nuts and coconut into pan. Pour batter over nuts and coconut. Bake for 45 minutes at 350° or until tests done.

Icing

1 (8-ounce) package cream cheese, softened	1 (16-ounce) box confectioners' sugar
1½ sticks butter or margarine, melted	1 teaspoon vanilla

Combine ingredients in order given and mix well. Chill and spoon on top of cake when cool.

Katherine Spears Hinton
Savannah, TN

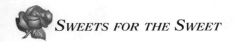

Upside Down German Chocolate Cake

1 box German chocolate cake mix	1 stick butter
1½ cups coconut	1 (8-ounce) package cream cheese,
1½ cups pecans, chopped	softened
1 (16-ounce) box confectioners' sugar	

Prepare cake as directed on box. Set aside. Spray a 13 x 9 x 2-inch pan with nonstick spray. Place coconut and pecans in bottom of pan. Pour prepared cake batter over this. Mix confectioners' sugar, butter and cream cheese until well blended and spoon over the batter. Bake at 350° for 55 minutes.

Rebecca Lewis
Savannah, TN

Wet Caramel Cake

This is a favorite of the men.

1   box cake mix, any flavor

Prepare cake according to package directions. Bake in a greased and floured 13 x 9 x 2-inch pan. As soon as cake is done, but into squares and leave in pan.

Sauce

1 stick butter	2 cups sugar
1 (12-ounce) can evaporated milk	1 teaspoon vanilla

Combine ingredients in 2-quart sauce pan and bring to a boil. Cook for 7 minutes stirring constantly. Pour over cake. Keep in refrigerator if there is any left.

Mary Nell Davis
Savannah, TN

Vanilla Wafer Pound Cake

1½ cups sugar	1 cup milk
2 sticks butter	1 can flaked coconut
6 eggs	1 cup chopped dates
5 cups crushed vanilla wafers	

Cream sugar and butter, add eggs, one at a time, beating well after each addition. Add vanilla wafers alternately with milk. Add coconut and dates. Put brown paper bag in bottom of 10-inch pan so it will not burn. Spray with nonstick spray. Bake at 350° for 1 hour and 20 minutes.

Charlotte Wolfe
Fort Lauderdale, FL

White Chocolate Layer Cake

1 cup butter	3 cups cake flour
2 cups sugar	1 teaspoon soda
4 eggs	1 cup buttermilk
4 ounces white chocolate	1 teaspoon vanilla
½ cup boiling water	

Cream butter and sugar until light and fluffy. Add eggs one at a time, beating well after each addition. Melt chocolate in boiling water and add to the egg mixture. Sift flour and soda and add alternately with the buttermilk. Stir in vanilla. Pour into 3 well greased and floured layer cake pans and bake for 30 minutes at 350° or until tests done. Frost with your favorite frosting.

You may vary by folding in 1 cup finely chopped pecans or 1 cup flaked coconut.

Charlotte Wolfe
Fort Lauderdale, FL

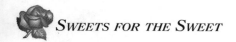

Buttermilk Frosting

1 cup buttermilk
2 cups sugar
½ stick butter

½ jar marshmallow cream, large jar
1 (6-ounce) package white baking chips
1 teaspoon vanilla

Combine buttermilk, sugar and butter and cook over low heat until mixture reaches 238° on thermometer, which takes about 10 minutes. Remove from heat and add marshmallow cream, white baking chips and vanilla. Stir until cool and of spreading consistency.

Charlotte Wolfe
Fort Lauderdale, FL

Caramel Icing

1 cup firmly packed light brown sugar
1 stick butter
⅓ cup milk

2 cups confectioners' sugar
1 cup chopped pecans

In saucepan heat brown sugar, butter and milk. Bring to a boil and cook for 2 minutes, stirring constantly. Cool 30 minutes. Gradually add confectioners' sugar and mix until smooth. Add more sugar to thicken or milk to thin if needed. Spread on cake and sprinkle with chopped pecans.

Charlotte Wolfe
Fort Lauderdale, FL

Chocolate Frosting

1 pound semi-sweet chocolate

2 cups sour cream

Melt chocolate in top of double boiler. Remove from heat. Mix ½ cup sour cream into approximately ½ cup of chocolate until well blended. Add to remainder of chocolate and add the rest of the sour cream, blending well until evenly mixed. Cool and frost cake. Store cake in refrigerator.

Charlotte Wolfe
Fort Lauderdale, FL

Yummy Cake

This is so good, yum, yum!

1 box German chocolate cake mix
1 (14-ounce) can sweetened condensed milk
1 can prepared chocolate icing

6 chocolate covered crunchy peanut butter candy bars, crushed
1 (12-ounce) container non-dairy frozen whipped topping, thawed

Prepare cake mix according to package directions. Bake as directed in a 13 x 9 x 2-inch pan. Cool for 15 minutes. Poke top of warm cake every ½-inch with the handle of a wooden spoon. Drizzle sweetened condensed milk evenly over top of cake and let stand until milk is absorbed. Heat icing in microwave oven for 1 minute to slightly soften. Spread over cake. Crush candy bars in a plastic bag or food processor until pieces are the size of a pea. Mix half of the crushed candy bars with the whipped topping and spread on cake. Sprinkle remainder of candy on top of cake. Refrigerate at least 2 hours prior to serving.

Linda Patterson
Savannah, TN

Divinity Nut Pie

23 round buttery crackers
3 egg whites
1 cup sugar
1 cup pecans, chopped
1 teaspoon vanilla

1 (8-ounce) carton heavy cream
2 teaspoons confectioners' sugar
3 teaspoon instant cocoa mix
1 square semisweet chocolate

Crush crackers in a zip-top plastic bag. Beat egg whites until firm. Gradually add sugar, beating well to incorporate. Fold in nuts, crushed crackers and vanilla. Place into a well buttered pie plate. Bake at 350° for 25 to 30 minutes. Cool away from draft. Whip heavy cream and gradually add confectioners' sugar and cocoa mix. Put cream on pie in dollops and grate a dusting of chocolate square on top.

Melinda Bennett
Corinth, MS

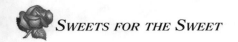

Wonderful Carrot Cake

Carrot Cake

3 cups all-purpose flour	2 (8-ounce) cans crushed pineapple, lightly drained
1¼ teaspoons baking powder	
¾ teaspoon baking soda	3 cups sugar
¾ teaspoon salt	1⅓ cups seedless raisins
2 teaspoons ground cinnamon, fresh is best	1½ cups chopped walnuts
	3 eggs
4 cups (about 1 pound) finely shredded carrots	1½ cups vegetable oil
	2 teaspoons pure vanilla extract

Whisk together flour, baking powder, soda, salt and cinnamon. Combine carrots, pineapple, sugar and raisins. Let stand about 8 minutes, stirring occasionally. Stir in dry ingredients. Add walnuts. In a separate bowl, beat eggs well and whisk in oil and vanilla. Stir into carrot mixture until well-combined. Spread evenly into a well greased and wax paper lined jelly-roll pan. Bake at 350° for 50 to 55 minutes or until tested done. Cool completely on wire rack.

Icing

6 ounces cream cheese, at room temperature	¾ cup (1½ sticks) unsalted butter, softened
6 ounces mascarpone cheese, at room temperature	Pinch salt
	1 tablespoon pure vanilla extract
	6 cups confectioners' sugar, sifted

Combine all ingredients except sugar in large mixing bowl and beat on medium speed of mixer. Gradually add sugar until icing becomes very thick and spreadable. When cake is completely cool invert onto a large cutting board. Cut cake in half crosswise to make 2 layers. Place first layer on plate and spread with a nice layer of frosting. Repeat with second layer and ice top and sides of cake. Refrigerate.

Charlotte Wolfe
Fort Lauderdale, FL

CC's Cherry Chocolate Cake

1 box German chocolate cake mix
1 (8-ounce) can cream of coconut
2 (8-ounce) cartons whipped cream cheese, softened
½ cup confectioners' sugar

1 (8-ounce) carton frozen whipped topping, thawed
1 can cherry pie filling
1 can prepared cake frosting

Prepare cake according to package directions except substitute the 8-ounce can of cream of coconut for 8 ounces of the water. Set batter aside. Combine softened cream cheese and beat in mixer. Add confectioners' sugar and blend well. Add whipped topping and beat until all ingredients are well blended. Reserve 1 cup of mixture. Pour half of the cake batter into a 13 x 9 x 2-inch greased and floured pan. Pour cream cheese mixture over batter and spread to within 1-inch of edges of pan. Carefully spoon pie filling over this. Pour remainder of cake batter over cherry pie filling. Bake at 350° for 45 minutes or until tested done. Cool completely. Over cooled cake spoon reserved cream cheese mixture on top of cake in dollops all over cake. Repeat with the chocolate icing. Take a knife or spoon and in swirling motion combine the two icings to form a white and brown pattern in icing. Enjoy.

Charlotte Wolfe
Fort Lauderdale, FL

Apple Dumplings

2 Granny Smith apples
1 (8-count) can crescent dinner rolls
⅛ teaspoon cinnamon
½ cup butter

1 cup sugar
1 cup orange juice
1 teaspoon vanilla

Peel and core apples, cut into fourths. Unroll and separate crescent rolls. Wrap each piece of apple in 1 crescent roll. Place in an 8-inch square baking dish. Sprinkle with cinnamon. Combine butter, sugar and orange juice in a saucepan; bring to a boil and remove from heat. Stir in vanilla. Pour over rolls; syrup will cook down as dumplings bake. Bake in 350° oven for 30 minutes.

Jo Ann Seaton and Betty Roberts
Savannah, TN

Bananas Foster

The key to success is to have all ingredients measured and ready to use.

1¼ pints vanilla ice cream	6 tablespoons unsalted butter
4 large bananas	¼ cup packed light brown sugar
¼ cup banana liqueur	½ teaspoon ground cinnamon
½ cup dark rum	

Cover a small rimmed baking sheet (one that will fit in your freezer) with wax or parchment paper and place in freezer for 10 minutes. When chilled, remove pan from freezer. Quickly scoop ice cream into 12 small balls and place on chilled lined baking sheet. Return to freezer until firm and ready to serve, at least 1 hour or up to 1 day ahead.

When ready to serve, peel bananas and quarter them, cutting lengthwise and then crosswise; set aside. Pour banana liqueur and dark rum into separate glass measuring cups; set aside, Heat 3 tablespoons butter in a large skillet over medium heat. Sprinkle sugar and cinnamon over butter and cook until sugar is dissolved. Remove pan from heat and carefully stir in banana liqueur. Add bananas, flat side down and cook until softened and lightly browned on the bottom. Remove pan from heat and add rum. Return to heat and cook about 10 seconds to allow rum to heat. If using a gas stove, carefully tip the pan away from you until the vapors from the rum ignite. (Alternatively, light the rum with a long match.) When the flames have subsided, remove pan from heat and gently stir in remaining 3 tablespoons butter. Place 3 scoops of ice cream in each of 4 serving bowls. Spoon the banana mixture and sauce over each. Serve immediately.

Pam Wolfe
Savannah, TN

Candy Bar Dessert

12 ounces ice cream, softened	1 small package butterscotch pudding, dry
1 (8-ounce) contained frozen non-dairy whipped topping, thawed	3 ounces crunchy wheat and barley type cereal
¼ cup chunky peanut butter	

Mix the ice cream, whipped topping, peanut butter and pudding mix in a mixer. Stir in cereal. Pour into an 8-inch square pan. Cover and freeze.

Dr. Lou Milciunis
Flowery Branch, GA

Cherry Delight

1	(16-ounce) can cherry pie filling	1	box butter flavored cake mix
1	(20-ounce) can crushed pineapple, drained	1	cup broken pecans
		1½	sticks melted butter

Pour cherry pie filling into oblong baking dish sprayed with nonstick spray. Next pour on pineapple. Sprinkle cake mix over fruit then add nuts. Pour melted butter over all. Bake at 325° for 45 minutes or until set. Serve warm with shipped topping if desired.

Annie Wolfe Bohler
Stone Mountain, GA

Easy Cherry Tart

1	package slice and bake sugar cookies, softened	4	tablespoons butter, softened
1	cup all-purpose flour	½	teaspoon almond extract
2	(8-ounce) packages cream cheese, softened	2½	cups confectioners' sugar
		1	(20-ounce) can cherry pie filling

Combined softened cookie dough and flour in mixer until well blended. Pat into a 13 x 9 x 2-inch greased pan. Bake 10 minutes at 375°. Cool and set aside, Combine cream cheese and butter until well blended. Add flavoring and confectioners' sugar. Blend well. When cookie is completely cool spread cream cheese mixture evenly over it. Spread cherry pie filling over top of cream cheese mixture. Refrigerate.

Charlotte Wolfe
Fort Lauderdale, FL

Christmas Salad

3	bananas, mashed	1	can whole berry cranberry sauce
1	cup miniature marshmallows	1	(12-ounce) contained frozen whipped topping, thawed
1	small can crushed pineapple, drained		

Combine bananas, marshmallows and pineapple together. Fold in whipped topping. Freeze.

Alice Slusher
Memphis, TN

151

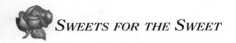

Chocolate Mint Frozen Dessert

27 chocolate sandwich cookies, crushed
¼ cup butter, melted

½ gallon mint flavored chocolate ice cream

Combine crushed cookies and butter and pat into a 13 x 9 x 2-inch pan. Freeze. Remove frozen crust from freezer. Slice and place ice cream on the frozen crust. Return to freezer.

Topping
1 large can evaporated milk
2 squares unsweetened chocolate

1 stick butter
1 cup sugar

Combine all ingredient and bring to a boil over medium heat. Cook until thick. Pour over frozen dessert and refreeze. Cut into squares and serve.

You can swirl melted ice cream on a serving plate and put square in center. Garnish with whipped topping and strawberry.

Becky Kerr
Savannah, TN

Chocolate Yums

2 small boxes instant vanilla pudding mix
3 cups milk
1 (8-ounce) container frozen whipped topping, thawed
1 box graham crackers

4½ tablespoons milk
3¾ tablespoons butter or margarine
¾ cup sugar
1 (12-ounce) bag chocolate chips

Combine pudding mix and milk. Fold in whipped topping. In a 13 x 9 x 2-inch pan, layer the bottom with graham crackers and then pour half of the pudding over the crackers. Repeat. Mix 4½ tablespoons milk, butter or margarine and sugar in saucepan. Boil 1 minute. Add chocolate chips and stir until mixture becomes thick. Pour over mixture and spread evenly.

Nanette N. Crowell
Murfreesboro, TN

Death By Chocolate

1 cup water	1½ cups semi-sweet chocolate chips
1 cup sugar	8 whole eggs
2 cups butter	2 teaspoons vanilla

Place water, sugar and butter in a heavy saucepan on medium high heat and bring to a boil. Remove from heat and stir in chocolate until smooth. Add eggs, one at a time, beating well after each addition. Add vanilla. Line a springform pan with foil (the batter is very thin and may leak) and spray lightly with cooking spray. Pour in batter and bake for 60 to 70 minutes in 350° oven. Let cool and place in refrigerator and chill well before serving.

Add any flavors to this, it's fun to experiment with coffee, orange or mint.

I like to wrap the outside with foil and bake in a water bath. I get a moister, sweeter result.

Janet Hickok
Chef, Simms Lodge
Nondalton, AK

Easy Chocolate Mousse

6 ounces sweet, eating chocolate	Whipped cream and berries for
6 eggs separated	garnish

Break the chocolate into squares and place in a heatproof bowl. Microwave on high for 1 minute. Stir and repeat until chocolate is melted. Beat egg yolks until thick and creamy (the thicker, the more firm the mousse will be). Bet melted chocolate into the egg yolks. Beat egg whites until stiff but not dry. Fold gently into chocolate mixture. Spoon into bowls and refrigerate until set. Garnish with whipped cream and berries.

Liz Rogers
Strubenvale, South Africa

Easy Fruit Salad

1 can peach pie filling
1 large can pineapple chunks
1 large can Mandarin oranges
1 bag whole frozen strawberries
2 large bananas, sliced

Mix all ingredients together in a bowl. Frozen strawberries keep the salad cold.

Vivian Epps
Adamsville, TN

Homemade Vanilla Ice Cream

2 pints heavy cream
2 cups sugar
1 can sweetened condensed milk
2 eggs
2 tablespoons vanilla
½ gallon milk

Mix all ingredients together. Freeze in ice cream freezer until frozen.

Carole Coats
Savannah, TN

Jon's Chocolate Dessert

A pretty dessert layered in a clear glass bowl.

1 box chocolate or devil's food cake mix
1 box chocolate instant pudding mix
1 large container frozen whipped topping, thawed
1 chocolate candy bar

Prepare cake mix according to box directions. Cool. Prepare pudding according to box directions. When cake is cool crumble. In a large glass bowl layer some of the crumbled cake, pudding and whipped topping. Repeat until all ingredients are used, ending with topping. Grate chocolate candy bar on top. Refrigerate for 12 hours before serving.

Beth Pippin
Savannah, TN

Homemade Chocolate Frosty

1 can sweetened condensed milk
1 (8-ounce) carton frozen whipped
   topping, thawed

1 (12-pack) of chocolate flavored cola

In a large mixing bowl, mix sweetened condensed milk, whipped topping and 2 or 3 of the chocolate colas until smooth. Pour mixture into ice cream freezer container. Add more chocolate colas to the fill line. Stir and freeze in ice cream freezer.

Pam Wolfe
Savannah, TN

Homemade Eggless Ice Cream

2 cans sweetened condensed milk
1 large can evaporated milk
1 (8-ounce) carton frozen whipped
   topping, thawed

1 cup sugar
1 teaspoon vanilla
½ gallon milk

Mix all ingredients together except ½ gallon of milk. Pour into ice cream freezer container. Add milk to the fill line on container. Freeze according to freezer directions. Any leftover ice cream can be kept in the freezer for several weeks.

Pam Wolfe
Savannah, TN

Ice Cream Sandwich Dessert

1 cup pecans pieces
¼ cup butter
1 can sweetened condensed milk
1 (8-ounce) package cream cheese

1 (8-ounce) container frozen whipped
   topping, thawed
12 frozen ice cream sandwiches
Chocolate and caramel sauce for garnish

Toast pecans in butter and cool. Beat together sweetened condensed milk and cream cheese until smooth. Fold in whipped topping. Place ice cream sandwiches in a 13 x 9 x 2-inch pan. Pour mixture over this and drizzle with chocolate and caramel sauce.

Carolyn Crunk
Marguerite Hughes
Savannah, TN

Mexican Chocolate Bread Pudding

10	cups large cubed white bread	10	chopped mission figs
½	cup rum		Rum to cover figs
3	cups half-and-half	3	whole eggs
½	cup granulated sugar	3	egg yolks
¼	cup orange flavored liqueur	8	ounces chopped Mexican chocolate

Soak bread in rum, set aside. Heat half-and-half, sugar and liqueur on medium heat just to boiling point. In a heat proof bowl, whisk whole egg and egg yolks until creamy in color. Add half-and-half mixture slowly to egg mixture until well combined. Cool quickly by placing bowl in cold water. Refrigerate until needed. In a large bowl add figs drained of rum, bread and chocolate. Slowly combine cooled custard mixture until bread is well saturated. Spoon into individual muffin pans. Place pan into a water bath in 350° oven. Bake until toothpick inserted into pudding comes out clean.

Cactus Pear Coulis

1	cup sugar	3	sprigs fresh mint
2	cups cranberry juice		Juice of 1 lemon
6	cactus pears, carefully cleaned and chopped		

Combine sugar and cranberry juice in saucepan. Simmer on medium heat until sugar is well dissolved. Add chopped cactus pears and mint. Simmer until pears are tender. Remove mint and puree remaining mixture until smooth. Run through sieve. Should be a vibrant red. To serve spoon ¼ to ½ cup coulis into serving dish. Center bread pudding in plate. Drizzle with additional coulis and mint if desired.

I obtained this from my friend, Chef Glenn Smith of Aspen, CO.

Donald L. Parris
Shelby, NC

Piña Colada Wedges

1 (8-ounce) package cream cheese, softened
⅓ cup sugar
2 tablespoons rum or ½ teaspoon rum extract

3½ cups frozen whipped topping, thawed
1 (8¼-ounce) can crushed pineapple, undrained
1 (7-ounce) can flaked coconut
Pineapple and cherries for garnish

Beat cream cheese with sugar and rum until smooth. Fold in 2 cups of the whipped topping, the pineapple with syrup and 2 cups of the coconut. Spread in an 8-inch layer pan lined with plastic wrap. Invert the pan into serving plate. Remove the pan and plastic wrap. Spread the remaining whipped topping and coconut. Freeze until firm, about 2 hours. Cut into wedges. Garnish with pineapple and cherries, if desired.

Rita Rasbach
Savannah, TN

Sawdust Salad

1 (3-ounce) package lemon jello
1 (3-ounce) package orange jello
2 cups boiling water
1¼ cups cold water
1 (15¼-ounce) can crushed pineapple, drained, reserve liquid
3 bananas, sliced
1 package miniature marshmallows

2 eggs, well beaten
4 tablespoons flour
1 cup sugar
2 cups pineapple juice
2 packages whipped topping mix
1 cup milk
1 (8-ounce) package cream cheese

Mix together lemon and orange jello in boiling water. Add cold water. To this mixture add pineapple, bananas and marshmallows and pour into a 13 x 9 x 2-inch dish. Chill. Combine eggs, flour sugar and pineapple juice and cook over medium heat until thick. Cool well and then spread on top of congealed mixture. Combine topping mix with milk and add cream cheese. Mix until well blended and spread on top.

Katherine Hinton
Savannah, TN

157

Peach Crisp

2 (15-ounce) cans peaches, drained
½ cup flour
⅓ cup firmly packed brown sugar

⅓ cup old-fashioned oats
⅓ cup chopped walnuts
⅓ cup butter, softened

Place fruit in an 8 x 8-inch baking dish. Combine flour, sugar, oats and walnuts. Mix in butter until mixture is crumbly. Sprinkle evenly over fruit. Bake at 425° for 15 to 20 minutes until light golden brown.

This is good served with ice cream.

Robaya Wolfe Ellis
Savannah, TN

South African Milk Tart

½ cup butter
½ cup sugar
1 egg

2 cups flour
1 teaspoon baking powder
Pinch salt

Cream butter and sugar well. Add egg and beat until light. Sift dry ingredients and work into creamed mixture. Press into greased pie plates thinly. Bake at 375° until golden.

Filling
Make in the microwave using a wire whisk.

4 cups milk
½ cup sugar
¼ ounce butter
⅓ cup cornstarch

2 tablespoons flour
2 eggs separated
2 tablespoons vanilla essence
Cinnamon

Mix 3 cups milk, sugar and butter and bring to a boil. In a separate container mix corn-starch and flour with remaining cup of milk and add 2 beaten egg yolks. Whisk hot milk into cold milk. Bring to boil, whisking frequently. Fold stiffly beaten egg whites into boiled mixture and whisk thoroughly until smooth. Add vanilla. Pour mixture into bake pastry shells. When cool, sprinkle surface of pies with cinnamon.

Liz Rogers
Strubenvale, South Africa

Pumpkin Cream Cheese Rollup

¾ cup all-purpose flour, sifted
1 teaspoon baking powder
2 teaspoons cinnamon
1 teaspoon pumpkin pie spice
½ teaspoon nutmeg
½ teaspoon salt

3 eggs, slightly beaten
1 cup sugar
⅔ cup canned pumpkin
1 cup chopped walnuts
¼ cup confectioners' sugar

Preheat oven to 350°. Grease a 15 x 10 x 1-inch pan. Line with wax paper and grease and flour. Sift first 6 ingredients onto a large piece of wax paper. Beat eggs and sugar until light and fluffy and then add pumpkin. Stir in sifted dry ingredients all at once. Spread evenly in pan and sprinkle with nuts. Bake 15 minutes or until center springs back. Loosen cake with knife. Invert onto damp clean towel dusted with confectioners' sugar. Peel off wax paper. Trim ¼-inch from all sides. Roll up cake and towel together from short sides. Place seam down on wire rack and cool completely. Unroll cake and spread with cream cheese filling. Re-roll cake.

Cream Cheese Filling

1 cup confectioners' sugar, sifted
1 (8-ounce) package cream cheese, softened

6 tablespoons butter
1 teaspoon vanilla

Combine all ingredients and beat until smooth.

This dessert was given to me by my close friend I grew up with, the late Caroline Joyce Gammill Adams. She always kept a dessert made in the freezer, just in case she had company. After living in Rhode Island many years she brought this back to Walkertown. The way she made it, it would melt in your mouth, a very fond memory of Carol.

Nancy Linam White
Adamsville, TN

159

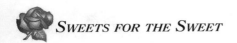

Red and White Delight

1 stick melted butter	1 pint sliced strawberries
1 cup pecans, finely chopped	1 package strawberry glaze
1½ cups flour	1 (12-ounce) carton frozen whipped
2 (8-ounce) packages cream cheese	topping, thawed
2 cups confectioners' sugar	

Combine melted butter, pecans and flour and press into the bottom of a 13 x 9 x 2-inch Pyrex dish. Bake at 375° for 15 minutes. Let cool. Mix cream cheese and confectioners' sugar and spread over crust. Mix strawberries and glaze together and spread on top of sugar mixture. Chill. Before serving spread with whipped topping.

Betty Roberts
Savannah, TN

Strawberry Soufflé

½ cup pecans, coarsely chopped	3 tablespoons lemon juice
1 cup flour	3 tablespoons orange flavored liqueur
⅓ cup firmly packed brown sugar	2 (10-ounce) packages frozen sliced
½ cup butter, melted	strawberries
4 egg whites	1 (12-ounce) carton frozen whipped
½ cup sugar	topping, thawed

Mix pecans, flour, sugar and butter to make crumb mixture. Spread into a 13 x 9 x 2-inch pan and bake at 350° for 20 minutes, stirring often. Remove from oven and let cool. Remove ⅓ of the crumbs and reserve for topping. Spread remaining crumbs evenly over bottom of pan. Beat egg whites until peaks form. Slowly add sugar and beat 5 more minutes. Fold in lemon juice, orange liqueur and strawberries. Fold in whipped topping. Spread mixture over crumbs. Sprinkle reserved crumbs on top. Cover and freeze at least 6 hours. Remove and let stand at room temperature for 20 minutes before serving.

Becky Kerr
Savannah, TN

Strawberry Angel Food Dessert

2 angel food cakes
1 (8-ounce) carton sour cream
1 cup milk
1 cup confectioners' sugar, sifted

1 (8-ounce) carton frozen whipped
   topping, thawed
2 pints strawberries, sliced
1 (16-ounce) package strawberry glaze

Tear cakes in small pieces and place in large bowl. Combine sour cream, milk and sugar. Fold in whipped topping and blend well. Pour over cake. Mix strawberries and glaze and pour over cake.

Bobbie Davis
Savannah, TN

Malva Pudding

1 cup refined sugar
2 large eggs
2 tablespoons apricot jam
½ cup milk

2 tablespoons butter
1 teaspoon white vinegar
12 ounces cake flour
1 teaspoon baking soda

Beat sugar and eggs until light. Beat in jam. Heat milk, butter and vinegar until warm and the butter has melted. Sift flour and soda and fold alternately with the milk into the egg mixture. Fold until just mixed. Pour into a greased ovenproof dish. Bake for 45 minutes at 350° or until skewer inserted comes our clean.

Sauce

1 cup cream
½ cup butter
½ cup sugar

⅓ cup water
¼ cup sherry

Heat sauce ingredients together in a saucepan over medium heat until sugar has melted. When pudding is done, remove from oven and make a few holes in the pudding using a fork. Pour the sauce over the pudding. Serve hot.

Liz Rogers
Strubenvale, South Africa

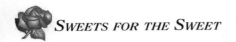

Telephone Pudding

The name originates from the old-fashioned telephone, which had to be connected by a telephone operator. Any recipe or gossip relayed over the phone was overheard and quickly passed on to others.

½	cup butter, softened	2	tablespoons apricot jam
1	cup sugar	1½	cups self-rising flour
1	extra large egg	¼-½	cup milk
1	teaspoon ground ginger	2	cups boiling water
1	teaspoon baking soda	1	cup sugar

Cream butter and 1 cup of sugar together until pale and fluffy. Add egg and beat well. Add ginger, soda and jam. Stir in flour and beat well. Add enough milk to make a soft, dropping consistency. Set aside. Make a syrup by stirring boiling water and sugar until sugar is dissolved. Pour syrup into base of a large, lightly greased ovenproof dish. Spoon reserved batter into syrup. Bake at 350° for 1 hour. Cover dish for first 10 minutes. Serve hot.

Add chopped cherries or raisins or fruit cake mix to syrup before adding the batter.

Liz Rogers
Strubenvale, South Africa

Tiramisu

1	(14-ounce) package ladyfingers	4	ounces sugar
2	cups espresso	14	ounces mascarpone cheese
4	eggs, separated	1	ounce cocoa powder

Soak ladyfingers in espresso. Line bottom of pan with half of the ladyfingers, set aside. Separate eggs. Beat yolks with sugar. Add mascarpone cheese and fold in stiffly beaten egg whites. Spread half of cream over ladyfingers. Repeat, ending with cream mixture. Dust top with cocoa powder.

Charlotte Wolfe
Fort Lauderdale, FL

Summer Delight

¼ cup fresh lemon juice
1 can sweetened condensed milk
1 (20-ounce) can crushed pineapple,
   drained

1 cup chopped pecans
1 (8-ounce) carton frozen whipped
   topping, thawed
2 graham cracker crusts

Mix lemon juice with sweetened condensed milk. Add pineapple and pecans. Fold in whipped topping. Pour into graham cracker crusts. Chill until firm.

Bobbie Davis
Savannah, TN

Caramel Sauce

1¼ cups sugar
½ cup water

1 cup heavy cream
3 tablespoons butter

In a large, heavy, deep saucepan, combine sugar and water. Cook over medium heat, stirring until sugar dissolves. Bring to a boil. Cook undisturbed until sugar turns golden brown and temperature on candy thermometer reaches 375°. Remove from heat and quickly pour in cream all at once. Be careful, it will bubble and spatter violently. When the caramel settles down, stir in butter until melted. To store, cool sauce for 10 minutes and store in a heatproof container.

Charlotte Wolfe
Fort Lauderdale, FL

Hot Fudge Sauce

8 ounces dark chocolate
7 tablespoons butter, softened
½ cup sugar
½ cup heavy cream

¼ cup hot water
1 teaspoon vanilla
Salt
Ice cream

Combine chocolate with butter, sugar, heavy cream and hot water in the top of a stainless steel double boiler. Melt chocolate mixture, stirring with a wooden spoon over simmering water on medium low heat, about 5 minutes. Remove from heat and stir in vanilla and salt. Serve warm over ice cream. Will keep in refrigerator for one week.

Charlotte Wolfe
Fort Lauderdale, FL

Raspberry Almond Tarts

This recipe is from Silverdale Bakery, a very good place for lunch.

2 (3-ounce) packages cream cheese
1 cup butter, cut into 1-inch pieces

2 cups all-purpose flour

Soften cream cheese and butter to room temperature, then mix until smooth. Add flour and mix well. Chill for 30 minutes. Roll into balls and press into small muffin pans.

Raspberry Almond Filling
½ cup red raspberry preserves
2 eggs
1 cup sugar

1 cup almond paste
Sliced almonds

Divide preserves among pastries (½ teaspoon each). Beat together eggs, sugar and almond paste in mixer until smooth. Spoon 1 level teaspoon almond mixture over the preserves. Sprinkle with sliced almonds. Bake at 350° for 25 minutes or until light brown and puffed. Cool. Will keep for 4 to 5 days in an air tight container.

Barbara Duryea
Poulsbo. WA

Caramel Walnut Tart

½ cup heavy cream
¼ cup butter
⅔ cup firmly packed brown sugar

¼ cup light corn syrup
2 cups walnuts or pecans
1 pre-baked pie shell

In small saucepan, combine cream, butter, brown sugar and syrup. Bring to a boil and simmer for 5 minutes. Add nuts and return to boil. Pour immediately into pre-baked crust. Put tart on cookie sheet into preheated 350° oven and bake for 5 minutes, or until bubbling all over. Remove from oven and cool.

May drizzle with chocolate sauce when serving.

Barbara Duryea
Poulsbo, WA

Lemon Tart

Crust

1 cup all-purpose flour
7 tablespoons butter, softened
  (no substitutions)

2 tablespoons confectioners' sugar

Combine ingredients and press into pie pan. Chill for 15 minutes. Bake for 15 to 18 minutes at 350°. Cool on rack for 15 minutes.

Filling

3 large eggs lightly beaten
1 cup sugar

⅓ cup fresh lemon juice
2 tablespoons flour

Whisk together all ingredients. Pour into tart shell. Bake for 15 to 18 minutes. Cool and refrigerate until ready to serve.

May garnish with fresh berries and whipped cream.

Barbara Duryea
Poulsbo, WA

Apple Cobbler Pie

2 cans apple pie mix
1 cup raisins
¼ teaspoon nutmeg
1 (6-ounce) ready crust shortbread crust

⅓ cup flour
¼ cup firmly packed brown sugar
3 tablespoons butter
¾ cup chopped walnuts

Preheat oven to 375°. Combine pie filling, raisins and nutmeg. Spoon into crust. Combine flour and sugar. Cut in butter. Add walnuts and sprinkle over filling. Bake for 35 to 45 minutes.

Annie Wolfe Bohler
Stone Mountain, GA

Apple Crisp

½ cup sugar	½ cup flour
3 tablespoons all-purpose flour	½ cup oats
1 teaspoon cinnamon	½ cup salted butter
½ teaspoon salt	½ cup chopped pecans
6 apples, peeled and sliced	Vanilla ice cream
1 cup firmly packed brown sugar	Caramel topping

Mix the first 4 ingredients with the apples. Place in a baking dish. Mix the next 5 ingredients with a pastry cutter or fork. Sprinkle on top of the apple mixture. Bake at 400° for 40 to 50 minutes or until done. Serve with ice cream and drizzle with topping.

To make a pie pour into an unbaked pie shell and bake until done.

Brigitte Elliott
Fort Lauderdale, FL

Aunt Dutchie's Chocolate Pie

6 tablespoons cocoa powder	3 eggs, separated
6 tablespoons all-purpose flour	1 teaspoon vanilla
1¾ cups sugar	2 tablespoons butter
Dash salt	1 baked pie shell
1 large can evaporated milk	6 tablespoons sugar

Sift together cocoa powder, flour and 1¾ cups flour, sugar and salt. Set aside. Combine evaporated milk with enough water to make 3 cups. Mix together dry ingredients with liquid and egg yolks and cook over low heat, stirring constantly until very thick. Add vanilla and butter. Pour into baked pie shell. Beat egg whites until stiff peaks form. Gradually whip in sugar. Spread over pie and bake in oven at 375° until meringue is brown.

Glenda Alexander
Savannah, TN

Apple Turnovers

1 (10-count) can biscuits
Sugar
5 apples, peeled and chopped
Cinnamon

1 cup sugar
1 stick butter
1 (12-ounce) can lemon-lime
carbonated beverage

Roll out each biscuit until thin. Put 1 tablespoon sugar and 2 tablespoons chopped apple on each biscuit. Sprinkle with cinnamon and fold over. Seal with fork and put in a 12 x 9-inch baking dish. Mix 1 cup sugar, butter and carbonated beverage and cook until butter melts. Pour over biscuits and bake at 400° until brown.

Betty Roberts
Savannah, TN

Apple Pie

This recipe was obtained from Mary Lou Newell in Adamsville, TN and is the best pie recipe for apples or peach pie I have ever eaten.

1 stick butter
3 cups peeled and sliced apples
½ cup sugar
1 teaspoon cinnamon
2 tablespoons cornstarch

1½ cups self-rising flour
½ cup shortening
⅓ cup milk
1½ cups sugar
1½ cups water

Melt butter in a large rectangular or oval dish. Add apples. Mix sugar, cinnamon and cornstarch together and pour over apples. Combine flour, shortening and milk to make a dough. Roll out on a lightly floured surface and cut into thin strips. Crisscross the strips over the apples. Combine remaining sugar and water and bring to a boil. Pour over the pie. Bake at 350° for 1 hour.

Vivian Epps
Adamsville, TN

Banana Split Pie

Crust

2 cups graham cracker crumbs
½ cup melted butter

¼ cup sugar

Mix together and press into the bottom of a 13 x 9 x 2-inch glass baking dish. Chill 1 hour.

Filling

2 cups confectioners' sugar
½ cup frozen egg product, thawed

1 teaspoon vanilla
1 cup butter

Cream together and spread over the crumb crust. Chill 1 hour.

Topping

4-5 ripe bananas, sliced
2 (10-ounce) packages frozen strawberries, drained
1 (16-ounce) can crushed pineapple, drained

1 cup heavy cream, whipped stiff (no sugar)
1 cup chopped pecans
1 (4-ounce) jar maraschino cherries, drained and chopped

Layer the toppings over the filling in the order listed. Cut into squares. Keep refrigerated.

Yield 12 to 15 servings

Charlotte Wolfe
Fort Lauderdale, FL

Bread and Butter Pudding

6 slices bread
6 tablespoons butter
6 tablespoons apricot jam
3 cups milk

4 eggs
4 tablespoons sugar
Raisins
Cinnamon and sugar for top

Remove crusts from bread. Spread with butter and jam. Cut into squares and place in baking dish. Combine milk, eggs, sugar and raisins. Pour over bread. Cover and bake for 60 to 75 minutes at 300°. If in a hurry, bake at 350° for less time. To test for doneness use a teaspoon and push into the middle of the pudding; if it comes out wet, it's not cooked.

Liz Rogers
Strubenvale, South Africa

Black Walnut Pie

3 eggs, lightly beaten	1 cup light corn syrup
1 cup firmly packed dark brown sugar	¼ cup butter, melted
1 tablespoon lemon juice	1 teaspoon vanilla
2½ cups black walnuts	1 (9-inch) unbaked pie crust

Preheat oven to 350°. Check pie crust to be sure the edges are at least ¼ to ½-inch above the rim of the pan to prevent the pie filling from bubbling over the edge. Gently combine all other ingredients in order listed. Stir enough to begin dissolving the sugar, but not enough to incorporate air into the filling. Do not beat or the pie will have air bubbles on the top, instead of black walnuts. Pour filling into crust. Place on a cookie sheet and bake for 60 minutes or until the center of the pie is no longer loose and black walnuts are browned. Serve either hot, cold or at room temperature.

Robaya Wolfe Ellis
Savannah, TN

Burnt Cream

This recipe is from a restaurant in Oakland, CA we visited many years ago.

1 pint heavy cream	1 tablespoon vanilla
4 egg yolks	Granulated sugar for topping
½ cup granulated sugar	

Preheat oven to 350°. Heat cream over low heat until bubbles form around edge of pan. Beat egg yolks and sugar together until thick, about 3 minutes. Gradually beat cream into egg yolks. Stir in vanilla and pour into 6 (6-ounce) custard cups. Place custard cups in baking dish that has about ½-inch water in the bottom. Bake until set, about 45 minutes. Remove custard cups from water and refrigerate until chilled. Sprinkle each custard with about 2 teaspoons granulated sugar. Place on top rack of oven under broiler and cook until topping is medium brown.

Yield 6 servings

Charlotte Wolfe
Fort Lauderdale, FL

Buttermilk Pie

1 cup buttermilk	1 stick butter
1½ cups sugar	1 teaspoon vanilla
3 tablespoons all-purpose flour	1 unbaked pie shell
3 eggs	

Combine all ingredients except pie shell. Do not use mixer. Pour into unbaked pie shell. Bake at 400° for 15 minutes. Then continue baking at 325° for 35 to 40 minutes. The pie will not look like it is done, however, it is. Let cool completely before cutting.

Vivian Epps
Adamsville, TN

Buttermilk Pie

3 cups sugar	1 cup butter, melted
6 tablespoons flour	2 teaspoons vanilla
1½ cups buttermilk	2 unbaked pie shells
5 eggs, beaten	

Mix sugar, flour and half of milk. Add beaten eggs. Add remainder of milk and fold in melted butter. Add vanilla. Pour into unbaked pie shells and bake at 425° for 10 minutes. Reduce oven to 350° and bake 45 to 55 minutes or until tested done.

Yield 2 pies

Charlotte Wolfe
Fort Lauderdale, FL

Chocolate Chess Pie

1½ cups sugar	1 (5-ounce) can evaporated milk
3 tablespoons cocoa	1 teaspoon vanilla
¼ cup butter, melted	¾ cup pecans, chopped
2 eggs, slightly beaten	1 unbaked pie shell
⅛ teaspoon salt	

Mix sugar, cocoa and butter. Stir well. Add eggs and beat with mixer for 2½ minutes. Add salt, milk, vanilla and pecans. Pour into unbaked pie shell. Bake at 350° for 35 to 45 minutes.

Nettye Beck
Savannah, TN

Caramel Coconut Cream Cheese Pies

¼ cup butter
1 (7-ounce) can coconut
1 cup chopped pecans
1 (8-ounce) package cream cheese
1 can sweetened condensed milk

1 (8-ounce) container frozen whipped topping, thawed
1 (12-ounce) jar caramel ice cream topping
2 deep crust graham cracker pie crusts

Melt butter in a large skillet. Add coconut and pecans. Stir until lightly browned. Set aside. Combine cream cheese and sweetened condensed milk. Mix until creamy. Fold in whipped topping. Layer ¼ of the cream cheese mixture in each pie crust. Drizzle on ¼ of the caramel topping. Sprinkle ¼ of the toasted coconut and pecans on top. Repeat each layer. Freeze until ready to serve.

Rita Rasbach
Savannah, TN

Caramel Custard

Butter
6 tablespoons sugar
4 tablespoons sugar
1 teaspoon vanilla

4 eggs
Salt
1⅓ cups hot evaporated milk

Butter insides of 4 (8-ounce) ceramic coffee mugs. Set aside. Melt 6 tablespoons sugar in a nonstick skillet over medium heat. Rock pan slowly without stirring until sugar becomes a golden brown syrup. Remove from heat. Divide equally among mugs. Sugar will harden. Mix 4 tablespoons sugar, vanilla, eggs and salt. Whisk in hot evaporated milk. Pour equal amounts of milk mixture into each mug. Place in a pan of boiling water and bake at 325° for 35 minutes. Rest in pan for 10 minutes. Remove from pan and refrigerate until cool. To serve, set mugs in warm water for 2 minutes. Loosen with knife. Invert onto serving plate and garnish if desired with fresh berries.

Yield 4 servings.

Charlotte Wolfe
Fort Lauderdale, FL

171

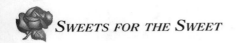
Caramel Pie

2 cups sugar, divided	1 teaspoon vanilla
3 tablespoons self-rising flour	2 tablespoons butter
1½ cups milk	6 tablespoons sugar
3 eggs, separated	1 baked pie shell

Combine 1 cup sugar, flour milk and egg yolks. Cook until thick. Remove from heat and add vanilla and butter. Brown 1 cup sugar until golden brown and syrupy. Add to milk mixture. Stir well. Pour into baked pie shell. Beat egg whites until stiff. Gradually add sugar. Put on top of pie and bake at 350° until meringue is lightly browned.

Charlotte Wolfe
Fort Lauderdale, FL

Cape Dutch Brandy Pudding

1 teaspoon soda	1 extra large egg
8 ounces chopped, pitted dates	1½ cups cake flour
¾ cup boiling water	1 tablespoon baking powder
1 tablespoon butter, softened	½ cup pecans, chopped
1½ cups refined sugar	

Sprinkle the soda over the dates. Cover with boiling water and leave to soak. Beat the butter and sugar. Add eggs and beat until very creamy. Sift flour and baking powder and add to the egg and sugar mixture. Pour into a prepared ovenproof dish, top with pecans and bake in preheated over at 350° for 45 minutes. Do not under bake.

Syrup

1½ cups sugar	1 teaspoon vanilla
1 cup water	⅓ cup brandy
1 tablespoon butter	

Place sugar in a saucepan with water. Slowly bring to a boil, stirring until sugar is dissolved. Add butter and vanilla. Cool slightly and add brandy. Remove the tart from the oven and prick the surface with a fork. Pour the sauce over the hot tart and allow to soak in.

May be served with whipped cream or ice cream.

Liz Rogers
Strubenvale, South Africa

Coconut Caramel Pie

This is a real hit in the summer.

1 can sweetened condensed milk
1 (16-ounce) container frozen whipped topping, thawed
1 (8-ounce) package cream cheese softened

¼ cup butter
1 cup coconut
1 cup chopped pecans
2 deep dish pie shells, baked and cooled
1 jar caramel ice cream topping

Combine sweetened condensed milk, whipped topping and cream cheese. Set aside. Combine butter, coconut and pecans. Layer milk mixture, then coconut mixture into pie shells. Drizzle with caramel. Repeat. Freeze until ready to use.

Yield 2 pies.

Mary Nell Davis
Robaya Wolfe Ellis
Savannah, TN

Chocolate Pie

This pie was a favorite of Vernon's uncle, Cleo Cooksey.
When he was plowing in the field, he'd always take time out to eat a big piece of this pie. I never make a chocolate pie that I don't think of him.

1 cup sugar
4 tablespoons flour
4 tablespoons cocoa powder
½ teaspoon salt
1½ cups milk

2 eggs, separated
4 tablespoons butter
1 teaspoon vanilla
4 tablespoons sugar
1 pie shell, baked

Mix sugar, flour, cocoa powder and salt. Add milk, beaten egg yolks, butter and vanilla. Cook over medium heat until mixtures becomes thick. Pour into baked pie shell. Beat egg whites until stiff. Gradually add sugar. Spread on pie and brown meringue in 350° oven until golden brown and set.

Nancy Linam White
Adamsville, TN

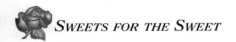

Chocolate Chess Pies

3 cups sugar
3 tablespoons flour
5 eggs, unbeaten
1 teaspoon vanilla
5 tablespoons cocoa powder

1 cup milk
1 stick butter, melted
2 (9-inch) unbaked pie shells
  Whipped topping or ice cream

Combine first 7 ingredients and beat thoroughly. Pour into the unbaked pie shells and bake at 375° for 45 minutes. Serve with whipped topping or ice cream.

Annie Wolfe Bohler
Stone Mountain, GA

Easy Lemon Chess Pie

1¾ cups sugar
2 tablespoons yellow cornmeal
¼ teaspoon salt
⅓ cup butter, melted

¼ cup evaporated milk
3 tablespoons lemon juice
4 large eggs
1 unbaked pie shell

Combine sugar, cornmeal and salt, stirring well. Add butter, milk and lemon juice, stirring well. Add eggs, one at a time, beating well after each addition. Pour into pie shell and bake at 350° for 35 to 45 minutes or until pie is set. Cool on wire rack.

Barbara Williams
Savannah, TN

Easy Pecan Pie

3 eggs
⅔ cup sugar
⅓ cup white syrup

¼ cup melted butter
1 cup pecans
1 unbaked pie shell

Combine first 5 ingredients and mix well. Pour into pie shell and bake at 350° for 40 minutes.

Nettye Beck
Savannah, TN

Easy Custard Pie

¾ cup sugar
2   tablespoons flour
¼   teaspoon salt
3   egg, well beaten
3   tablespoons butter, melted

1½ cups milk
1   teaspoon vanilla
1   unbaked pie shell
½   teaspoon nutmeg

Combine sugar, flour and salt. Add well beaten eggs, butter, milk and vanilla. Pour into pie shell and sprinkle with nutmeg. Bake in a preheated 375° oven for 30 minutes. Let cool before serving.

Neda Chester Hargis
Franklin, TN

Egg Custard Pie

1   cup sugar
2   eggs
3   tablespoons all-purpose flour
1   large can evaporated milk
3   tablespoons butter

1   teaspoon vanilla
⅛   teaspoon nutmeg
1   (9-inch) pie shell, unbaked
½   teaspoon cinnamon

Mix sugar and eggs together. Add flour (use whisk.) Add milk, butter, vanilla and nutmeg. Pour into pie shell and sprinkle cinnamon on top. Place on cookie sheet and bake on bottom rack of 325° oven for 30 minutes, or until firm. Do not over bake.

Annie Wolfe Bohler
Stone Mountain, GA

Fresh Peach Pie

4-5 cups sliced fresh peaches
1   (9-inch) pie shell, unbaked
⅓   cup butter, melted

1   cup sugar
⅓   cup all-purpose flour
1   egg

Placed peaches in pastry shell. Combine remaining ingredients and pour over peaches. Bake at 350° for 1 hour and 10 minutes.

This is also good with fresh blackberries.

Brenda Cornelius
Savannah, TN

Egg Nog Pie

1 (9-inch) pie shell, unbaked	1 teaspoon vanilla
3 eggs	¼ teaspoon salt
1 can sweetened condensed milk	⅛ teaspoon nutmeg
1¼ cups very hot tap water	

Preheat oven to 425°. Bake pie shell for 8 minutes. Remove from oven. In a bowl, beat eggs, sweetened condensed milk, water, vanilla, salt and nutmeg. Pour into pie shell. Bake at 425° for 10 minutes, reduce heat to 350° and continue baking for 25 minutes.

Carole Appleby
Fort Lauderdale, FL

Grandmother White's Key Lime Pie

1 can sweetened condensed milk	1 (8-ounce) package cream cheese, softened
1 (8-ounce) container frozen whipped topping, thawed	½ cup Key lime juice
	2 graham cracker pie crust

Mix milk, topping, cream cheese and lime juice until smooth and pour into pie crusts. Refrigerate.

Pam Wolfe
Savannah, TN

Key Lime Pie

2 cans sweetened condensed milk	1 graham cracker pie shell
½ cup sweetened lime juice	Whipped topping

Combine milk and lime juice and pour into pie shell. Garnish with whipped topping just before serving. Refrigerate.

Jo Ann Leike
Germantown, TN

South Florida Key Lime Pie

2 (14-ounce) cans sweetened condensed milk
5 egg yolks
½ cup Key lime juice
Lime zest
1 graham cracker pie shell

Combine milk, egg yolks, lime juice and lime zest. Pour into crust. Bake for 10 minutes in preheated 350° oven. Freeze for 1 hour before serving.

Charlotte Wolfe
Fort Lauderdale, FL

Lemon Rub Pie

2 cups sugar
1 tablespoon flour
2 tablespoons cornmeal
4 unbeaten eggs
¼ cup butter, melted
¼ cup milk
¼ cup lemon juice
3 tablespoons grated lemon rind
1 unbaked pie shell

Combine sugar, flour and cornmeal. Add eggs, butter, milk, lemon juice and rind. Beat until blended and pour into pie shell. Bake at 375° for 45 minutes. This is a very thick pie.

Laverne Calvert
Savannah, TN

Marie's Apple Pie

3 tablespoons all-purpose flour
1 cup sugar
½ teaspoon cinnamon or allspice
1 stick melted butter
1 egg, beaten
2 cups grated apples
1 unbaked pie shell

Mix flour, sugar and spices together. Melt butter and pour into flour mixture. Add beaten egg, then the apples. Pour into pie shell and bake in 350° oven for 60 minutes.

Barbara Linam
Muscle Shoals, AL

177

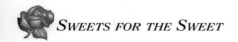

Hot Lemon Sauce Pudding

2	ounces cake flour	1⅔	cups milk
1¾	cups refined sugar	3	ounces butter, melted and cooled
6	egg yolks	6	egg whites
4	large lemons, juiced	3½	ounces sugar
	Grated lemon peel from 4 lemons		

Sift flour and sugar together. Set aside Beat egg yolks, peel, lemon juice and milk. Stir flour mixture and melted butter into lemon mixture until smooth. Beat egg whites until stiff. Beating constantly, add the sugar gradually to make a meringue. Fold smooth lemon mixture into meringue using a metal spoon. Pour into ungreased 4-cup baking dish. Place in a roasting pan, add water to come halfway up sides of dish and bake at 300° for 45 minutes or until golden brown. Cool on rack.

May dust with confectioners' sugar and serve with whipped cream, if desired.

Liz Rogers
Strubenvale, South Africa

Millionaire's Pie

⅔	cup dark corn syrup	1	unbaked 9-inch pie shell
½	cup sugar	1	(6-ounce) package semisweet
½	cup butter		chocolate pieces
4	eggs	1⅓	cups flaked coconut
¼	cup all-purpose flour	1	cup pecans
1	teaspoon vanilla		Whipped cream, optional

In a small saucepan, stir together corn syrup and sugar. Cook and stir over medium heat until sugar is melted and mixture boils, remove from heat. Stir in butter until melted. Set aside to cool slightly, about 10 minutes. Meanwhile, in a large mixing bowl, beat eggs, flour and vanilla on medium speed with electric mixer until mixture is blended and smooth. Add corn syrup mixture in a slow, steady stream, beating constantly. Set aside. In unbaked pie shell, layer chocolate pieces, coconut and pecans. Pour egg mixture over all, spreading smoothly. Cover edge of pie shell with aluminum foil. Bake at 325° for 1 hour. Remove foil, bake for 20 minutes more or until filling is set in center and slightly puffed. Cool and serve with whipped cream.

Yield 8 to 10 servings.

Ted Fowler
Raleigh, NC

Millionaire Pie

1 (15-ounce) can sweetened condensed
   milk
⅓ cup lemon juice
⅓ cup maraschino cherries, drained and
   chopped
⅓ cup pecans, chopped
⅓ cup crushed pineapple, drained
1 (9-inch) graham cracker pie shell
1 (8-ounce) carton frozen whipped
   topping, thawed

Pour condensed milk into a bowl. Gradually add lemon juice, stirring constantly. Fold in cherries, pecans and pineapple. Pour into pie shell: chill 2 hours. At serving time, spread with whipped topping.

Yield 6 servings.

Mary Ellen Parks
Bartlett, TN

Mother's Egg Custard

1 tablespoon butter
½ cup sugar
2 tablespoons all-purpose flour
3 eggs
1 cup milk
½ teaspoon vanilla or lemon flavoring
1 unbaked pie shell

Mix butter and sugar; add flour, eggs, milk and flavoring. Pour into unbaked pie shell and bake at 400° for 10 minutes. Reduce heat to 350° for 30 minutes.

Barbara Linam
Muscle Shoals, AL

Chess Pie

2 cups sugar
2 heaping teaspoons flour
1 heaping teaspoon yellow cornmeal
1 stick butter, melted
3 eggs, well beaten
½ cup buttermilk
1 teaspoon vanilla
1 (12-inch) pie shell, unbaked

Combine sugar, flour and cornmeal and mix well. Combine melted butter, eggs, buttermilk and vanilla. Blend thoroughly. Pour mixture into pie shell and bake at 425° for 10 minutes. Reduce heat to 325° and bake for 30 minutes. When pie begins to brown, cover with a sheet of foil to prevent burning.

Muriel Smith
Savannah, TN

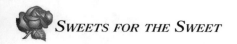

Mother's Old-Fashioned Coconut Pie

2	extra large eggs, separated	1	tablespoon butter
1½	cups milk	1	(7-ounce) can flaked coconut
2	tablespoons flour	1	pie shell, baked
¾	cup sugar	2	tablespoons sugar

Mix beaten egg yolks add milk and place in double boiler over medium heat. Stir until mixture is hot. Mix flour and sugar and add to hot milk mixture. Cook until thick. Remove from heat and add butter and half of the coconut. Stir thoroughly. Pour into cooked pie shell. Beat egg whites until stiff and gradually add sugar. Spread on pie and sprinkle with remaining coconut.

Carole Coats
Savannah, TN

Mrs. Katye's Pecan Tarts

1	(3-ounce) package cream cheese, softened	1	egg
			Dash salt
1	stick butter, softened	1	tablespoon butter, melted
1	cup flour	½	cup chopped pecans
¾	cup brown sugar	1	teaspoon vanilla

Cream together the cream cheese, butter and flour. Take small amount and pat into bottom of 2 (12-count) miniature muffin pan. Refrigerate. Combine brown sugar, egg, salt, melted butter, pecans and vanilla. Drop by teaspoonfuls into chilled pastry lined muffin pans. Bake at 350° for 25 minutes. Cool before removing from pan.

Yield 24 pies.

Katye Beckham Ellis
Waterloo, AL

Mother's Chocolate Pie

½ cup sugar
2 tablespoons cornstarch
1 tablespoon flour
2 tablespoons cocoa powder
3 eggs, separated

2 cups milk
1 tablespoons butter, melted
1 teaspoon vanilla
1 baked pie shell
6 tablespoons sugar

Mix sugar, cornstarch, flour and cocoa powder. Set aside. Beat egg yolks and gradually add milk. Whisk dry ingredients into milk mixture until smooth. Add butter and vanilla. Pour into pie shell. Beat egg whites until stiff. Gradually add sugar to meringue. Spread on top of pie and bake in 375° oven until lightly browned.

Nettye Beck
Savannah, TN

Old-Fashioned Chess Pie

My great aunt, Ethel Stansell, baked
this pie for me every week when I was a child.

2 cups sugar
4 eggs
4 tablespoons cornmeal
1½ tablespoons vinegar
1 stick butter, melted

1 teaspoon vanilla
½ teaspoon nutmeg
5 tablespoons milk
1 (9-inch) pie shell, unbaked

Combine all ingredients except milk and pie shell. Beat ingredients, the longer the better. Add milk. Pour mixture into pie shell. Bake at 350° for 45 minutes.

Dr. Suzanne Thomas
Savannah, TN

Old-Fashioned Chocolate Pie

2	large eggs, separated	¾	cup sugar
1½	cups milk	1	tablespoon butter
3	teaspoons cocoa powder	1	pie shell, baked
2	tablespoons flour	4	tablespoons sugar

Beat egg yolks and add milk. Mix cocoa, flour and ¾ cup of sugar and add to milk mixture. Cook in double boiler until thick: add butter and pour into baked pie shell. Beat egg whites until stiff. Gradually add 4 tablespoons sugar until sugar is dissolved. Spread on pie and bake at 300° until brown.

Carole Coats
Savannah, TN

Peanut Butter Pie

1	(8-ounce) package cream cheese, softened	¾	cup peanut butter
1	can sweetened condensed milk	1	(8-ounce) container frozen whipped topping, thawed
2	teaspoons vanilla	1	(10-inch) graham cracker pie shell

Combine cream cheese, milk, vanilla and peanut butter. Mix with mixer until smooth. Fold in whipped topping and pour into pie shell. Refrigerate or may be frozen.

Angeline Gray
Savannah, TN

Pecan Pie Tarts

3	eggs, slightly beaten	1	teaspoon vanilla
1	cup sugar	1¼	cups pecans, chopped
1	cup light corn syrup		Frozen tart shells, thawed
2	tablespoons butter, melted		

Preheat oven to 350°. In a large bowl, stir eggs, sugar, corn syrup and butter until well blended. Add vanilla. Stir in pecans and pour into tart shells. Bake for 25 to 30 minutes.

Jo Ann Taylor
Dyersburg, TN

Pecan Pie

¼ cup butter	1 teaspoon vanilla
1 cup sugar	1 cup chopped pecans
½ cup white corn syrup	1 unbaked pie shell
3 eggs, beaten	

Melt butter; add sugar and syrup. Add beaten eggs, vanilla and nuts. Pour into crust and bake at 350° for 50 minutes.

This is the best pecan pie I have ever eaten. Mrs. Calvert always gave us one of these at Christmas. Charlotte.

Laverne Calvert
Savannah, TN

Pecan Tarts

This is my mom, Jane Shutt's recipe and it is our favorite for the holidays.

3 eggs	¼ cup butter, melted
1 cup white corn syrup	1 teaspoon vanilla flavoring
1 cup chopped pecans	16 tart shells
1 cup sugar	

Mix eggs, corn syrup, pecans, sugar, butter and vanilla in large mixer bowl. Pour into tart shells and bake slowly at 300° to 325° for 30 to 40 minutes. Yummy.

Diane Hardin
Savannah, TN

Perfect Pie Crust

1 cup solid shortening	1 egg
3 cups flour	3 tablespoons vinegar
1 teaspoon salt	3-4 tablespoons cold water

Cut shortening into flour and salt until mealy fine. Beat together egg, vinegar and water. Pour over flour mixture while tossing with a fork. Shape into a ball and refrigerate. Roll out and put in pie plate for use with favorite pie recipe.

Yield 2 pie shells.

Charlotte Wolfe
Fort Lauderdale, FL

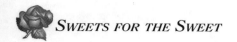

Piña Colada Pie

1 (8-ounce) can cream of coconut
1 (14-ounce) can sweetened condensed milk
1 (15½-ounce) can crushed pineapple, drained
1 (8-ounce) carton frozen whipped topping, thawed
¼ cup light rum
2 graham cracker pie shells

Blend coconut, milk, pineapple, topping and rum together and pour into pie shells. Freeze. Set out about 20 minutes before serving.

Patty Morris
Dyersburg, TN

Pineapple Delight Pie

1 (15-ounce) can crushed pineapple
1 (8-ounce) package cream cheese, softened
1 large package instant vanilla pudding mix
1 graham cracker pie shell

Combine pineapple, cream cheese and pudding mix. Pour into pie shell and chill overnight. Serve with whipped topping if desired.

Annie Wolfe Bohler
Stone Mountain, GA

Sooo Easy Chocolate Pie

1 (8-ounce) solid chocolate candy bar with almonds
1 (12-ounce) carton frozen whipped topping, thawed
1 graham cracker pie shell

Melt candy bar in top of double boiler. Fold in whipped topping and pour into pie shell. Refrigerate.

Add extra chocolate bars for darker chocolate.

Hilda Riggins
Naples, FL

Pineapple Cloud Pie

1 (8½-ounce) box cake mix
½ stick butter, melted
2 (8-ounce) packages cream cheese, softened
½ sugar
2 tablespoons rum
1 (8-ounce) container frozen whipped topping, thawed

1 (16-ounce) can crushed pineapple with syrup
1 (6-ounce) package frozen coconut, thawed
1 cup chopped nuts
Cherries and mint leaves

Mix cake mix and melted butter together until all butter is absorbed. Pat into bottom of a 9-inch cake pan or Pyrex pie pan. Bake at 375° until brown, about 7 or 8 minutes. Remove from oven and with metal spatula pat crust down flat. Leave in pan and cool thoroughly. Beat cream cheese with sugar and rum until very smooth. Fold in whipped topping, pineapple with syrup, coconut and nuts. Spread over cooled crust. Garnish with cherries and mint leaves. Keep covered in refrigerator.

Charlotte Wolfe
Fort Lauderdale, FL

Cracker Pie

50 round buttery crackers
1 stick margarine, melted
2 small packages instant vanilla pudding
2 cups milk
1 quart vanilla ice cream, softened

1 (16-ounce) carton frozen whipped topping, thawed
1 package frozen coconut, thawed
½ cup crushed pecans

Crush crackers and mix with melted margarine. Press into a 12 x 9 x 2-inch glass dish. Cool 10 minutes in freezer. Mix instant pudding and milk. Beat for 1 minute. Add softened ice cream to pudding and milk mixture. Spread over cooled cracker crust. Chill until set, overnight. Cover with whipped topping, coconut and pecans.

Shirley Huddleston
Booneville, TN

185

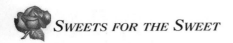

Strawberry Custard Pie

1⅓ cups sugar, divided	1 teaspoon pure vanilla
6 tablespoons cornstarch, divided	1 (9-inch) pie shell, baked
¼ teaspoon salt	1 cup water, divided
2 cups milk	1 tablespoon lemon juice
2 egg yolks, lightly beaten	½ teaspoon liquid red food coloring
1 tablespoon butter	6 cups fresh strawberries, sliced

Combine ⅔ cup sugar, 4 tablespoons cornstarch and salt in a saucepan. Stir in milk. Bring to a boil over medium heat. Cook for 1 minute, stirring constantly. Whisk milk mixture gradually into egg yolks until blended. Return mixture to saucepan. Cook over medium heat, whisking constantly until thickened, about 1 minute. Remove from heat; stir in butter and vanilla. Spoon hot mixture into pie shell. Stir together remaining ⅔ cup sugar, remaining 2 tablespoons cornstarch and 2 tablespoons water. Set aside. Bring remaining water to a boil. Whisk in sugar mixture and cook, whisking constantly, until mixture is thickened and clear, 2 to 3 minutes. Remove from heat. Stir in lemon juice and food coloring. Cool. Fold strawberries into syrup mixture and spoon over custard mixture. Refrigerate 4 hours prior to serving.

Charlotte Wolfe
Fort Lauderdale, FL

Sweet Potato Pie

2 cups boiled and mashed sweet potatoes	2 eggs, well beaten
2 cups sugar	1 teaspoon vanilla
3 tablespoons all-purpose flour	1 teaspoon lemon juice
1 stick butter	1 large can evaporated milk
	2 pie shells, unbaked

Combine all ingredients except pie shells. Beat well and pour into pie shells. Bake at 325° for 30 to 35 minutes or until set.

Robaya Wolfe Ellis
Savannah, TN

Sweet Potato Pie

I really like sweet potato pie, but my husband, Vernon does not.
So I bake my pie and cut into 6 pieces and freeze separately.
Then I have pie as long as it lasts.

1 cup brown sugar
2 egg yolks, beaten
1 stick butter, softened
2 cups cooked and mashed sweet
    potatoes
½ teaspoon ginger
½ teaspoon cinnamon

½ teaspoon salt
½ teaspoon nutmeg
½ cup evaporated milk
2 egg whites
½ cup sugar
1 pie shell, unbaked

Combine brown sugar, egg yolks, butter and sweet potatoes. Add ginger, cinnamon, salt, nutmeg and milk. Blend well. Beat egg whites until stiff. Gradually add sugar, beating until sugar is dissolved. Pour into pie shell and bake in 350° oven until pie is set.

You can sprinkle a small amount of sugar and nutmeg on top before baking.

Nancy Linam White
Adamsville, TN

Turtle Pie

1 (8-ounce) package cream cheese
1 can sweetened condensed milk
1 (16-ounce) carton frozen whipped
    topping, thawed
8 ounces flaked coconut

1 cup chopped nuts
½ stick butter
3 pie shells, baked
1 (12-ounce) jar caramel ice cream
    topping

Mix the first 3 ingredients together. Toast the coconut, nuts and butter in oven until coconut is golden. Layer half of each mixture in the baked pie shells. Drizzle with topping. Repeat. Freeze until ready to use.

This works well with chocolate ice cream topping too.

Bobbie Lou Peck
Florence, AL

Two-Minute Pie

1 (8-ounce) carton sour cream
1 (20-ounce) can crushed pineapple,
  with syrup

1 (5-ounce) package instant vanilla
  pudding mix
½ cup toasted almonds
1 graham cracker pie shell

Mix sour cream, pineapple and syrup, pudding mix and almonds together until well blended. Pour into pie shell. Refrigerate.

Jane Nied

Applesauce Salad

1 (25-ounce) jar applesauce
1 (6-ounce) package cherry jello

1 can lemon-lime carbonated beverage

Heat applesauce and jello until the jello dissolves. Add lemon-lime beverage until all foam is gone. Pour in mold or glass rectangular dish.

1 (8-ounce) can of crushed pineapple, well drained, may be added if desired.

Robaya Wolfe Ellis
Savannah, TN

Broccoli-Raisin Salad

1 cup mayonnaise
¼ cup sugar
2 tablespoons red wine vinegar
1 head broccoli, cut into bite-size pieces

½ red onion, diced
1 cup sunflower seeds
1 cup raisins
6 slices bacon, fried and chopped

Whisk together mayonnaise, sugar and vinegar. Combine remainder of ingredients in a large bowl and pour dressing over. Stir well and refrigerate.

Janet Hickok
Forest Grove, OR

Wolfe's Dairy Bar Coconut Pie

Submitted in memory of my parents, Robert and Jean Wolfe.

1 cup sugar	1 teaspoon vanilla
2 heaping tablespoons flour	½ stick butter
Dash salt	1 pie shell, baked
2 cups milk	¼ cup sugar
3 eggs, separated	¼ teaspoon egg stabilizer (cream of tartar)
1 cup flaked coconut	Coconut to sprinkle

Mix sugar, flour and salt together. Add milk and egg yolks and cook in a double boiler until thick. Add coconut, vanilla and butter. Pour into pie shell. Beat egg whites until stiff. Gradually add sugar and stabilizer. Spread on pie. Sprinkle coconut on top and bake at 350° until meringue is golden brown.

Robaya Wolfe Ellis
Savannah, TN

Wolfe's Dairy Bar Chocolate Pie

This is another pie my late parents,
Robert and Jean Wolfe, served in their restaurant.

1 cup sugar	1 teaspoon vanilla
2 heaping tablespoons flour	½ stick butter
Dash salt	1 pie shell, baked
2 ounces cocoa powder	¼ cup sugar
2 cups milk	¼ teaspoon egg stabilizer (cream of tartar)
3 eggs, separated	

Mix sugar, flour, salt and cocoa together. Add milk and mix. Add the egg yolks. Cook in double boiler until thick. Add vanilla and butter and pour into pie shell. Beat the eggs whites until stiff . Gradually add ¼-cup sugar and stabilizer. Spread on pie and bake at 350° until golden brown.

Robaya Wolfe Ellis
Savannah, TN

Orange Pineapple Salad

1 (3-ounce) package lemon jello
1 (3-ounce) package orange jello
1 cup boiling water
2 (4½-ounce) cans Mandarin oranges
1 (20-ounce) can crushed pineapple

1 (6-ounce) package miniature
    marshmallows
1 (8-ounce) carton heavy cream, whipped
1 cup mayonnaise
1 cup grated cheese

Dissolve both packages of jello into boiling water. Add oranges, pineapple and marshmallows. Stir well and pour into glass casserole dish. Combine heavy cream and mayonnaise. Spread over top and sprinkle with grated cheese.

Gladys Coaker
Savannah, TN

Frozen Fruit Cups

1 (16-ounce) carton sour cream
¾ cup sugar
3 bananas, peeled and cubed
¼ cup chopped maraschino cherries
¼ cup chopped pecans

2 tablespoons lemon juice
⅛ teaspoon salt
1 (8¼-ounce) can crushed pineapple,
    drained

Mix all ingredients together and pour into muffin tins lined with cupcake papers. Freeze until firm. Store in plastic bags in freezer.

Yield 18 servings.

Demetrice Winters Hart
Savannah, TN

Creamsicle Salad

1 small box orange jello
1 small box instant vanilla pudding
1 small can Mandarin oranges, drained,
    reserve liquid

2 cups miniature marshmallows
1 (12-ounce) carton frozen whipped
    topping, thawed

In a large bowl, mix jello and vanilla pudding. Add 2 to 4 tablespoons reserved Mandarin orange liquid. Stir well. Stir in Mandarin oranges and marshmallows. Fold in whipped topping until well blended. Chill.

Charlotte Wolfe
Fort Lauderdale, FL

Grape Party Salad

1 (8-ounce) package cream cheese, softened
¼ cup sour cream
¼ cup mayonnaise

3 tablespoons sugar
1 teaspoon vanilla
2 pounds seedless grapes, cut in half
1 cup chopped pecans

Combine cream cheese, sour cream, mayonnaise, sugar and vanilla in a bowl and blend well. Place grapes in a bowl and add cream cheese mixture. Add pecans.

Yield 8 servings.

Robaya Wolfe Ellis
Savannah, TN

Hot Spiced Fruit

1 (16-ounce) can peach halves
1 (16-ounce) can pear halves
1 (16-ounce) can pineapple spears
½ cup pure orange marmalade

2 tablespoons butter
1 stick cinnamon
⅛ teaspoon nutmeg
⅛ teaspoon ground cloves

Drain fruit, reserving 1½ cups combined syrup, set aside. Combine marmalade, butter, spices and reserved syrup in a saucepan. Bring to a boil, reduce heat and cook 20 to 30 minutes. Gently stir in fruit. Heat 20 minutes.

Yield 8 servings.

Charlotte Wolfe
Fort Lauderdale, FL

Mucho Good Fruit Compote

2 cups diced mangoes
3 passion fruit, pulp only
4 peaches, peeled and sliced

½ cup guava syrup
3 teaspoons lime juice

Combine and refrigerate.

Glenda Fowler
Raleigh, NC

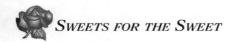

Lemon Strawberry Salad

1 (3-ounce) package lemon jello
1 (20-ounce) can crushed pineapple,
     drained, reserve liquid
1 (8-ounce) package cream cheese
     softened
½ cup chopped celery

½ cup chopped nuts
⅛ teaspoon salt
1 (8-ounce) carton frozen whipped
     topping, thawed
1 (3-ounce) package strawberry jello

Prepare lemon jello according to package directions using drained pineapple juice for the cold water. Add cold water as needed to get correct amount. Mix softened cream cheese with celery, nuts, salt and crushed pineapple. Fold in whipped topping, then fold all into lemon jello. Refrigerate until completely congealed. Prepare strawberry jello according to package directions. When cool gently pour over top of congealed lemon mixture and refrigerate 2 hours.

Peggy and Dave Dickinson
Sarasota, FL

Orange Cream Fruit Salad

1 (20-ounce) can pineapple tidbits,
     drained
1 (16-ounce) peach slices, drained
1 (11-ounce) can Mandarin oranges,
     drained
2 medium firm bananas, sliced

1 medium apple, chopped
1 (3.4-ounce) package instant vanilla
     pudding mix
1½ cups milk
⅓ cup frozen orange juice concentrate
¾ cup sour cream

In a large salad bowl, combine fruits and set aside. In small mixing bowl, beat pudding mix, milk and orange juice for about 2 minutes. Add sour cream and mix well. Spoon over fruit and toss to coat. Cover and refrigerate for 2 hours.

Yield 8 to 10 servings.

Sheryl Wolfe
Savannah, TN

Pineapple Delight

2 (20-ounce) cans pineapple tidbits or crushed pineapple	1½ cups grated Cheddar cheese
¼ cup cornstarch	2 tubes round buttery crackers
1½ cups sugar	2 sticks butter, melted

Drain pineapple. Put into Pyrex dish. Mix cornstarch, sugar and cheese. Sprinkle over pineapple. Crush crackers and mix with the melted butter. Put on top of pineapple mixture. Bake at 325° for 30 to 40 minutes.

Charlotte Wolfe
Fort Lauderdale, FL

Piña Colada Wedges

1 (8-ounce) package cream cheese	1 (8-ounce) can crushed pineapple, undrained
⅓ cup sugar	
½ teaspoon rum extract	2⅔ cups coconut
1 (8-ounce) container frozen whipped topping, thawed	

Beat cream cheese with sugar and rum extract until smooth. Fold in 2 cups of the whipped topping, pineapple and 2 cups coconut. Spread in pan. Spread with remaining coconut. Freeze until firm, at least 2 hours.

Bobbie Lou Peck
Florence, AL

Buckeyes

1 (16-ounce) box confectioners' sugar	¼ bar paraffin
1 stick butter, melted, no substitute	1 (6-ounce) package chocolate chips
1 (18-ounce) jar peanut butter	

Mix sugar, butter and peanut butter together and shape into small balls. Melt paraffin and chocolate chips in top of double boiler. Dip balls in melted chocolate and place on waxed paper.

Johnna Pippin Shaw
Savannah, TN

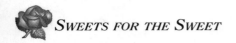

Strawberry Nut Salad

2 small packages strawberry jello
1 cup boiling water
2 (10-ounce) packages sliced
   strawberries, thawed and drained

1 (20-ounce) can crushed pineapple,
   drained
3 medium bananas, sliced
1 cup chopped pecans
1 (16-ounce) carton sour cream

Dissolve jello in water and fold in strawberries, pineapple, bananas and nuts. Pour half of mixture into a 12 x 8 x 2-inch glass dish and refrigerate until firm, about 1 hours. Then spread sour cream evenly over congealed salad. Gently spoon remainder of mixture on top. Refrigerate.

Charlotte Wolfe
Fort Lauderdale, FL

Candy Bar Fudge

6 (2.07-ounce) chocolate nougat
   caramel candy bars
3 cups sugar
¾ cup butter, no substitutes
⅔ cup evaporated milk

1 (12-ounce) package semisweet
   chocolate chips
1 (7-ounce) jar marshmallow cream
1 teaspoon vanilla

Line a 9-inch square pan with foil. Butter the foil and set pan aside. Cut candy bars into ½-inch slices; set aside. In a heavy saucepan, bring sugar, butter and milk to a boil over medium heat. Cook and stir until candy thermometer reads 234°, about 3 minutes. Remove from heat. Stir in chocolate chips, marshmallow cream and vanilla until smooth. Pour half into prepared pan. Sprinkle with candy bar slices. Top with remaining chocolate mixture and spread evenly. Let stand at room temperature to cool. Lift out of pan and remove foil. Cut into squares.

Yield 4 pounds.

Charlotte Wolfe
Fort Lauderdale, FL

Double Chocolate Cookies

1 (8-ounce) package Belgian chocolate semisweet squares
¾ cup firmly packed brown sugar
¼ cup butter
2 eggs
½ cup flour

¼ teaspoon chili powder
¼ teaspoon baking powder
1 tablespoon bourbon
1 (6-ounce) package semisweet chocolate chips
2 cups chopped pecans

Heat oven to 350°. Break chocolate squares into pieces and microwave on high for 1 to 2 minutes. Stir and repeat until chocolate is melted and smooth. Stir in sugar, butter and eggs. Stir in flour, chili powder, baking powder and bourbon. Add chocolate chips and nuts, stir well. Drop by ¼ cupfuls onto ungreased cookie sheet. Bake 12 or 13 minutes. Cool on cookie sheet 1 minute. Transfer to wire rack to cook completely.

Yield 1½ dozen.

Charlotte Wolfe
Fort Lauderdale, FL

Chocolate Chip Cookies

5 cups oatmeal
2 cups butter
2 cups firmly packed brown sugar
2 cups sugar
4 eggs
2 teaspoons vanilla
4 cups flour

1 teaspoon salt
2 teaspoon baking powder
2 teaspoons baking soda
2 (12-ounce) packages semisweet chocolate chips
1 (8-ounce) solid chocolate bar, grated
3 cups chopped nuts

Measure oatmeal and blend in a blender to a fine powder. Cream the butter and both sugars. Add eggs and vanilla. Combine flour, salt, baking powder and soda. Add to egg and sugar mixture. Add chocolate chips, grated chocolate bar and nuts. Roll into balls and place 2 inches apart on a cookie sheet. Bake for 10 minutes at 375°.

Yield 112 cookies.

Sheryl Wolfe
Savannah, TN

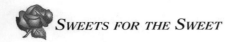

Chow Mein Candy Clusters

1 (12-ounce) package butterscotch morsels
1 cup chow mein noodles
1 cup cocktail peanuts

Melt morsels over hot, not boiling, water until thoroughly dissolved. Remove from heat, stir in noodles and nuts. Mix well. Drop by teaspoonfuls on wax paper. Cool until firm.

You may use other nuts, such as walnuts or pecans.

Hilda Riggins
Naples, FL

Coconut Bonbons

1 stick butter or margarine
1 can sweetened condensed milk
7 cups confectioners' sugar
3 cups coconut
1 tablespoon vanilla
2 pounds vanilla bark

Mix butter, milk, sugar, coconut and vanilla. Roll into 1-inch balls and chill for 1 to 2 hours (best if frozen.) Melt vanilla bark in microwave or double boiler. Dip coconut balls into melted bark and place onto wax paper to harden. Store in refrigerator.

Yield 100 candies.

Diane DeBerry
Savannah, TN

English Toffee

3 sticks butter
1 cup sugar
1 cup walnuts
1 (12-ounce) package milk chocolate chips
1 cup almonds

Melt butter and sugar together. Stir until mixture becomes a golden brown. Lay walnuts evenly in a 13 x 9 x 2-inch pan. Pour sugar mixture over walnuts. Spread chocolate chips over mixture. When chocolate melts spread with spatula. Sprinkle almonds over the chocolate. Chill overnight.

Ruth Hughes
Alta Loma, CA

Date Bourbon Crispies

½ cup butter, softened
1 cup sugar
1 (10-ounce) package chopped nuts
1 large egg, slightly beaten

1 cup toasted, chopped pecans
1 ounce bourbon
5 cups crisp rice cereal
Confectioners' sugar

Combine first 4 ingredients in a saucepan. Cook over low heat 6 to 8 minutes, stirring constantly until sugar dissolves. Add pecans and cook, stirring constantly for 10 minutes. Remove from heat and stir in bourbon. Stir in cereal and cool slightly. Pour into prepared 9 x 12 x 2-inch pan. Sprinkle with confectioners' sugar. Cut into squares after completely cooled.

For thinner squares, use larger pan.

Charlotte Wolfe
Fort Lauderdale, FL

Divinity

This is so easy and always turns out perfectly.

2 cups sugar
½ cup light corn syrup
½ cup hot water
¼ teaspoon salt

2 egg whites
1 teaspoon vanilla
½ cup chopped nuts

In a 2-quart saucepan combine sugar, corn syrup, hot water and salt. Cook and stir until sugar dissolves and mixture comes to a boil. Cook to hard ball stage, 250° on a candy thermometer, without stirring. Remove from heat. Immediately beat the egg whites until stiff peaks form. Slowly pour hot syrup over the beaten egg whites beating constantly at high speed on mixer. Add vanilla and beat until mixture forms soft peaks and begins to lose its gloss. Add chopped nuts and drop from teaspoon onto wax paper.

Charlotte Wolfe
Fort Lauderdale, FL

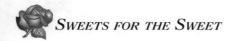

Chocolate Balls

This freezes well so it can be made ahead of time for Christmas.

2 sticks butter
1 (16-ounce) box confectioners' sugar
½ cup peanut butter
1 tablespoon vanilla

1 cup chopped nuts
1 cup graham cracker crumbs
1 stick paraffin
1 (6-ounce) package chocolate chips

Melt butter over low heat. Add sugar and mix well. Add peanut butter, vanilla, chopped nuts and graham cracker crumbs. Mix well and form into balls the size of a walnut. Chill until firm. Melt paraffin and chocolate chips. Dip balls in chocolate and place on wax paper to dry.

Loral Wolfe White, 1915-2001
Fort Myers, FL

Chocolate Candy

My mother always made these for Christmas, Charlotte.

1 stick butter
1 can sweetened condensed milk
1 tablespoon vanilla
2 (16-ounce) boxes confectioners' sugar

1 (7-ounce) can flaked coconut
1 cup chopped pecans
1 stick paraffin
1 (12-ounce) package chocolate chips

Mix butter, sweetened condensed milk, vanilla, confectioners' sugar, coconut and pecans together. Chill. Roll into 1-inch balls. Chill again. Melt paraffin in top of double boiler. Add chocolate chips. Put candy balls on toothpick and dip in melted mixture. Keep in refrigerator.

Jo Ann Linam Johnson, 1926-1999
Florence, AL

Buttermilk Fudge

1 teaspoon soda	2 tablespoons light corn syrup
1 cup buttermilk	½ cup butter
2 cups sugar	1 cup chopped nuts

Blend soda and buttermilk together in a large saucepan. Add sugar, corn syrup and butter. Bring to a boil and cook to 240° on candy thermometer. Remove from heat and beat well. Stir in nuts. Drop by spoonfuls onto wax paper.

Jo Ann Linam Johnson, 1926-1999
Florence, AL

Microwave Candy

1 (12-ounce) package semisweet chocolate chips	3 cups miniature marshmallows
1 cup chunky peanut butter	1 cup pecans, chopped

Microwave chocolate and peanut butter in a 2-quart bowl on medium heat for 2 to 3 minutes or until melted. Stirring after each minute. Fold in marshmallows and nuts. Pour into foil lined 8-inch square pan. Chill until firm and cut into pieces.

Charlotte Wolfe
Fort Lauderdale, FL

Homemade Toffee Bars

1 pound butter	1 (8-ounce) solid chocolate bar
1 (16-ounce) box light brown sugar	1 cup chopped nuts

In heavy saucepan, cook butter and brown sugar slowly to hard crack stage, 300° on candy thermometer. Stir occasionally. While cooking, melt chocolate bar in double boiler. Grease a 15 x 10 x 1-inch jelly-roll pan and sprinkle with pecans. Pour sugar mixture over chopped pecans. Spread melted chocolate over the pecans. Allow to cool and break into pieces.

Charlotte Wolfe
Fort Lauderdale, FL

199

English Toffee

2 sticks butter
1 cup sugar
2 tablespoons water

1 tablespoon light corn syrup
½ cup coarsely slivered almonds or other nuts, toasted

Lightly butter a 10 x 15-inch pan. Set aside. Melt the butter in a heavy 3-quart saucepan over low to medium heat. Stir in sugar and cook, stirring constantly until the mixture comes to a full rolling boil. Add the water and corn syrup and mix well. Cook to 290° on candy thermometer. Add the nuts. Stir and immediately pour into the prepared pan, tipping back and forth to spread the toffee and distribute the nuts evenly. When the toffee is cool, break into random serving size pieces. Store in airtight container.

Linda Patterson
Savannah, TN

Holiday Orange Vodka Truffles

¼ cup heavy cream
2 tablespoons citron vodka
6 ounces sweet chocolate, broken up

2 tablespoons orange zest
4 tablespoons unsalted butter
Powdered unsweetened cocoa powder

Boil cream in a small heavy pan until reduced by half. Remove from heat. Stir in vodka, chocolate and orange zest and mix until completely melted and smooth. Cut butter into chunks and whisk in. When mixture is smooth, pour into a shallow dish and refrigerate until firm. Scoop chocolate up with a teaspoon and shape into rough 1-inch balls. Roll the truffles in the cocoa to coat lightly. Store truffles covered in refrigerator. Serve at room temperature.

Chef Jill K. Bosich, CEC, CCE
Dean of Culinary Education
Culinard, The Culinary Institute of Virginia College

Peanut Brittle

1½ cups sugar	1 teaspoon vanilla
½ cup water	1 tablespoon butter
½ cup light corn syrup	1 teaspoon baking soda
3 cups raw peanuts	

Place sugar, water and corn syrup in a large saucepan. Stirring constantly bring to a boil and boil for 5 minutes. Add peanuts and cook 10 minutes longer, continue to stir constantly. Add vanilla, butter and soda. Pour on a buttered cookie sheet and cool. When cool, break into pieces.

Mabel Callins
Memphis, TN

Microwave Peanut Brittle

1 cup white sugar	1 teaspoon vanilla
½ cup light corn syrup	4 tablespoons butter
1 cup salted peanuts	1 teaspoon baking soda

Mix sugar and syrup in a large glass bowl. Cook in microwave on high for 2 minutes. Stir, using a wooden spoon, and cook another 2 minutes. Add peanuts and cook another 4 minutes. Add vanilla and butter. Mix well and cook 3 minutes. Add baking soda and stir. Pour onto a greased cookie sheet and chill for 30 minutes.

Ruth Hughes
Alta Loma, CA

Millionaires

1 (14-ounce) package caramel candy squares	2 cups pecans
	3 teaspoons evaporated milk
6 (1½-ounce) solid milk chocolate candy bars	¼ bar paraffin

In double boiler melt caramels and milk. Stir in pecans. Drop rounded teaspoonfuls on greased cookie sheet. Chill overnight. Next day, melt chocolate candy bars and paraffin in double boiler. Keep the mixture hot and dip each candy piece in chocolate and coat. Place on wax paper to let chocolate harden.

Pam Wolfe
Savannah, TN

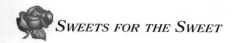

Peanut Butter Treats

1 cup light corn syrup
1 cup sugar

1 cup peanut butter
4 cups plain cereal squares

Combine syrup and sugar and bring to a boil. Boil for 30 seconds and add peanut butter. Remove from heat and add cereal. Drop onto waxed paper in small mounds. Store in airtight container.

Charlotte Wolfe
Fort Lauderdale, FL

Peanut Butter Snowballs

1 cup confectioners' sugar
½ cup creamy peanut butter

3 tablespoons margarine, softened
1 pound vanilla bark

Mix sugar, peanut butter and softened margarine. Shape into 1-inch balls. Place in freezer for 1 to 2 hours. Melt vanilla bark in microwave or double boiler. Dip balls and place on wax paper to harden. Store in airtight container.

Yield 20 to 24 candies.

Diane DeBerry
Savannah, TN

Cheese Fudge

1 (8-ounce) box processed cheese loaf
2 sticks butter
1⅓ teaspoons vanilla

2 (16-ounce) boxes confectioners' sugar
½ cup cocoa powder
3 cups pecans, chopped

Heat cheese loaf, butter and vanilla in microwave until melted. Set aside. Combine sugar, cocoa powder and pecans in a large bowl. Combine 2 mixtures, using mixer. When completely mixed, spread in a buttered 13 x 9 x 2-inch dish. Chill for 1 hour and slice.

Charlotte Wolfe
Fort Lauderdale, FL

Penuche

Butter
1½ cups sugar
1 cup firmly packed brown sugar
⅓ cup light cream

⅓ cup milk
2 tablespoons butter or margarine
1 teaspoon vanilla
½ cup chopped pecans or walnuts

Line an 8 x 4 x 2-inch or a 9 x 5 x 3-inch loaf pan with foil; extend foil over the edges. Butter foil and set aside. Butter the sides of a heavy 2-quart saucepan. Combine sugars, cream and milk. Cook and stir over medium-high heat to boiling. Reduce heat to medium-low and cook until mixture reaches 236° on candy thermometer, about 15 to 20 minutes. Remove from heat. Add butter or margarine but do not stir. Cool without stirring to 110°, about 50 minutes. Remove thermometer and beat mixture vigorously until penuche just begins to thicken. Add nuts. Continue beating until mixture gets very thick and just starts to lose its gloss, about 10 minutes. Spread into pan. Score into squares. Cut when firm.

Yield 32 servings.

Robaya Wolfe Ellis
Savannah, TN

Rum Balls

2½ cups finely crushed vanilla wafers
1 cup confectioners' sugar
2 tablespoons cocoa powder
½ cup finely chopped walnuts or pecans

¼ cup rum, light or dark
¼ cup light corn syrup
Confectioners' sugar

Combine wafer crumbs, sugar, cocoa powder and nuts. Stir in rum and syrup. Form mixture into ¾-inch balls, adding a small amount of water if necessary. Roll in confectioners' sugar. Store in tightly covered container.

This can be made with brandy or bourbon also.

Yield 4 dozen.

Neda Chester Hargis
Franklin, TN

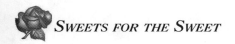

Quick Candy Bars

1   package sugar free hot cocoa mix
1   tablespoon peanut butter

¾   ounces quick cooking oats

Mix all ingredients together with a small amount of water. Drop by spoonfuls and freeze. Eat frozen or partially frozen.

Yield 3 servings.

Robaya Wolfe Ellis
Savannah, TN

Brownies with Caramel Sauce

8   ounces unsalted butter
12   ounces bittersweet chocolate
1½   cups all-purpose flour
1   teaspoon baking powder

Pinch salt
4   eggs
2   cups sugar
2   cups walnuts

Melt butter and chocolate in a heat-proof bowl over simmering water until melted. Combine flour, baking powder and salt; set aside. Whisk together eggs and sugar until pale yellow. Add chocolate and combine. Fold in flour mixture until just combined. Add walnuts and place in greased and floured pan. Bake at 350° for 40 minutes. Cool.

Brandy Caramel Sauce

1   cup water
2   cups granulated sugar
½   cup brandy

1   vanilla pod, split in half
3   cups heavy cream

Place water and sugar in heavy-bottom pot and resolve at low heat. Then turn temperature to medium-high to caramelize to a light golden brown. When caramelized, set aside. Simmer brandy with vanilla pods, burning off alcohol. Add cream and bring to a low boil. Slowly add cream mixture to caramel. Bring to a low boil. Reduce to consistency, which will coat spoon. Remove from heat and cool to room temperature.

Donald Parris
Shelby, GA

Unbaked Chocolate Oatmeal Cookies

2 cups sugar	1 (4-ounce) box chocolate instant
⅔ cup evaporated milk	pudding
1½ sticks butter, softened	3⅓ cups oatmeal

Combine sugar, milk and butter in large pan. Bring to a rolling boil, stirring often. Remove from heat and add pudding. Add oatmeal and mix thoroughly. Drop by spoonfuls onto wax paper. Store in airtight container.

Diane DeBerry
Savannah, TN

Brown Sugar Pecan Cookies

1 cup butter, softened	2 cups all-purpose flour
½ cup firmly packed brown sugar	½ teaspoon baking powder
1 egg	¼ teaspoon salt
1 teaspoon vanilla	½ cup finely chopped pecans

Beat butter at medium speed on mixer until light and fluffy. Gradually add sugars and egg, mixing well. Combine flour, soda and salt. Gradually add to creamed mixture. Stir in pecans. Chill dough 30 minutes. Shape dough into 1-inch balls and place on ungreased cookie sheet. Bake at 350° for 10 to 12 minutes. Cool on wire racks.

Brown Sugar Frosting

1 cup firmly packed brown sugar	1½ cups confectioners' sugar
½ cup half-and-half	Pecan halves
1 tablespoon butter	

Combine brown sugar and half-and-half in a saucepan. Cook over medium heat, stirring constantly until mixture comes to a boil. Boil for 4 minutes. Remove from heat. Stir in butter. Add confectioners' sugar and beat at medium speed on mixer until smooth. Spread on each cookie and top with a pecan half.

Barbara Linam
Muscle Shoals, AL

Cracker Cookies

1 cup butter, softened
1 cup firmly packed brown sugar
2 eggs
1 (16-ounce) package club crackers, crushed
1 cup chopped nuts
1 cup miniature marshmallows cut in half
Confectioners' sugar

Cream butter and sugar together. Add eggs and beat well. Add crackers, nuts and marshmallows and stir until blended. Bake in 350° oven for 7 to 10 minutes until light golden brown.

Charlotte Wolfe
Fort Lauderdale, FL

CC's White Chocolate Chunk Cookies

¾ cup sugar
¾ cups firmly packed brown sugar
1 cup butter
3 eggs
1 teaspoon vanilla
1 ounce bourbon
2½ cups all-purpose flour
1 teaspoon baking powder
1 teaspoon baking soda
½ teaspoon salt
1 cup coconut
½ cup rolled oats, not instant
1½ cups chopped walnuts or pecans
2 (6-ounce) packages white chocolate bars, cut into ¼-inch chunks

Heat oven to 350°. In a large bowl combine sugar, brown sugar and butter. Beat until light and fluffy. Add eggs one at a time, beating well after each. Add vanilla and bourbon and blend well. Combine flour, baking powder, baking soda and salt. Gradually add to sugar mixture. Stir in remaining ingredients. Drop by rounded tablespoonfuls on ungreased cookie sheet. Bake for 10 to 15 minutes. Cool.

Yield 5 dozen cookies.

Charlotte Wolfe
Fort Lauderdale, FL

Butterscotch Muffins

2 cups all-purpose flour	1 cup milk
½ cup sugar	1½ teaspoons butter flavoring
1 tablespoon baking powder	1 teaspoon vanilla extract
½ teaspoon salt	¼ cup vegetable oil
1 egg	¾ cup butterscotch morsels

Preheat oven to 400°; grease or paper line 12 muffin cups. In a large bowl whisk together flour, sugar, baking powder and salt until well blended. Set aside. In a medium size bowl beat together egg, milk, flavoring and oil until blended. Add to dry mixture along with butterscotch chips and stir just until blended. Do not over beat. Fill muffin cups ⅔ full and bake for 20 to 25 minutes.

Yield 12 muffins.

Charlotte Wolfe
Fort Lauderdale, FL

Cake Mix Cookies

1 box cake mix, any flavor	2 eggs
¼ cup oil	

Combine all ingredients. Roll out, cut with cookie cutter and bake for 8 to 10 minutes in a 350° oven.

Linda Neill
Savannah, TN

Chocolate Chews

1 box fudge cake mix	1 (6-ounce) package mint chocolate chips
2 eggs	1 cup chopped nuts
½ cup butter, melted	1 can prepared chocolate icing

Preheat oven to 350°. Grease 13 x 9 x 2-inch pan. Combine cake mix, eggs and butter in a large bowl. Stir until thoroughly blended. Stir in chips and nuts. Press mixture into pan. Bake 25 to 30 minutes. Cool completely. Drizzle with icing.

Charlotte Wolfe
Fort Lauderdale, FL

Chewy Oatmeal Cookies

When my dad was a little boy, he made a recipe book for his mother.
This recipe was in it. I have entered these in the Hookstown Fair in PA, as
well as the Hardin County Fair, winning First Place, a blue ribbon each time.
I also submitted them in a contest in the Houston Chronicle in Texas was
sponsoring and won. I always think of my late Maw Maw when I bake them.

1¾	cups self-rising flour	½	cup shortening, melted
1½	cups sugar	¼	cup molasses
½	teaspoon salt	2	eggs
½	teaspoon cinnamon	1	teaspoon vanilla
½	teaspoon allspice	1½	cups quick cooking oats
½	teaspoon nutmeg	1	cup chopped nuts

Combine flour, sugar, salt, cinnamon, allspice and nutmeg. Add melted shortening, molasses, eggs and vanilla and mix until smooth. Stir in oats and nuts. Drop by spoonfuls onto lightly greased cookie sheet. Bake at 350° for 8 to 10 minutes.

Arian Epps
Adamsville, TN

Chocolate Chip Cookies

⅔	cup butter, softened	½ teaspoon baking soda
½	cup sugar	½ teaspoon salt
⅓	cup firmly packed brown sugar	½ cup chopped pecans
1	egg	1 (6-ounce) package milk chocolate
1	teaspoon maple flavoring	chips
1½	cups flour	

Preheat oven to 375° Mix butter, sugars, egg and maple flavoring. Mix flour, soda and salt. Add to sugar mixture and mix thoroughly. Add nuts and chocolate chips. With teaspoon drop 2 inches apart on ungreased cookie sheet. Bake 8 to 10 minutes. Cool slightly before removing from cookie sheet.

Johnna Pippin Shaw
Savannah, TN

Chocolate Coconut Bars

*With a middle layer of coconut, these
sweet chocolaty treats are similar to a Mounds candy bar.*

2 cups graham cracker crumbs
½ cup butter, melted
¼ cup sugar
2 cups flaked coconut
1 (14-ounce) can sweetened condensed
   milk

½ cup chopped pecans
1 (7-ounce) solid milk chocolate candy
   bar
2 tablespoons creamy peanut butter

Combine the crumbs, butter and sugar. Press into a greased 13 x 9 x 2-inch pan. Bake at 350° for 10 minutes. Meanwhile, combine coconut, milk and pecans. Spread over the baked crust. Bake at 350° for 15 minutes. Cool completely. In a small saucepan melt candy bar and peanut butter. Spread over bars. Cool until set.

Yield 3 dozen bars.

George Ann Ingram
Fort Myers, FL

Chocolate Oatmeal Bars

This recipe won honorable mention in a 1995 national recipe contest.

1 box German chocolate cake mix
2 cups old-fashioned oats
1 stick butter, melted
2 teaspoons pure vanilla, divided
3 eggs
1 cup flaked coconut

1 cup chopped pecans
1 (16-ounce) box confectioners' sugar
1 (8-ounce) package cream cheese
1 teaspoon vanilla
3 eggs

Combine cake mix, oats, butter, vanilla and eggs. Pat into a 13 x 9 x 2-inch pan. Sprinkle with coconut and nuts. Set aside. Mix confectioners' sugar, cream cheese vanilla and egg. Beat on medium speed of mixer until smooth. Pour over oat mixture. Bake at 350° for 45 minutes until lightly browned and crusty. Cool completely and cut into bars.

Yield 18 to 24 bars.

You may substitute egg substitute for the eggs and fat free cream cheese if desired.

Charlotte Wolfe
Fort Lauderdale, FL

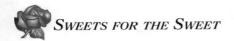

Chocolate Oatmeal Cookies

1 stick butter	1 teaspoon maple flavoring
2 cups sugar	3 cups oats
½ cup milk	½ cup peanut butter
4 tablespoons cocoa powder	

Mix butter, sugar, milk and cocoa powder in a saucepan. Bring to a rolling boil. Boil for 2 minutes. Remove from heat. Add flavoring, oats and peanut butter. Drop by spoonfuls on waxed paper.

Johnna Pippin Shaw
Savannah, TN

Cinnamon Buttons

1 package sugar cookie dough	1 tablespoon cinnamon
4 tablespoons sugar	½ cup wheat germ

Cut dough into 12 pieces and cut each piece into 4 pieces. Roll each piece into a ball. Mix sugar, cinnamon and wheat germ together and put into a plastic zip top bag. Put 6 of the cookie balls in bag at a time and shake until well coated. Repeat until all pieces are used. Place on ungreased cookie sheet 2 inches apart. Bake at 375° for 8 to 10 minutes or until light golden brown.

Charlotte Wolfe
Fort Lauderdale, FL

Cream Cheese Cookies

1 stick butter	1 cup all-purpose flour
1 (3-ounce) package cream cheese	½ teaspoon vanilla
1 cup sugar	½ cup chopped pecans

Cream butter and cheese. Add sugar and mix well. Add flour, vanilla and nuts. Drop by teaspoonfuls on ungreased cookie sheet. Bake at 375° until light brown. Watch carefully, do not let them burn.

Yield 3 dozen.

Charlotte Wolfe
Fort Lauderdale, FL

Creamy Cashew Brownies

1 (1-pound, 5.5-ounce) package fudge
   brownie mix
⅓ cup water
¼ cup oil
1 egg
1 cup chocolate chips

Heat oven to 350°. Grease the bottom of a 13 x 9 x 2-inch pan. In a large bowl, combine brownie mix, water, oil and egg. Beat 50 strokes with spoon. Stir in chocolate chips. Spread in prepared pan. Bake at 350° for 24 to 27 minutes. Do not over bake. Cool completely.

Topping

2 (8-ounce) packages cream cheese
1 cup confectioners' sugar
1 teaspoon vanilla
1½ cups cashews
½ cup hot fudge topping, warmed

Beat cream cheese, sugar and vanilla until smooth. Set aside. Sprinkle half of cashews over brownies. Spread cream cheese mixture over brownies. Sprinkle cashews over cream cheese mixture. Drizzle hot fudge topping over cashews. Store in refrigerator.

Yield 24 bars.

Robaya Wolfe Ellis
Savannah, TN

Crystal's Cookies

5 cups blended oatmeal
2 cups butter
2 cups sugar
2 cups firmly packed brown sugar
4 eggs
2 teaspoons vanilla
4 cups flour
1 teaspoons salt
2 teaspoons baking powder
2 teaspoons baking soda
5 cups chocolate chips
1 (6-ounce) solid milk chocolate candy
   bar
3 cups chopped nuts

Blend oatmeal in blender until it is a fine powder. Cream butter and both sugars. Add eggs and vanilla. Mix together with flour, oatmeal, salt, baking powder, baking soda. Add chips, candy and nuts. Roll into balls and place 2 inches apart on a cookie sheet. Bake for 6 minutes at 350°.

Crystal Dollahite
Memphis, TN

Date Bars

1 stick butter
1 cup sugar
1 (8-ounce) box chopped dates
2 cups crisp rice cereal

1 cup chopped nuts
2 teaspoons vanilla
Confectioners' sugar

Melt butter, sugar and dates. Cook slowly about 10 minutes, stirring all the time. Remove from heat and pour over the other ingredients. Press into a pan or dish that has been greased and sprinkled with confectioners' sugar. Let cool and cut into squares. Dust top with confectioners' sugar.

Janice Hooper
Whitwell, TN

Date Bars

1 (8-ounce) package pitted dates, coarsely chopped
1½ cups orange juice
2½ cups all-purpose flour
1½ cups firmly packed brown sugar
½ teaspoon salt, optional

1½ cups butter, chilled
2 cups old-fashioned rolled oats
1½ cups flaked, sweetened coconut, divided
1 cup chopped nuts

Heat oven to 350°. In a medium nonreactive saucepan combine dates and orange juice. Bring to a boil over medium heat; reduce heat and simmer 15 to 20 minutes or until thickened, stirring occasionally. Remove from heat; cool slightly. Combine flour, sugar and salt. Cut in butter until mixture is crumbly. Stir in oats, 1 cup coconut and nuts. Mix well. Reserve 4 cups of the oat mixture, set aside. Press remaining oat mixture into bottom of ungreased 13 x 9 x 2-inch baking pan. Spread date mixture evenly over crust to within ¼-inch of edges. Sprinkle with reserved oat mixture. Sprinkle with remaining ½ cup coconut, patting down gently into oat mixture. Bake 35 to 40 minutes or until light golden brown. Cool completely. Cut into bars and store in tightly covered container.

Charlotte Wolfe
Fort Lauderdale, FL

Della's Butter Cookies

The late Mindy English was a special friend I met online.
Sadly she died in May 2000. She had sent me this recipe and it is delicious.

1 cup butter	Dash salt
1 cup sugar	1 teaspoon soda
2 cups flour	1 teaspoon vanilla

Cream butter and sugar. Sift flour, salt and soda into creamed mixture. Mix well. Roll into a roll and wrap in wax paper. Refrigerate until chilled. Cut into slices and bake at 350° for 10 to 12 minutes or until lightly brown around the edges.

Mindy English
Atlanta, GA

Double Chocolate Bars

½ cup butter	2 tablespoons unsweetened cocoa powder
¾ cup sugar	¼ teaspoon baking powder
2 eggs	¼ teaspoon salt
1 teaspoon vanilla	2 cups miniature marshmallows
¾ cup all-purpose flour	
½ cup chopped pecans	

Cream together butter and sugar. Beat in eggs and vanilla. Set aside. Stir together flour, chopped nuts, cocoa powder, baking powder and salt. Stir into egg mixture. Spread in bottom of greased 13 x 9 x 2-inch baking pan. Bake at 350° for 15 to 20 minutes or until bars test done. Sprinkle marshmallows evenly on top; bake 3 more minutes. Cool.

Topping

1 (6-ounce) package semisweet chocolate chips	1 cup creamy peanut butter
	1½ cups crisp rice cereal

In small saucepan, combine chocolate chips and peanut butter. Cook and stir over low heat until chocolate is melted. Stir in cereal. Spread mixture on top of cooled bars. Chill. Cut into bars. Refrigerate.

Yield 3 to 4 dozen bars.

Linda Patterson
Savannah, TN

213

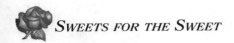

Dream Bars

1 cup butter	4 eggs, well beaten
1 teaspoon salt	4 tablespoons all-purpose flour
3 cups firmly packed brown sugar	1 teaspoon baking powder
2 cups sifted all-purpose flour	3 cups shredded coconut
2 teaspoons vanilla	2 cups chopped nuts

Combine butter and salt, add 1 cup brown sugar and cream well. Add flour and blend. Press mixture firmly into an 8 x 12-inch greased pan and bake for 20 minutes at 325°. Add remaining 2 cups brown sugar and vanilla to well beaten eggs until mixture is thick and foamy. Add 4 tablespoons flour, baking powder, coconut and nut meats and blend. Spread over baked mixture. Return to oven and bake 25 minutes. Cool and cut into squares.

Joyce Sandler
Gloucester, Ontario, Canada

Fudge Brownies

My friends Genevieve and Bill Toupal of Stonewall, CO
gave me this recipe. It is a hit at the lodge with the fishermen.

2 eggs	½ cup butter, softened
1 cup sugar	2 ounces unsweetened chocolate
⅛ teaspoon salt	¾ cup flour
1 teaspoon vanilla	½ cup nuts

Mix eggs, sugar and salt together in mixing bowl, add vanilla. Melt butter and chocolate together in a saucepan. Cool slightly before stirring into egg mixture. Add flour ½ cup at a time. Fold in nuts. Turn into a lightly greased 8 x 8-inch baking pan. Bake in a 350° oven for 25 to 30 minutes. Do not over bake.

Janet Hickok, Simms Lodge
Nondalton, AK

Extra Good Cookies

1 cup butter, softened
1 cup sugar
1 egg, separated

2 cups all-purpose flour
1 teaspoon cinnamon
1 cup chopped pecans

Combine butter and sugar and beat until smooth. Add egg yolk. Blend well. Add flour and cinnamon. Blend. Press mixture into a greased jelly-roll pan. Beat egg white and spread on top of mixture. Sprinkle with pecans. Bake at 350° for 20 minutes. Cut into squares.

Millie Ungren
Crump, TN

Graham Cracker Bars

Graham Crackers
2 sticks butter
1 beaten egg
1 cup sugar

½ cup milk
1⅓ cups coconut
1 cup chopped pecans
1 cup graham cracker crumbs

Line a 9 x 12 x 2-inch pan with whole graham crackers. Combine butter, egg, sugar and milk in a saucepan. Cook, stirring constantly, over medium heat, until it boils. Remove and add coconut, pecans and cracker crumbs. Spread over crackers in pan. Place another layer of whole crackers on top and spread with topping. Refrigerate 24 hours and cut into small bars.

Topping
1 stick butter, softened
4 tablespoons evaporated milk

1 teaspoon vanilla
2½ cups confectioners' sugar

Combine all ingredients and beat until fluffy.

Diane Hardin
Savannah, TN

Freckles

These are called freckles because after baking the
wheat germ looks like the freckles that were once on my nose.

2   sticks butter, softened
1¾ cups sugar
½   cup egg substitute
2¾ cups sifted all-purpose flour
2   teaspoons cream of tartar

1   teaspoon baking soda
¼   teaspoon salt
1   cup chopped nuts
¾   cup wheat germ

Heat oven to 400°. Cream shortening and sugar until smooth. Add egg substitute and mix well. Sift together flour, cream of tartar, soda and salt. Stir into sugar mixture. Add nuts and wheat germ. Form dough into balls the size of walnuts. Roll in topping mixture and place 2 inches apart on ungreased baking sheet. Bake 8 to 10 minutes.

Topping
4   tablespoons sugar
1   tablespoon cinnamon

½ cup wheat germ

Mix together in small bowl.

Charlotte Wolfe
Fort Lauderdale, FL

Gene's Tea Cakes

1½ sticks butter or margarine, softened
1   cup sugar
2   eggs, beaten
2   teaspoons vanilla

3   cups flour
1   teaspoon baking powder
½   teaspoon salt

Cream butter or margarine and sugar. Add eggs and vanilla and blend well. Add flour, baking powder and salt. Blend well. Drop by teaspoonfuls onto a sprayed cookie sheet about 2 inches apart. Press down with bottom a glass dipped in small amount of flour. Bake at 350° for 10 to 12 minutes.

Gene Churchwell
Crump, TN

Gingersnaps

These are my favorite cookies.

¾ cup shortening
1 egg
1 cup firmly packed brown sugar
¼ cup molasses
2¼ cups all-purpose flour
2 teaspoons soda

1 teaspoon cinnamon
1 teaspoon ginger
½ teaspoon cloves
¼ teaspoon salt
Granulated sugar

Cream together shortening, brown sugar, egg and molasses. Blend in remaining ingredients except sugar. Cover and chill 1 hour. Heat oven to 375°. Shape dough by rounded teaspoonfuls into balls. Dip tops in granulated sugar. Place balls sugar side up 3 inches apart on lightly greased cookie sheet. Bake 10 to 12 minutes or until just set. Immediately remove from cookie sheet and cool.

Yield 4 dozen cookies.

Barbara Duryea
Poulsbo, WA

LJ's Chocolate Peanut Butter Oatmeal Cookies

1 stick butter
2 cups sugar
1 teaspoon vanilla extract
⅓ cup peanut butter

4 tablespoons cocoa powder
½ cup milk
3 cups oats
½ cup plus 1 tablespoon peanut butter

Combine butter, sugar, vanilla, peanut butter, cocoa powder and milk in a saucepan and bring to a boil. Boil 2 minutes. Pour into a large bowl. Add oats and peanut butter. Stir and drop onto wax paper.

Robaya Wolfe Ellis
Savannah, TN

Kim Wolfe Nelson
Kansas City, MO

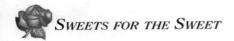

Hedgehogs

1 (7-ounce) package chopped dates
2 cups chopped pecans
2 cups flaked coconut

2 eggs
1 cup firmly packed brown sugar
Confectioners' sugar

Grind dates, pecans and coconut with coarse blade of food processor. Beat eggs and add brown sugar, blending well. Add ground mixture and stir together. With dampened hands, shape into oblong pieces about 1-inch long. Place on greased cookie sheet. Bake at 350° for 12 minutes. Roll in confectioners' sugar.

Charlotte Wolfe
Fort Lauderdale, FL

Lemon Squares

1 cup flour
½ cup butter
¼ cup confectioners' sugar
2 eggs

1 cup granulated sugar
½ teaspoon baking powder
¼ teaspoon salt
2 tablespoons lemon juice

Heat oven to 350°. Cream flour, butter and confectioners' sugar. Press evenly into bottom of an ungreased 9-inch square pan. Bake 20 minutes. Beat remaining ingredients together until light and fluffy, about 3 minutes. Pour over hot crust and bake about 25 minutes longer or until no imprint remains when touched lightly in center.

Charlotte Wolfe
Fort Lauderdale, FL

Lollipop Cookies

Kids just love these!

1 box cake mix, any flavor	24 wooden sticks with rounded ends
⅓ cup vegetable oil	1 container ready to spread frosting
2 eggs	

Heat oven to 375°. Stir together dry cake mix, oil and eggs in a large bowl, using spoon. Drop dough by rounded tablespoonfuls about 3 inches apart onto ungreased cookie sheet. Insert wooden stick in edge of dough until tip is in the center. Bake 8 to 11 minutes or until puffed and almost no indention remains when touched. Cool 1 minute before removing from cookie sheet. Cool completely. Frost and decorate as desired.

Yield 2 dozen cookies.

Charlotte Wolfe
Fort Lauderdale, FL

Mexican Wedding Cookies

1 cup butter, softened	2¼ cups all-purpose flour
¾ cup confectioners' sugar, divided	½ teaspoon salt
1 teaspoon vanilla extract	¼ cup chopped almonds
1 teaspoon almond extract	

Cream together butter, ⅔ of the confectioners' sugar, vanilla and almond extracts in a medium bowl. In a small mixing bow, sift flour and salt together. Blend into creamed mixture and stir in nuts. Refrigerate 1 hour. Preheat oven to 400°. Roll dough into 1-inch balls and place on lightly greased cookie sheet. Bake 9 to 10 minutes or until set, not brown. Roll in remaining confectioners' sugar while warm. Roll again after cooled.

Diane Hardin
Savannah, TN

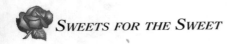

Mackie Nell's 100 Cookies

1	cup butter, softened	3½	cups all-purpose flour
1	cup oil	1	teaspoon salt
1	cup firmly packed brown sugar	1	teaspoon baking soda
1	cup white sugar	1	cup oats
1	egg	1	cup flaked coconut
1	teaspoon vanilla	1	cup crisp rice cereal

Cream together butter, oil, brown sugar, white sugar, egg and vanilla. Combine remaining ingredients and add to sugar mixture. Drop by teaspoonfuls on lightly greased cookie sheet. Bake at 325° for 10 minutes or until slightly brown around edges.

Lynette Linam
Savannah, TN

Mint Sugar Cookies

1	cup butter	2¼	cups all-purpose flour
⅔	cup sugar	1	(28-piece) box thin mint candies,
1	large egg, lightly beaten		each cut in half
1	teaspoon pure vanilla	¼	cup confectioners' sugar
	Dash salt		

In a large mixing bowl, cream butter and sugar until light. Add egg, vanilla and salt and mix well. Stir in flour. Dough should not be too moist, but one that can easily worked with fingers. Add more flour if necessary. Preheat oven to 350°. Use a scant tablespoon of dough to shape around each piece of mint, evenly all around. Place seam down on an ungreased cookie sheet and bake in center of oven for 18 to 20 minutes or until lightly browned. Remove to wire racks to cool. Put confectioners' sugar in a sieve and shake over tops of cooled cookies.

Yield 56 cookies.

Charlotte Wolfe
Fort Lauderdale, FL

Mother's Brownies

1 box butter pecan cake mix
1 stick butter, melted
1 egg, well beaten
1 stick butter, melted

1 (8-ounce) package cream cheese, softened
1 (16-ounce) box confectioners' sugar
2 eggs, well beaten
1 cup chopped nuts

Combine cake mix, 1 stick melted butter and egg. Press into a 13 x 9 x 2-inch pan. Mix remaining stick of butter, cream cheese, confectioners' sugar and eggs. Pour over brownie mixture. Sprinkle with nuts. Bake at 325° for 35 to 40 minutes.

Muriel Smith
Savannah, TN

Nana Bars

½ cup butter
¼ cup sugar
5 tablespoons cocoa powder
1 egg, slightly beaten

¼ teaspoon vanilla
2 cups graham cracker crumbs
¾ cup flaked coconut
½ cup chopped walnuts

In a double boiler melt together butter, sugar and cocoa powder. Add egg and vanilla. Cook, stirring constantly, until mixture thickens. Stir in cracker crumbs, coconut and nuts. Press firmly into a 9-inch square pan. Chill.

Middle Layer
4 tablespoons butter
2 tablespoons milk
2 tablespoons instant vanilla pudding mix

2 cups confectioners' sugar
1 teaspoon pure peppermint extract

Cream together butter, milk and pudding mix. Add confectioners' sugar and blend well. Spread over crumb layer.

Top Layer
2 squares semisweet chocolate

1 tablespoon butter

Melt in double boiler. Cool to room temperature. Spread over middle layer. Chill until top layer hardens. Cut into squares.

Yield 20 squares.

Linda Patterson
Savannah, TN

Oatmeal Chess Bars

2 cups oatmeal
1 box yellow cake mix
1 stick butter, softened
½ teaspoon vanilla
2 eggs
1 cup flaked coconut

1 cup chopped nuts
1 box confectioners' sugar
1 (8-ounce) package cream cheese
½ teaspoon vanilla
3 eggs

Combine oatmeal, cake mix, butter, vanilla and eggs. Press into a 13 x 9 x 2-inch pan. Sprinkle with coconut and nuts. Set aside. Mix together confectioners' sugar and cream cheese. Add vanilla and eggs and beat 3 minutes on medium speed of mixer. Pour over cake mixture and bake 45 minutes at 350°. Cool and cut into squares.

A flavored cake mix can be used. I find that German chocolate makes an interesting taste.

Charlotte Wolfe
Fort Lauderdale, FL

Oatmeal Cookies

2½ sticks butter, softened
¾ cup firmly packed brown sugar
½ cup granulated sugar
1 egg
1 teaspoon vanilla
1½ cups all-purpose flour

1 teaspoon baking soda
1 teaspoon salt
1 teaspoon cinnamon, optional
¼ teaspoon nutmeg, optional
3 cups old-fashioned oats, uncooked

Heat oven to 375°. Beat butter and sugars until fluffy. Beat in egg and vanilla. Combine flour, baking soda, salt and spices. Gradually blend into egg mixture. Stir in oats. Drop by rounded tablespoonfuls onto ungreased cookie sheet. Bake 8 to 9 minutes for a chewy cookie; 10 to 11 minutes for a crisp cookie. Cool 1 minute on cookie sheet; remove to wire rack. Store tightly covered.

Yield 4½ dozen cookies.

Charlotte Wolfe
Fort Lauderdale, FL

Orange Blossoms

1 box lemon cake mix
2 lemons, juice and rind

2 oranges, juice and rind
1 (16-ounce) box confectioners' sugar

Prepare cake mix as directed on box and bake in prepared miniature muffin tins. Cool. Mix juice of lemons and oranges, grated rind of 1 lemon and 1 orange and confectioners' sugar. As cakes come out of oven, dip individually in glaze and place on wax paper to cool. These freeze well.

Yield 12 dozen cakes.

Beth Pippin
Savannah, TN

Peachy Potato Cookies

2 cups all-purpose flour
1 teaspoon baking soda
3 cups potato buds, dry
½ cup butter
¾ cup firmly packed brown sugar
½ cup granulated sugar

1 teaspoon vanilla
2 eggs, slightly beaten
2 cups chopped pecans
1 cup flaked coconut
1 ounce peach schnapps

Heat oven to 350°. Stir together flour and baking soda. Set aside. Reserve 1 cup of the potato buds. Microwave butter uncovered, on high until melted. Stir in sugars, flour mixture, vanilla, eggs, remaining potato buds, nuts, coconut and schnapps. Let dough stand for 5 minutes. Shape into 1-inch balls and roll balls in reserved potato buds. Place 2 inches apart on ungreased cookie sheet. Bake 9 to 11 minutes, until light golden brown. Remove immediately from cookie sheet. Cool.

Charlotte Wolfe
Fort Lauderdale, FL

Overnight Cookies

2 egg whites	¼ teaspoon vanilla
Pinch salt	1 cup chopped nuts
¼ teaspoon cream of tartar	1 cup chocolate morsels
⅔ cup sugar	

Preheat oven to 350°. Beat egg whites until foamy. Add salt and cream of tartar and beat until stiff. Add sugar, 2 tablespoonfuls at a time, beating well after each addition. Stir in vanilla, nuts and chocolate morsels. Drop by teaspoonfuls on cookie sheet lined with aluminum foil. Put in oven. Turn off heat immediately. Do not open door for at least 8 hours. Carefully remove cookies from foil.

Jo Ann Johnson 1926-1999
Florence, AL

Peanut Butter Bars

⅔ cup unsalted butter	1½ cups finely crushed graham crackers
1 cup peanut butter, smooth or chunky	1 (12-ounce) package semisweet
2 cups confectioners' sugar, sifted	chocolate chips

Butter a 13 x 9 x 2-inch baking pan. Set aside. In a heavy saucepan, melt butter over medium heat. Add peanut butter and stir until melted. Stir in sugar and cracker crumbs. Press into bottom of prepared pan. In top of double boiler over barely simmering water, melt chocolate chips, stirring constantly. Pour over crumb mixture, smoothing evenly. Refrigerate for 3 hours until chocolate is set. Remove and cut into bars. Do not store in refrigerator.

Yield 36 bars.

Charlotte Wolfe
Fort Lauderdale, FL

Peanut Butter Oat Bars

⅔ cup butter, melted
¼ cup peanut butter
1 cup firmly packed brown sugar

¼ cup light corn syrup
¼ teaspoon vanilla extract
4 cups quick-cooking oats

In a mixing bowl, combine the butter, peanut butter, brown sugar, corn syrup and vanilla; gradually add the oats. Press into a greased 13 x 9 x 2-inch baking pan. Bake at 400° for 12 to 14 minutes or until the edges are golden brown. Cool on wire rack for 5 minutes.

Topping
1 cup milk chocolate chips
½ cup butterscotch chips

⅓ cup peanut butter

Melt chips and peanut butter in microwave or saucepan. Stir until blended. Spread over warm bars. Cool completely and refrigerate 2 to 3 hours before cutting.

Robaya Wolfe Ellis
Savannah, TN

Pecan Pie Muffins

Every time I take these somewhere, someone wants the recipe.

1 cup firmly packed light brown sugar
½ cup flour
1 cup chopped pecans

⅔ cup butter, softened
2 beaten eggs
½ teaspoon vanilla

Stir together brown sugar, flour and pecans. Set aside. In a separate bowl, beat the butter until smooth; add eggs and vanilla. Stir into the dry ingredients just until combined. Spoon batter into medium-size muffin cups with paper liners. Fill ⅔ full. Bake at 350° for 20 minutes.

Vivian Epps
Adamsville, TN

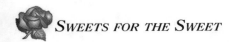

Pecan Tassies

½ cup butter, softened
1 (3-ounce) package cream cheese,
   softened
2 tablespoons sugar
1 teaspoon vanilla
1 cup all-purpose flour

⅓ cup light corn syrup
¼ cup firmly packed brown sugar
2 tablespoons butter
1 large egg
1 teaspoon vanilla
1 cup chopped nuts

Beat butter, cream cheese, sugar and vanilla for 2 minutes until fluffy. At low speed add flour. Chill for 1 hour. Preheat oven to 350°. In a saucepan over medium heat, stir corn syrup and brown sugar until boiling and sugar is dissolved. Remove from heat and let cool for 3 minutes. Whisk in egg and vanilla. Add nuts. Divide dough in 24 portions of 1 tablespoon each. Press into ungreased mini muffin tins, making a shell. Spoon 1 tablespoon of filling into each shell. Bake 18 minutes or until edges are golden. Cool for 15 minutes on wire rack. Remove from pans to finish cooling process. These can be frozen.

Becky Culver
Counce, TN

Potato Chip Cookies
These are "Velly Good"

1 cup brown sugar
1 cup white sugar
1 cup solid vegetable shortening
2 eggs, well beaten
2 cups all-purpose flour

1 teaspoon soda
1 (6-ounce) package butterscotch
   morsels
2 cups crushed potato chips

Cream sugars and shortening together. Add eggs and beat until smooth. Add flour and soda. Gradually add butterscotch morsels and potato chips. Drop by teaspoonfuls on greased cookie sheet. Bake at 325° for 15 minutes.

Hilda Riggins
Naples, FL

Potato Chip Cookies

2 sticks butter, softened	3½ cups all-purpose flour
2 sticks margarine, softened	1 cup crushed potato chips
1 cup sugar	Confectioners' sugar
2 teaspoons vanilla	

Cream butter, margarine, sugar and vanilla. Add flour gradually and mix well. Stir in potato chips. Drop by tablespoonfuls onto cookie sheet. Bake at 350° for 10 to 12 minutes. Sprinkle with confectioners' sugar.

Yield 5 dozen cookies.

Jo Ann Johnson, 1926-1999
Florence, AL

Potato Chip Cookies

Do not use low sodium chips.
This recipe needs the salt that is on regular chips.

1½ cups butter, softened	2 teaspoons pure vanilla
½ cup firmly packed light brown sugar	3 cups all-purpose flour
¾ cup granulated sugar	2 cups crushed potato chips
2 large egg yolks	½ cup nuts, chopped

Preheat oven to 350°. In a large bowl cream butter and sugars on medium speed of mixer. Beat in egg yolks and vanilla. With a spoon stir in flour, potato chips and nuts. Mixture will be thick. Shape into walnut sized balls. Place 2 inches apart on ungreased cookie sheet. Flatten with fork or bottom of glass. Bake 10 to 12 minutes.

Yield 60 cookies.

Charlotte Wolfe
Fort Lauderdale, FL

Pumpkin Squares

These are great for the holidays.

Crust

1 package yellow cake mix, reserve 1 cup for topping

½ cup margarine, melted
1 egg, beaten

Combine ingredients and spread in a 13 x 9 x 2-inch pan.

Filling

1 (15-ounce) can pumpkin
½ cup sugar
1½ teaspoons cinnamon
¾ teaspoon nutmeg

½ teaspoon salt
2 eggs, beaten
⅔ cup evaporated milk

Combine ingredients and stir until smooth. Pour over crust.

Topping

Reserved cake mix
¼ cup sugar

½ teaspoon cinnamon
2 tablespoons margarine, not melted

Mix together and sprinkle over top. Bake at 350° for 50 minutes.

Ruth Hughes
Alta Loma, CA

Rocky Road Clusters

2 cups semisweet chocolate chips
¾ cup white raisins

16 marshmallows, cut into pieces
1½ cups chopped walnuts

Melt chocolate over warm water, stirring to keep smooth. Add remaining ingredients and when coated, drop by teaspoonfuls onto wax paper. Cool.

Yield 3 dozen.

Charlotte Wolfe
Fort Lauderdale, FL

228

Russian Tea Cakes

¾ cup butter, softened
4 tablespoons confectioners' sugar
2 cups cake flour
1 cup chopped nuts

2 teaspoons water
1 teaspoon vanilla
Confectioners' sugar

Beat butter and 4 tablespoons confectioners' sugar until smooth. Add flour, nuts, water and vanilla and blend well. Chill until firm enough to shape with fingers. Form into balls and bake at 400° for 10 to 12 minutes. Roll in confectioners' sugar as soon as removed from oven.

Charliene Baird
Counce, TN

Sinful Squares

These are sinfully delicious

1 (29-ounce) can pumpkin
1 large can evaporated milk
1 cup sugar
½ teaspoon cinnamon

3 eggs
1 box yellow cake mix
1 cup chopped pecans
2 sticks butter, melted and cooled

Preheat oven to 350°. Line a 13 x 9 x 2-inch pan with wax paper. Mix the first 5 ingredients together and pour into pan. Then pour half of the dry cake mix over this. Sprinkle nuts over and top with remaining dry cake mix. Evenly spoon melted butter over this. Bake for 50 to 60 minutes. Cool. Invert onto tray and remove paper. Cool completely. Frost.

Frosting
1 (8-ounce) package cream cheese
¾ cup frozen whipped topping, thawed

1½ cups confectioners' sugar

Combine ingredients and frost. Keep refrigerated.

Charlotte Wolfe
Fort Lauderdale, FL

229

Skinny Hermits

There are only 70 calories in each cookie.

½ cup pecans, toasted
¼ cup butter, softened
1 cup brown sugar
½ cup unsweetened applesauce
¾ cup egg substitute or 4 egg whites
½ teaspoon baking soda
2 teaspoons water
2 cups all-purpose flour

1 cup old-fashioned oats
1 teaspoon baking powder
1 teaspoon ground cinnamon
1 teaspoon allspice
1 teaspoon ground nutmeg
½ teaspoon ground cloves
1½ cups raisins

Spread pecans on a cookie sheet and place in oven for 5 to 8 minutes at 350°. Cool. In a large bowl combine the butter and brown sugar. Add applesauce, egg substitute or egg whites and baking soda dissolved in water. Set aside. In another bowl combine flour, oats, baking powder, cinnamon, allspice, nutmeg and cloves. Add the flour mixture to the liquid mixture all at once. Stir to moisten then add the raisins and toasted nuts and mix. Drop the cookies by rounded teaspoonfuls onto a prepared cookie sheet. Bake for 12 minutes.

Barbara Duryea
Poulsbo, WA

Tea Cakes

2 eggs
1 cup sugar
½ cup solid vegetable shortening
1 teaspoon vanilla

2 cups all-purpose flour
1½ teaspoons baking powder
½ teaspoon salt
2 teaspoons milk

Cream eggs, sugar, shortening and vanilla until smooth. Set aside. Sift together flour, baking powder and salt. Add to creamed mixture along with milk. Blend well. Form into a ball and refrigerate for at least 1 hour. Remove from refrigerator and knead a couple of times. Roll out to desired thickness and cut into desired shapes with cookie cutter. Bake at 375° until edges are slightly brown. Do not brown tops.

Nyoka Beer
Cordova, TN

Sandies

1 cup butter
⅓ cup sugar
2 teaspoons water
2 teaspoons vanilla

2 cups flour
1 cup chopped nuts
   Confectioners' sugar

Cream butter and sugar. Add cold water and vanilla then flour and pecans. Chill 3 to 4 hours. Shape into balls or fingers and bake at 325° for 20 minutes. Cool slightly and roll in confectioners' sugar.

Gladys Coaker
Savannah, TN

Sour Cream Cookies

1 cup all-purpose flour
1 cup cake flour
2 teaspoons baking powder
½ teaspoon baking soda
½ teaspoon salt
½ teaspoon nutmeg

1 cup firmly packed light brown sugar
½ cup butter
1 egg
½ cup sour cream
1 cup chopped nuts

Sift flours, baking powder, soda, salt and nutmeg. Set aside. Put brown sugar through a coarse sieve. Cream butter and sugar until light and fluffy. Beat in egg, continuing to beat well. Add the dry ingredients alternately with the sour cream and beat well. Stir in pecans. Drop by heaping teaspoonfuls 2 inches apart onto a greased cookie sheet. Bake 8 to 10 minutes at 400° or until no imprint is left when pressed lightly. Remove and cool on rack.

Yield 3 dozen cookies.

Sue Morgan
Pickwick Dam, TN

Toffee Bars

2 sticks butter	½ teaspoon salt
1 cup firmly packed light brown sugar	1 teaspoon vanilla
1 egg yolk	12 solid milk chocolate candy bars
1 cup sifted all-purpose flour	Chopped pecans

Grease a 13 x 9 x 2-inch pan. Preheat oven to 350°. Cream butter, sugar and egg yolk. Add flour, salt and vanilla. Spread in greased dish. Bake 20 to 25 minutes. Have candy bars unwrapped. As soon as dish is removed from oven, lay chocolate bars on top lengthwise, breaking as needed to fit. Spread with spatula when melted. Sprinkle with chopped pecans.

Marilyn Qualls
Savannah, TN

Walnut Bars

½ cup butter, softened	1 cup sifted all-purpose flour
½ cup firmly packed light brown sugar	

Mix butter, sugar and flour and press into an ungreased 9 x 12-inch pan. Mixture will be stiff. Bake 15 minutes in a preheated 350° oven or until lightly brown. Do not over cook.

Topping

1 cup firmly packed light brown sugar	¼ teaspoon salt
1 teaspoon vanilla	1½ cups flaked coconut
2 eggs, well beaten	1 cup chopped black walnuts
2 tablespoons flour	

Combine sugar, vanilla and eggs and beat well. Add flour and salt. Blend well. Fold in coconut and walnuts. Spread over baked layer and return to oven and bake 15 to 20 minutes. Cool and cut into bars.

Neda Chester Hargis
Franklin, TN

Vienna Bars

2   sticks butter, softened
1½ cups sugar, divided
2   egg yolks
2½ cups all-purpose flour

¼   teaspoon salt
1   (10-ounce) jar strawberry preserves
4   egg whites
2   cups finely chopped pecans

In mixing bowl, cream butter and half of the sugar. Beat in egg yolks. Add flour and salt. Knead with fingers. Pat batter out on greased 9 x 9-inch pan. Bake at 350° for 15 to 20 minutes or until lightly browned. Remove from oven and spread with preserves. Beat egg whites until stiff. Fold in remaining sugar and nuts. Gently spread on preserves. Return pan to oven and bake 25 minutes. Cut into squares.

Yield 2 dozen bars.

Charlotte Wolfe
Fort Lauderdale, FL

Walnut Whoppers

2   sticks butter, softened
1   (8-ounce) package cream cheese,
      softened
1¼ cups granulated sugar
¼   cup firmly packed light brown sugar
2   eggs
1   teaspoon pure vanilla

2½ cups all-purpose flour
1   teaspoon baking soda
1   teaspoon salt
2   teaspoons cream of tartar
1½ cups black walnuts
½   cup sugar

Combine butter, cream cheese, sugars and cream until light and fluffy. Add eggs, one at a time, beating well after each addition. Add vanilla and mix well. Sift together flour, soda, salt and cream of tartar. Add gradually to sugar mixture. Add walnuts and blend. Refrigerate 1 hour. Roll into walnut size balls. Roll balls in sugar. Place on ungreased cookie sheet and bake at 375° for 9 to 11 minutes or until light golden brown.

Yield 5 dozen cookies.

Charlotte Wolfe
Fort Lauderdale, FL

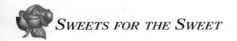

Baked Popcorn

2 cups firmly packed light brown sugar
½ cup light corn syrup
1 cup butter

½ teaspoon cream of tartar
1 teaspoon baking soda
16 cups popped corn, lightly salted

Mix brown sugar, corn syrup, butter, cream of tartar in a saucepan. Dissolve over low heat, stirring constantly. Bring to a boil and boil for 5 minutes on high. Remove from heat; add soda and pour over popped corn in a large pan or bowl. Mix well and place in a shallow baking pan in oven. Bake at 250° for 30 minutes, stirring every few minutes. Store in tightly covered plastic or metal container.

Charlotte Wolfe
Fort Lauderdale, FL

Chocolate Dipped Peppermint Crunch

1 box confectioners' sugar
3 tablespoons butter
10 drops peppermint flavoring

8 ounces crushed peppermints
24 ounces semi-sweet chocolate chips
2 tablespoons shortening

Mix sugar, butter, peppermint flavoring and crushed peppermints. Roll into 1-inch balls. Chill for 30 minutes. Flatten with a glass to ¼-inch thickness. Chill for an additional hour. Melt chocolate chips and shortening. Dip flattened patties in the chocolate and place on waxed paper to harden. Store in airtight container.

Yield 40 to 50 candies.

Diane DeBerry
Savannah, TN

Fruit Juice Pops

1 (6-ounce) can frozen juice concentrate	1 (16-ounce) container plain yogurt
2 tablespoons sugar	1 teaspoon vanilla

Blend ingredients in a blender. Pour into small plastic cups and insert sticks into each when mixture is partially frozen.

Charlotte Wolfe
Fort Lauderdale, FL

Jigglers

Great to have for grandchildren's visits.

2 large boxes jello, any flavor	2½ cups boiling water or apple juice

Completely dissolve jello in boiling water or juice. Pour into a 13 x 9 x 2-inch pan. Chill until firm, about 3 hours. To unmold dip pan in warm water about 15 seconds. Cut into squares or use cookie cutters. Lift from pan.

Ruth Hughes
Alta Loma, CA

Party Pecans

1 egg white	¾ cup light brown sugar
1 teaspoon vanilla	2 cups pecan halves

Beat egg white until stiff. Fold in brown sugar and vanilla. Add pecans and dip out one at a time onto a greased cookie sheet. Bake at 250° for 20 to 25 minutes until golden brown. Store in airtight container.

Yield 2 cups.

Charlotte Wolfe
Fort Lauderdale, FL

235

Nuts and Corn

3 quarts popped corn	¼ teaspoon salt
½ cup peanuts or pecans or almonds	½ teaspoon soda
1 cup brown sugar	1 tablespoon butter flavoring
1 stick margarine	½ tablespoon vanilla
¼ cup light corn syrup	

Spread popped corn on large cookie sheet and add nuts. Mix brown sugar, margarine, light corn syrup and salt and bring to a boil. Boil for 5 minutes. Remove from heat; add soda, butter flavoring and vanilla. Stir. Dribble over popcorn and stir well. Place in 200° oven for 1 hour, stirring every 15 minutes. Remove and let cool.

Pattye Morris
Dyersburg, TN

Party Popcorn

2 cups miniature marshmallows	3 quarts unsalted popcorn
½ cup melted butter	1 (3-ounce) package jello, any flavor

Combine marshmallows and butter in top of a double boiler. Cook over simmering water until marshmallows have melted. Pour over popped corn and stir to mix well. Sprinkle jello powder over popcorn and stir to coat each kernel.

Charlotte Wolfe
Fort Lauderdale, FL

Cornflake Crunch

1 cup sugar	1 cup crunchy peanut butter
1 cup white corn syrup	10 cups corn flake cereal

Boil sugar and corn syrup just until sugar is dissolved. Remove from heat and stir in peanut butter. Pour over cereal and mix thoroughly. Press into a greased cookie sheet and cut into squares while warm.

Charlotte Wolfe
Fort Lauderdale, FL

Snowflake Pecans

1 stick butter	1 cup sugar
3 egg whites	3 cups pecan halves

Preheat oven to 325°. Cut butter into small pieces and put in oven to melt. Meanwhile beat egg whites in mixer, gradually adding sugar until stiff meringue forms. Fold in pecans. Very carefully add the nut mixture to the melted butter. Combine well. Bake for 30 minutes, stirring every 10 minutes. Cool nuts on wax paper, separating them. Store in tightly covered container.

Charlotte Wolfe
Fort Lauderdale, FL

Chocolate Chip Truffles

1 stick butter	1 (8-ounce) package chocolate chips
½ cup brown sugar, packed	¾ cup pecans
¼ cup sugar	1 (12-ounce) package chocolate chips
1 teaspoon vanilla	1½ tablespoons shortening
1¼ cups all-purpose flour	

Mix butter, brown sugar, sugar, vanilla, flour and 8-ounce package chocolate chips. Add pecans and mix thoroughly. Roll into 1-inch balls and freeze for 1 to 2 hours. Melt 12-ounce package chocolate chips and shortening. Dip chocolate chip balls in the chocolate mix. Place on wax paper to harden. Store in airtight container.

Yield 30 to 40 candies.

Diane DeBerry
Savannah, TN

Sweet Nothings

1 stick butter
½ cup creamy peanut butter
1 (6-ounce) package semisweet
   chocolate chips

1 box bite-size, crispy-rice or corn cereal
   squares
1 (16-ounce) box confectioners' sugar

Melt butter, peanut butter and chocolate chips over medium heat. Pour cereal into a large bowl. Pour chocolate mixture over and stir gently until well coated. Pour confectioners' sugar over mixture and stir until all is well coated.

Charlotte Wolfe
Fort Lauderdale, FL

Snack Attack

½ cup dried apricots, chopped
½ cup dried banana chips
½ cup dried peaches, chopped
2 cups granola
½ cup dates, chopped

½ cup small, round, multicolored
   chocolate candies
½ cup chopped pecans
½ cups raisins

Combine all ingredients and stir to mix. Cover and store unrefrigerated.

Charlotte Wolfe
Fort Lauderdale, FL

Notions 'n Potions

Signs of The Times 241

Cooking Tips 242

Vegetables and Side Dishes 248

Breads, Cakes and Cookies 250

Household Hints 254

Beverages 255

Party Tips 255

Other Stuff 256

Signs of The Times

❧ If there is thunder at night in February, beware of a cold spell in April.

❧ Rub a mixture of buttermilk and salt water on a rash or poison ivy to stop the itching.

❧ Only 6 weeks until frost when goldenrods bloom.

❧ When smoke hovers close to the ground, there will be a weather change.

❧ When animals and birds are excessively active, the weather will change for the worse.

❧ Stars inside a ring around the moon indicate the number of days before rain.

❧ When it clouds up on a frost, rain is in the near future.

❧ When spiders spin webs on heavy dew, rain is on the way.

❧ When blackberry blooms are heavy, the winter will be severe.

❧ When the katydids start to sing, only 90 days until a heavy frost.

❧ The twelve days after Christmas will indicate the weather for each of the following months.

❧ The weather will be fair if a screech owl hoots.

❧ When the sun shines while raining, it will rain the following day at the same time.

❧ When the wind blows from the West, fish bite the best. When the wind blows from the East, fish bite the least.

❧ When the points of the moon hang down, it will rain within 3 days.

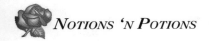

Cooking Tips

✤ 300 strokes by hand will equal approximately 2 minutes on medium speed on a mixer.

✤ Place greased pans into the oven for a few minutes before adding batter to make lighter muffins.

✤ A clean toothbrush is a handy gadget for removal of excess rind from your grater.

✤ Chill individual salad plates for one hour in freezer before using. This will keep salad crisper.

✤ Never cook a roast directly from the refrigerator. Let stand for 45 minutes at room temperature. Brush with oil before and during roasting to seal in natural juices.

✤ Asparagus stems are delicious slivered thinly and stir-fried quickly in hot oil.

✤ Cakes test done when they spring back when lightly touched in center and pull away slightly from the edge of the pan.

✤ Chocolate that has turned gray still retains its flavor when melted.

✤ Cooking meat at low temperatures retains juice and flavor and reduces shrinkage.

✤ On a hot, humid day, cook candy 2 degrees higher than on a cold, dry day.

✤ Every Southerner knows for crusty cornbread, heat bacon drippings in an iron skillet before pouring in the batter.

✤ Tear greens for salads, never cut them. Prevents bruising and edges turning brown. To store already torn lettuce, toss with a small amount of oil and refrigerate in a large plastic bag.

✤ Walnuts or pecans toasted in garlic salt and butter add a delicious taste to salads.

✤ Do not wash lettuce until the day it is used. Dry lettuce stores longer.

✤ Freeze fresh mint leaves in ice cubes for use in tea.

✤ A fresh egg sinks in a bowl of cold water. A bad egg floats.

❧ For moist and fluffy scrambled eggs, add one tablespoon of sour cream for each egg.

❧ Marshmallows can be cut easily with scissors that are dipped in hot water.

❧ If soup is too salty, add raw potato pieces. Remove before serving.

❧ Leftover soups are great used as the liquids in casseroles.

❧ To be sure your yeast is active, "proof" it. Pour 1 package dry yeast into one half cup warm water (100 to 115 degrees F.) and add 2 teaspoons granulated sugar. Stir and set aside for a few minutes. If mixture swells and bubbles appear on the surface, it is good.

❧ A few drops of lemon juice in the water will whiten boiled potatoes.

❧ Remove pulp from lemon halves and use them as cups to hold tartar or cocktail sauce for seafood dishes.

❧ Add a pinch of baking soda along with the milk and butter when mashing potatoes to make them fluffy. Using hot milk keeps them from becoming soggy and heavy.

❧ To make baking powder, mix 2 tablespoons cream of tartar, 1 tablespoon baking soda and 1 tablespoon cornstarch. Measure the same as commercial baking powder.

❧ To insure nutmeats come out whole, soak whole nuts in salted water overnight before cracking.

❧ One medium lemon yields 2 to 3 tablespoons juice. Five to eight medium lemons yield 1 cup.

❧ Put lemons in hot water for several minutes before squeezing and they will yield more juice.

❧ To ripen tomatoes, put them in a brown paper bag in a dark cupboard and they will ripen overnight.

❧ Fresh tomatoes will keep longer when they are stored upside down. Cut them vertically instead of horizontally and they will tend to bleed less.

❧ The usual proportion in salad dressings is one part acid (either vinegar or lemon juice) to two or three parts oil. Mix herbs with acid portion first. Add the oil last as it has a tendency to coat herbs and lessen the release of flavors. Garlic lovers, put a clove of garlic in a bottle of your favorite dressing to improve its flavor.

❧ Citrus peel can be grated and then frozen for later use.

❧ Melt cheese over low heat; high heat will make it stringy.

❧ One pound hard cheese yields four to five cups grated cheese.

❧ Use a vegetable peeler to shave fresh Parmesan. It is easier to clean than a grater and safer than a knife.

❧ Fresh herbs are only half as potent as dried herbs, so use twice as much.

❧ When using glass-baking dishes, always lower the temperature by 25 degrees F.

❧ Always serve cheese at room temperature.

❧ A hollowed out pineapple makes a unique container for fruit dip. Spear pieces of fruit with toothpicks and stick them into the side of the pineapple. Looks great in the center of the table.

❧ Freeze meatballs on a cookie sheet. Then store in a ziplock bag. They are easy to remove as many or as few as you need.

❧ Stuff tiny red and green peppers with cream cheese. Chill and slice.

❧ For crystal clear ice molds, set aside the water to be frozen, stirring 4 to 5 times during a 15-minute period. This breaks up the air bubbles in tap water.

❧ Ice Molds: Fill mold about ⅓ full of liquid and freeze. Add fruit chunks or slices. Cover with cold liquid and freeze. Repeat process making sure that each layer is completely surrounded by clear ice.

❧ A leaf of lettuce dropped in a pot of soup absorbs the grease from the top.

❧ To thicken a sauce, knead together flour and butter and add small balls of this mixture to the sauce. This is called *beurre manie*.

❧ A pinch of salt will make water boil quicker.

❧ Slice tomatoes lengthwise instead of crosswise for firmer slices.

❧ Remove corn silk from fresh corn more easily by using a dry vegetable brush or a dampened paper towel.

❧ For a tastier soup or stew, rub the inside of the pot with a cut garlic clove.

❧ To prevent the white membrane from adhering to peeled fruit sections, soak the fruit in hot water for five minutes before peeling.

❧ One tablespoon of gelatin sets 2 cups of liquid. Never boil gelatin.

❧ Fresh potatoes should be cooked in boiling water. Old potatoes should be placed in cold water and brought to a boil.

❧ To frost grapes, dip in slightly beaten egg whites and then in granulated sugar.

❧ Do not use metal bowls when mixing salads. Use wooden or glass or china.

❧ Whipping cream may be substituted for the oil in almost any vinaigrette dressing.

❧ For crunchy coleslaw, cut cabbage in half and soak in salted water for an hour before chopping.

❧ Add a little instant coffee powder when making gravy to give it a rich brown color and a deeper flavor.

❧ A tablespoon of vinegar in hot water will remove the onion odor from the pot where it was cooked.

❧ A bowl of vinegar sitting around will absorb smoke odors.

❧ When cooking cabbage, place a small bowl of vinegar on the stove near the cabbage. It will absorb all odors from it.

❧ Rub hands with salt or vinegar and rinse in cold water to remove onion smell.

❧ Add 1-teaspoon molasses to pancake batter for well-browned pancakes.

❧ When unmolding a congealed salad, sprinkle a few drops of water on the serving plate. It will be easy to move the salad around to position it correctly.

❧ Make garlic flavored potato chips by placing a peeled clove of garlic in a container with regular chips for several hours. Discard garlic before serving.

❧ After boiling chicken for a casserole, let cool in broth before cutting into chunks. It will have twice the flavor.

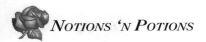

❧ Add 1 teaspoon ground ginger or several slices fresh ginger to dried beans when cooking to prevent those gas attacks.

❧ Use dental floss to truss a stuffed chicken or turkey. It will not tear the skin.

❧ Freeze fish and shrimp in water to ensure fresher taste when cooked. Game should be frozen quickly and kept at a temperature of 9 degrees.

❧ Use ungreased muffin tins as molds when baking stuffed green peppers.

❧ Before separating and beating egg whites, bring them to room temperature.

❧ The fresher and colder the eggs, the better they retain their shape while poaching.

❧ If beaten egg whites do not slide when the bowl is turned upside down, they are stiff enough.

❧ Baking sheets with little or no sides will let your cookies bake evenly and quickly. Use shiny pans for more even browning. Dark or Teflon coated pans cause items to brown quicker and be crustier.

❧ 2-inches clearance around baking pans insures better heat circulation and more even baking.

❧ To fish out a piece of pasta from the pot to test it, use a serrated knife, held with the notches facing up. They keep the pasta from sliding back into the pot.

❧ For an unripe avocado, place in a plastic bag with a piece of banana peel to ripen faster.

❧ To prevent boiled eggs from having the gray color when boiled, place eggs in cold water and bring to a boil. Cover, remove from heat and let stand for 15 minutes. To peel, place eggs in ice water for exactly 1 minute. Then return to the hot water for 10 seconds.

❧ A boiled egg spins beautifully. A raw egg wobbles as it spins.

❧ Lemon juice is a natural tenderizer for beef.

❧ Seasoned butters freeze well and can be used on any grilled meat.

❧ Cook tougher cuts of meat in tea instead of water. The tannin in tea is a tenderizer.

❧ To prevent breaded meats from sticking to the pan and losing their coating when frying, bread the meat ahead of time and let stand on wax paper for at least 20 minutes before frying.

❧ Before opening a package of bacon, roll it into a long tube. This loosens the slices, keeping them from sticking together.

❧ Meat loaf will not stick if you place a slice of bacon on the bottom of the pan.

❧ Mayonnaise with fresh dill and capers and lemon juice make a wonderful sauce for salmon.

❧ Canned shrimp loses its canned taste by soaking in 2 tablespoons vinegar and 1 tablespoon of sherry for 15 minutes.

❧ Rubbing the inside of a cooking pan with vegetable oil will prevent noodles and other starches from boiling over.

❧ One pound of fresh mushrooms sliced and cooked equals one 8-ounce can of sliced mushrooms.

❧ A roast with the bone in will cook faster than a boneless roast. The bone carries the heat to the inside of the meat quicker.

❧ To sear meat to a rich brown color, add 1 tablespoon of sugar to heated oil, stir until it browns, then add the meat.

❧ Cooked chicken should be refrigerated soon after cooking and used within 3 days.

❧ Turning only once while frying, broiling or charcoal-cooking meats will insure maximum juiciness.

❧ Flour or breading mix used for meat or chicken will adhere better during cooking if first allowed to chill for an hour or two.

❧ Rub chicken with a good brandy before roasting along with other seasonings for extra flavor.

❧ To reduce the gamey taste of venison, soak in milk overnight.

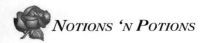

Vegetables and Side Dishes

❧ Do not add salt to the water when boiling corn. It will toughen it. Salt when serving.

❧ If your garlic cloves sprout, don't discard. Plant them close together in a pot. The young shoots that will soon appear are garlic chives. They will have a faint garlic taste, perfect for eggs and salads.

❧ Add ½ teaspoon sugar to vegetables such as corn, peas or carrots when cooking to bring out their flavor.

❧ Add lettuce to a pot of soup to absorb grease. (Remove) Add ice cubes to solidify grease. Floating a paper towel on top also works.

❧ Store garlic cloves in olive oil. After the cloves are used, the oil will have a garlic flavor that's good for using in salad dressings or cooking.

❧ Any fresh or frozen vegetable can be cooked in the oven. Place vegetable in covered dish; add salt and 2 tablespoons of butter. Cook at 350° to desired doneness.

❧ Add a little milk to the water where cauliflower cooks. This makes the florets especially white.

❧ Cook vegetables in chicken or vegetable stock or consommé for a different flavor.

❧ Always simmer soup, never boil.

❧ Vegetables and spices should be added lastly to soup to avoid over-cooking and losing flavor and color.

❧ To prevent a quiche crust from becoming soggy, wait to fill it until just before baking.

❧ A little vinegar or lemon juice added to potatoes, to be mashed, just before draining off water will make them beautifully white.

❧ Let raw potatoes stand in cold water for at least half an hour before frying to improve crispness.

❧ Never cook with what you would not drink. Avoid buying "cooking wines" as they have too much salt. Use the real thing.

❧ To keep celery crisp, stand it in a pitcher of cold salted water and refrigerate.

- Homemade celery salt: Thoroughly dry celery leaves, crush into a powder or rub through a sieve, then mix with salt.

- When preparing party sandwiches for freezing, spread first with butter (never salad dressing) then spread with filling. No more soggy bread.

- To make large ice cubes for pitchers of drinks, fill empty frozen orange juice cans with water and freeze. Large cubes do not melt as quickly.

- When making iced tea, pour boiling water "over" the tea bags. Do not add the bags to the water.

- Use ginger ale or lemon-lime carbonated beverage to reconstitute frozen juices for a fizzy taste.

- Mix crumbled, fried bacon to dry ingredients of biscuits for a different taste.

- Use the cover of a cake server to cover a pan of rolls while they are rising.

- Do not wiggle the cutter while cutting biscuits. This will cause them to topple while baking.

- Homemade baking powder: Combine 6-ounces cream of tartar, 2⅔ ounces bicarbonate of soda and 4½ ounces flour and mix well. Store tightly covered.

- For "scalded milk" use canned evaporated milk diluted with equal parts of HOT water.

- Store washed celery in aluminum foil in refrigerator instead of plastic bags.

- To peel tomatoes easily, dip for a few seconds into boiling water.

- To keep cooked rice warm (if you don't use a rice cooker) place in a colander over simmering water and cover with a cloth or paper towel.

- Rice will be drier and fluffier if a slice of dry bread is placed on top of it after cooking and draining.

- Toss rice with two forks or stir with one fork as the use of a spoon bruises the grains and makes them sticky.

- The flavors of garlic, pepper and cloves get stronger when frozen. Salt, onion and sage get milder when frozen.

- To curl fresh vegetables such as celery and carrots, cut thinly lengthwise and soak in ice water until ready to use.

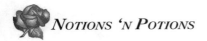

Breads, Cakes and Cookies

❧ Rolls and breads brushed with olive oil before baking will have tender crusts. Those brushed with milk or a combination of egg and milk will have crisp crusts.

❧ Over-beating breads will cause the dough and bread to contain too many air pockets.

❧ A loaf of frozen bread should be taken out of plastic wrap before thawing so that it does not become soggy. Thaw for about 1 hour.

❧ Almost all bread should be baked in the center of a preheated oven. For a hard crust, put the bread pan on the bottom rack of the oven after 15 minutes of baking.

❧ A rib of celery in a bread bag keeps the bread fresher longer.

❧ Put a whole sprig of rosemary in the oven to flavor baking bread.

❧ One pound of apples yields 3 cups pared or diced or sliced.

❧ Save time by chopping raisins and marshmallows by using scissors.

❧ Freeze fresh bread to trim crust more easily. Cook nut breads several hours before cutting for easier, more even slices.

❧ Mix cream cheese and apricot preserves as a spread for date nut bread.

❧ Soak raisins in water for 5 minutes before using in cookies. They will not be dry after baking.

❧ To prevent raisins, dates and other fruits from sticking together in a solid mass when put through a food chopper, place fruit in a strainer and hold under the cold water tap before chopping.

❧ When selecting a pineapple, pluck a leaf from the pineapple's crown. If the leaf pulls out easily, it is ripe and ready to eat.

❧ If you grease more muffin cups than you need, fill the empty ones with water to keep the grease from baking on.

❧ Ingredients for cakes, butter, cream cheese and eggs, should be at room temperature. Ingredients for pastry should be ice cold.

❧ If you are short 1 egg for making a box cake, use scant ¼ cup mayonnaise (not fat free). Follow package directions.

❧ Immediately after removing a cake from the oven, set it on a wet towel to cool, to prevent sticking.

❧ Raw eggs separate more easily while still cold from the refrigerator, but let egg whites come to room temperature to get maximum volume when beating.

❧ Biscuits and rolls will open more easily if the dough is rolled thin and folded over once before cutting.

❧ Coat nuts with a very light dusting of flour prior to adding to a batter to prevent them from settling to the bottom.

❧ When slicing cake, dip knife into water before slicing each piece.

❧ Cake flour produces larger, lighter and more even grain cakes than all-purpose flour.

❧ Dust a little flour or cornstarch on light cakes before icing to prevent icing from sliding off. Use cocoa powder on a chocolate cake.

❧ When baking a chocolate cake, use cocoa powder for dusting greased pan instead of flour. This will help eliminate the white coloration on the cake.

❧ Using waxed paper (or round coffee filters) on a greased cake pan helps prevent cake from falling apart when removing from pan.

❧ After pouring cake batter into pans, bang pan on counter top to prevent air holes in cake when done. Angel food cakes are the exception.

❧ Store cream cheese and cottage cheese upside down in the refrigerator to stay fresh longer.

❧ To measure syrup or molasses, grease cup in which it is to be measured.

❧ When making cookies, mix dry ingredients thoroughly with creamed mixture to prevent crumbly dough.

❧ Hull strawberries after washing to keep them from absorbing too much water and becoming mushy. Do not wash until ready to use.

❦ Try curry sprinkled on apples, plums or thick slices of bananas.

❦ Always use a wire whisk, not electric mixer when making a sauce.

❦ Roll pastry dough out between 2 sheets of waxed paper; peel one layer off, turn dough upside down in pie shell and carefully peel off other sheet. Simple and easy.

❦ Chill pie dough 10 minutes in the refrigerator to reduce the amount of flour needed on the board when rolling out.

❦ To keep the bottom crust of a pie from getting soggy, brush surface with beaten egg white.

❦ To prevent juices in berry pies from running over, stick a few pieces of large macaroni through top of crust. Remove after baking.

❦ Handle pie dough as little as possible after adding water to dough. Excess handling results in a tough crust that is not flaky.

❦ Apples will not crack while they are baking if you peel a 1-inch band around the middle of the top. Core the apples, stuff the centers and add a little water to the pan and bake.

❦ To make a purchased pie crust more "homemade" brush the bottom with milk and sugar before baking.

❦ To keep the juices in a fruit pie from penetrating the bottom crust, mix 2 tablespoons sugar and 2 tablespoons flour together and sprinkle over the crust before adding the filling.

❦ Substitute corn flakes for pecans in pecan pie. They will rise to the top and be crisp.

❦ Put a layer of marshmallows in the bottom of a pumpkin pie then add the filling. The marshmallows will come to the top and make a very nice topping.

❦ For extremely flaky pie pastry, measure flour and shortening into a bowl and chill at least 1 hour before mixing.

❦ Use a serrated knife when slicing a pie with meringue – it will not pull or tear.

❦ Ripen avocados, bananas, melons and pears at room temperature.

❧ Mix 8-ounces of cream cheese with ½ cup fresh fruit and 2 teaspoons grated fruit peel as a dressing for fresh fruit salad.

❧ Melt marshmallow cream in the microwave. Half of a 7-ounce jar will melt in 35 to 40 seconds on high. Stir to blend.

❧ A little butter on the tip of a cream pitcher will eliminate the usual drip when pouring. Try it on the bowl spout when pouring pancakes.

❧ Baked cookies or dough may be frozen for up to nine months.

❧ Press plastic wrap directly onto the surface of custards, puddings and white sauces after cooking to prevent the formation of film.

❧ Pineapple strips marinated in Grand Marnier make an easy and elegant appetizer.

❧ When alternating liquids with dry ingredients, always begin and end with dry ingredients.

❧ A pinch of salt added to whipping cream just before whipping strengthens the fat cells and makes the cream thicken faster.

❧ For gumdrop flowers, roll gumdrops between 2 sheets of sugared waxed paper. Cut into petals and leaves and arrange on cake in the shape of a flower.

❧ Add a pinch of baking powder to confectioners' sugar icings. Icing will not get hard or crack and will stay moist.

❧ To help prevent cakes layers from sticking to the pans, place pans on a wet towel as soon as they come out of the oven.

❧ Substitute confectioners' sugar for flour when preparing buttered cake pans. They will be less sticky. Use cocoa powder for chocolate cakes.

❧ Glass, enamel and dark metal pans absorb more heat than shiny ones, therefore oven temperatures should be lowered 25° when using them.

❧ Store soft cookies in an airtight container along with a slice of bread to keep them soft. Store crisp cookies in containers with loose-fitting tops.

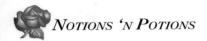

Household Hints

❧ Save your children's broken crayons. Put pieces in muffin tins and bake at 350° for 5 minutes. After cooling you children have big fat cookie crayons.

❧ To test your microwave for accuracy, place 8-ounces of tap water in the oven and microwave for 3 minutes. Water should boil in this time at sea level.

❧ Water houseplants with the cooled water where eggs or vegetables have been boiled. The nutrients are good for the plants.

❧ To remove candle wax from your tablecloth, stick it in the freezer. The wax shrinks and you can peel it off.

❧ Pouring a strong solution of salt and hot water down the sink will help eliminate odors and remove grease from drains.

❧ To clean your microwave, place a wet towel in the oven and microwave for 3 to 4 minutes. It will easily wipe clean with the towel after the steam has set for a few minutes.

❧ Stains or discoloration on aluminum utensils can be removed by boiling a solution of 2 to 3 tablespoons cream of tartar, lemon juice or vinegar to each quart of water in the utensil for 5 to 10 minutes.

❧ Vinegar brought to a boil in a new frying pan will prevent foods from sticking.

❧ If postage stamps get stuck together, freeze them for 1 hour and they will come apart.

❧ To dry up a cold sore, dab a bit of vanilla extract on it.

❧ Put 1-gallon of vinegar in washing machine and run full cycle to remove mineral deposits from washer and drain lines.

❧ Add a cup of water to the bottom portion of the broiling pan before sliding into the oven to absorb smoke and grease.

❧ Run out of furniture polish? Mix one part vinegar and 3-parts olive oil.

❧ To remove oil stains from driveways or garages, pour cola over them and let stand for 5 minutes. Then rinse with the water hose. The acids in the cola break down the oil.

Beverages

❧ A pinch of salt added to over-perked coffee will eliminate the bitter taste. For a more delicate flavor, add a little cinnamon to the grounds before perking.

❧ Ice tea requires half as much sugar if sweetened while hot.

❧ Only Irish Coffee provides in a single glass all four-food groups. Alcohol, caffeine, sugar and fat.

❧ To eliminate the "bleach smell" from your clothes, add ¼ cup vinegar to the final rinse. It neutralizes the sodium hypochlorite in the bleach.

Party Tips

❧ Store extra ice in the washing machine. It is clean and easy to get to. No mess to clean up.

❧ Crisp stale chips or crackers in a microwave oven on full power for 45 to 60 seconds.

❧ Marinate honeydew balls in sherry and apricot brandy for a simple appetizer.

❧ Pecan halves spread with sharp cheese and put together are a quick and tasty appetizer.

❧ When planning food for an afternoon party, allow 3 to 4 cups of punch, 2 to 3 cups of tea and coffee, ½ bottle of wine or champagne (unless Charlotte is coming, then have more) and 10 "bites" (finger sandwiches, etc.) per person.

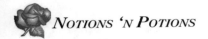

Other Stuff

❧ When your child needs to take a vile-tasting medicine, put an ice cube on their tongue for a moment beforehand. This temporarily paralyzes the taste buds.

❧ To permanently preserve a newspaper clipping of your child, let it stand overnight in a solution of Milk of Magnesia tablet to 1-quart club soda. The next day, submerge newspaper in water for 1-hour. Remove and pat dry.

❧ Cover and decorate an empty potato chip can. Cut and bake fresh cookies to stack perfectly inside the can. Works with drink mix or coffee cans.

❧ Using a large Mason jar, "dump" the measured dry ingredients for your favorite cookie recipe in neat layers inside the jar. The different layers look interesting. Cap tightly and tie with a ribbon. Include the recipe card and instruct friends to simply add the wet ingredients and mix for a perfect batch of cookies.

❧ For the New Family in the neighborhood, fill an attractive address book with the names (include all the family members), addresses and telephone numbers of the neighbors. Also include the best doctors, baby sitters, dry cleaners, florists, etc. in town. They will think of you every time it is used.

A

Alligator Eyes 37
APPETIZERS *(also see Dips & Spreads)*
Almond Ham Rollups 36
Ann's Tomato Tart 37
Asparagus Rolls 38
Bacon Filled Cherry Tomatoes 39
Bacon Wrapped Water Chestnuts 39
Buried Treasures 69
Carrot Sandwiches 40
Caviar Pie 40
Cream Cheese Pastry Cups 45
Cucumber Sandwiches 44
Drunken Wieners 46
Encrusted Brie 45
Festive Bruschetta with a
    Three Tomato Salsa 63
Fruit Kabobs with Margarita Dip 74
Grilled Salmon Summer Rolls
    with Spicy Citrus Dipping Sauce 47
Ham Rollups 48
Ham-Pickle Rollup 48
Hanky Panky Party Pizzas 49
Hawaiian Grab Bag 74
Mahogany Chicken Wings 49
Miniature Quiches 50
Mushroom Turnovers 50
Olive Cheese Balls 51
Party Pizzas 52
Pepper Cheesecake 52
Pizza Burgers 54
Rumaki 53
Sausage Balls 53
Sausage Crescents 55
Scalloped Sweet Potatoes and Apples 57
Smoky Barbecue Chicken Pizza 54
Snappetizer 55
Spinach Balls 56
Stuffed Mushrooms 57
Taco Appetizer Platter 58
Tortilla Rollups 59
Warm Welcome Appetizer 60
APPLES
Apple Brickle Dip 68
Apple Cake with Caramel Sauce 91
Apple Crisp 166
Apple Dumplings 149
Apple Nut Cake 92
Apple Pie 167
Apple Sour Cream Streusel Tart 93
Apple Turnovers 167
Canadian Slipper 20
Four Cheese Pâté 46
Marie's Apple Pie 177
Orange Cream Fruit Salad 192
Peaches and Cream 24
Scalloped Sweet Potatoes and Apples 57

Spicy Apple Cider 17
Wassail 18
Applesauce Salad 188
APRICOTS
Frosty Fruit Cooler 11
Miracle Fruit Cake 123
Snack Attack 238
ARTICHOKE
Russian Dip 79
Spinach and Artichoke Dip 80
Spinach Artichoke Dip 56
ASPARAGUS
Asparagus Rolls 38
AVOCADO
Fresh Vegetable Mexican Dip 73
Hawaiian Grab Bag 74

B

Baked Popcorn 234
BANANAS
Banana Nut Bread 62
Banana Nut Cake 94
Banana Punch 9
Banana Split Pie 168
Bananas Foster 150
Christmas Salad 151
Easy Fruit Salad 154
Four Fruit Cooler 11
Frozen Fruit Cups 190
Grand Mama's Banana Pudding 116
Orange Cream Fruit Salad 192
Punch Bowl Cake 133
Sawdust Salad 157
Snack Attack 238
Strawberry Nut Salad 194
Barbecued Chicken Dip 67
Bavarian Mint Coffee Mix 28
BEANS & PEAS
Black Bean Dip 39
Country Caviar 43
Layered Mexican Dip 75
Layered Tamale Dip 77
Mexican Corn Bread Salad 65
Russian Dip 79
Texas Caviar 57
BEEF
Dried Beef
    El-Brenda's Dunk 73
    Linda's Cheese Ball 42
Ground Beef
    Bumpy Road Dip 69
    Chili Cheese Dip 70
    Hanky Panky Party Pizzas 49
    Pacesetter Picante Dip 78
    Party Pizzas 52
    Pizza Burgers 54
    Taco Appetizer Platter 58

Beer Rolls 60

BEVERAGES

Aromatic Beverages
Christmas Brew for the Senses 7

Cold Beverages
Afternoon Delight 8
Banana Punch 9
Beach Bubble 19
Brave Bull 19
Bride's Pink Punch 8
Brunch Juice 9
Bucking Bronco 19
Bulldog 19
Canadian Slipper 20
Caribbean Chiller 20
Carpet Tax 20
Charlotte's Bloody Marys 21
Christmas Eve Punch 10
Coffee Punch 10
Cool Splash 9
Dew Drop 20
Dizzy Blond 21
Dreamcicle Orange Punch 11
Dwanna Pusser 25
Fantastic T 22
Flirtini 29
Four Fruit Cooler 11
Frosty Fruit Cooler 11
Frozen Margaritas 21
Frozen Russian 22
Grand Pete's Summer Tea 12
Happy Undertaker 32
Holly's Here 22
Irish Cream Liqueur 24
Island Bubbly 23
Key Lime Shake 14
Luscious Lips 27
Make-Ahead Lemonade Mix 14
Mama Rock's Boiled Custard 15
Martimmy 32
Mock Champagne 14
Monkey Wrench 24
P K's Sting 25
Party Lemonade 16
Party Punch 16
Pink Pussycat 25
Raspberrytini 32
Ruby Martini 26
Sea Breeze Cocktail 31
Silver Monkey 26
Slush Punch 17
Southern Breeze 30
Southern Lemonade 16
Stacey's Cosmopolitans 27
Suffering Bastard 27
The Art of Champagne 7
The Infamous Chocolate Martini 31
Tropical Tea 15

Watermelon Margaritas 31
White Sangría 18
Wicked Woo Woo 28

Hot Beverages
Bavarian Mint Coffee Mix 28
Cappuccino Mix 28
Coffee Nog 29
Holiday Cocoa 12
Homemade Amaretto 12
Homemade Kahlúa 13
Hot Buttered Rum 23
Hot Buttered Rum Mix 23
Hot Spiced Tea 13
Instant Russian Tea 13
Peaches and Cream 24
Snow Bunny 26
Spicy Apple Cider 17
Tipsy Coffee 29
Vanilla Coffee 30
Wassail 18

BLACKBERRIES
White Sangría 18
Blackberry Wine Cake 94
Bread and Butter Pudding 168

BREADS
Baked French Toast 61
Banana Nut Bread 62
Basic Starter 64
Beer Rolls 60
Broccoli Cornbread 62
French Toast 61
Green Meadows Six-Week Bran Muffins . . . 115
Italian Flat Bread 64
Jalapeño Cheese Bread 65
Marshmallow Rolls 62
Monkey Bread 63, 64
Onion Walnut Muffins 66
Rolls 66
Sally Lunn 67
Skillet Coffee Cake 136
Sour Cream Coffee Cake 138

BROCCOLI
Broccoli Cornbread 62
Broccoli-Raisin Salad 188
Buckeyes 193
Buried Treasures 69
Burnt Cream 169
Buttermilk Cake 96
Buttermilk Frosting 146
Buttermilk Fudge 199
Buttermilk Pie 170
Butternut Pound Cake 97
Butterscotch Muffins 207

C

CABBAGE
Grilled Salmon Summer Rolls with
Spicy Citrus Dipping Sauce 47

Cactus Pear Coulis 156
Cake Mix Cookies 207
CANDY & SNACKS *(also see Desserts and Chocolate)*
  Baked Popcorn 234
  Buckeyes 193
  Buttermilk Fudge 199
  Candy Bar Fudge 194
  Cheese Fudge 202
  Chocolate Balls 198
  Chocolate Candy 198
  Chocolate Chip Truffles 237
  Chocolate Dipped Peppermint Crunch ... 234
  Chow Mein Candy Clusters 196
  Cocktail Pecans 85
  Coconut Bonbons 196
  Cornflake Crunch 236
  Date Bourbon Crispies 197
  Divinity 197
  English Toffee 196, 200
  Fruit Juice Pops 235
  Hedgehogs 218
  Holiday Orange Vodka Truffles 200
  Homemade Toffee Bars 199
  Jigglers 235
  Microwave Candy 199
  Microwave Peanut Brittle 201
  Millionaires 201
  Nuts and Corn 236
  Party Mix 85
  Party Pecans 235
  Party Popcorn 236
  Peanut Brittle 201
  Peanut Butter Snowballs 202
  Peanut Butter Treats 202
  Penuche 203
  Quick Candy Bars 204
  Rocky Road Clusters 228
  Rum Balls 203
  Snack Attack 238
  Snowflake Pecans 237
  Sweet Nothings 238
Candy Bar Dessert 150
Cape Dutch Brandy Pudding 172
Cappuccino Cake 97
Cappuccino Chocolate Layer Cake 98
Cappuccino Mix 28
Caramel Coconut Cream Cheese Pies 171
Caramel Custard 171
Caramel Frosting 99
Caramel Icing 146
Caramel Pie 172
Caramel Pound Cake 99
Caramel Sauce 91, 163
Caramel Walnut Tart 164
Carpet Tax 20
CARROTS
  Carrot Sandwiches 40
  College Carrots 43
  Wonderful Carrot Cake 148
CAULIFLOWER
  Buried Treasures 69
Caviar Pie 40
Charlotte's Bloody Marys 21
CHEESE
  Another Mexican Dip 78
  Asparagus Rolls 38
  Bacon and Cheddar Dip 67
  Bumpy Road Dip 69
  Cheese Ball 41
  Cheese Fudge 202
  Cheese Ham Log 42
  Cheese Wafers 43
  Chili Cheese Dip 70
  Chili Dip 70
  Crab Dip 70
  Crab Dip with Crackers 71
  Four Cheese Pâté 46
  Fresh Vegetable Mexican Dip 73
  Hanky Panky Party Pizzas 49
  Jalapeño Cheese Bread 65
  Layered Mexican Dip 75
  Layered Tamale Dip 77
  Mediterranean Dip 76
  Mexican Corn Bread Salad 65
  Mexican Dip 77
  Miniature Quiches 50
  Olive Cheese Ball 51
  Olive Cheese Balls 51
  Onion Dip 78
  Onion Soufflé 51
  Pacesetter Picante Dip 78
  Party Pizzas 52
  Pepper Cheesecake 52
  Pineapple Delight 193
  Pizza Burgers 54
  Russian Dip 79
  Sausage Balls 53
  Smoked Salmon Spread 82
  Smoky Barbecue Chicken Pizza 54
  Spinach and Artichoke Dip 80
  Spinach Artichoke Dip 56
  Spinach Balls 56
  Stuffed Mushrooms 57
  Sunset Dip 82
  Surprise Spread 58
  Taco Appetizer Platter 58
  Taco Dip 83
  Tamale Dip 83
  Tangy Grecian Spread 83
  Warm Welcome Appetizer 60
  White Cheese Dip 85
Cheese Fudge 202
CHERRIES
  Banana Split Pie 168

Brazil Nut Date Cake 96
CC's Cherry Chocolate Cake 149
Cherry Cheese Cake 100
Cherry Delight 151
Easy Cherry Tart 151
Frozen Fruit Cups 190
Linda's Surprise 119
Millionaire Pie 179
Party Lemonade 16
Pecan Cake 127
Chess Pie 179
CHICKEN (see Poultry)
Chicken Livers, Rumaki 53
Chili Cheese Dip 70
Chili Dip 70
CHOCOLATE (also see Candy & Snacks, and Desserts)
Aunt Dutchie's Chocolate Pie 166
Bavarian Mint Coffee Mix 28
Brownies with Caramel Sauce 204
Buckeyes 193
Buttermilk Frosting 146
Candy Bar Fudge 194
Cappuccino Chocolate Layer Cake 98
Cappuccino Mix 28
CC's White Chocolate Chunk Cookies . . 206
Cheese Fudge 202
Chocolate Balls 198
Chocolate Cake 102, 116
Chocolate Candy 198
Chocolate Chess Pie 170
Chocolate Chess Pies 174
Chocolate Chews 207
Chocolate Chip Cake 102
Chocolate Chip Cookies 195, 208
Chocolate Chip Truffles 237
Chocolate Coconut Bars 209
Chocolate Coconut Cake 100
Chocolate Cookie Cake 126
Chocolate Delight Cake 101
Chocolate Dipped Peppermint Crunch . . 234
Chocolate Frosting 146
Chocolate Kahlúa Cheesecake 103
Chocolate Mint Frozen Dessert 152
Chocolate Oatmeal Cookies 210
Chocolate Pie 173
Chocolate Sheet Cake 104
Chocolate Yums 152
Creamy Cashew Brownies 211
Crunchy Upside Down Cake 109
Crystal's Cookies 211
Death By Chocolate 153
Divinity Nut Pie 147
Double Chocolate Bars 213
Double Chocolate Cookies 195
Easy Chocolate Mousse 153
English Toffee 196
Frozen Russian 22

Fudge Brownies 214
German Chocolate Cake 112
Holiday Cocoa 12
Holiday Orange Vodka Truffles 200
Homemade Toffee Bars 199
Hot Fudge Sauce 163
Jon's Chocolate Dessert 154
LJ's Chocolate Peanut Butter Oatmeal
Cookies 217
Mexican Chocolate Bread Pudding 156
Microwave Candy 199
Milk Chocolate Bar Cake 122
Millionaires 201
Millionaire's Pie 178
Mint Chocolate Chip Cake 123
Mother's Chocolate Pie 181
Nana Bars 221
Old-Fashioned Chocolate Pie 182
Overnight Cookies 224
Peanut Butter Bars 224
Peanut Butter Oat Bars 225
Rocky Road Clusters 228
Rum Balls 203
Shirley's Favorite Chocolate Cake 136
Shock Cake 137
Snack Attack 238
Snow Bunny 26
Sweet Nothings 238
Swiss Chocolate Cake 140
Swiss Chocolate Sheet Cake 139
Texas Sheet Cake 141
The Infamous Chocolate Martini 31
Tiramisu 162
Toffee Bars 232
Triple Chocolate Mess for the Crockpot . . 140
Turtle Cake 142
Unbaked Chocolate Oatmeal Cookies . . . 205
Upside Down Chocolate Cake 143
Upside Down German Chocolate Cake . . 144
Vanilla Coffee 30
White Chocolate Layer Cake 145
Wolfe's Dairy Bar Chocolate Pie 189
Christmas Brew for the Senses 7
Christmas Eve Punch 10
Christmas Rum Cake 106
Christmas Salad 151
Chutney Shrimp Dip 71
Cinnamon Buttons 210
Cocktail Pecans 85
COCONUT
Caramel Coconut Cream Cheese Pies . . . 171
CC's Cherry Chocolate Cake 149
Cherry Berry Cake 106
Chocolate Candy 198
Chocolate Coconut Bars 209
Chocolate Coconut Cake 100
Chocolate Oatmeal Bars 209
Chutney Shrimp Dip 71

Coconut Bonbons 196
Coconut Caramel Pie 173
Cracker Pie 185
Crunchy Upside Down Cake 109
Date Bars 212
Dream Bars 214
Dreamcicle Orange Punch 11
Dwanna Pusser 25
Earthquake Cake 111
Fresh Coconut Sheet Cake 111
Graham Cracker Bars 215
Hawaiian Fruit Dip 75
Hedgehogs 218
Mackie Nell's 100 Cookies 220
Millionaire's Pie 178
Miss Daisy's Five Flavor Pound Cake
  with Glaze 124
Mother's Old-Fashioned Coconut Pie 180
Nana Bars 221
Oatmeal Chess Bars 222
Peachy Potato Cookies 223
Pecan Cake 127
Pecan Mango Coconut Cake 129
Piña Colada Cake 130
Piña Colada Pie 184
Piña Colada Wedges 157, 193
Pineapple Cloud Pie 185
Punch Bowl Cake 133
Senator Fred Thompson's Mother's Fresh
  Coconut Cake 136
Sweet and Sour Cake 139
Tropical Salsa 59
Turtle Pie 187
Upside Down Chocolate Cake 143
Upside Down German Chocolate Cake ... 144
Vanilla Wafer Pound Cake 145
Walnut Bars 232
Wolfe's Dairy Bar Coconut Pie 189
Coffee Nog 29
Coffee Punch 10
Cola Cake 107

CORN
Mexican Corn Bread Salad 65
Mexican Dip 77
Cornflake Crunch 236
Cornmeal Pound Cake 108
Country Caviar 43
Cracker Cake 110
Cracker Cookies 206
Cracker Pie 185

CRANBERRY OR CRANBERRY JUICE OR SAUCE
Brunch Juice 9
Christmas Eve Punch 10
Christmas Salad 151
Luscious Lips 27
Martimmy 32
Mexican Chocolate Bread Pudding ... 156
Pineapple Cranberry Upside-Down Cake . 131

Sea Breeze Cocktail 31
Cranberry-Horseradish Sauce
  and Cream Cheese 44
Cream Cake 107
Cream Cheese Cookies 210
Cream Cheese Filling 159
Cream Cheese Pastry Cups 45
Cream Cheese Pound Cake 108, 109
Cream Cheese Sheet Cake 110
Creamsicle Salad 190
Creamy Cashew Brownies 211
CROCKPOT DISHES
Chili Cheese Dip 70
Mexican Dip 77
CUCUMBERS
Brenda's Cucumber Salad 41
Cucumber Sandwiches 44

D

DATES
Brazil Nut Date Cake 96
Cape Dutch Brandy Pudding 172
Date Bars 212
Date Bourbon Crispies 197
Date Cheese Ball 44
Hedgehogs 218
Pecan Cake 127
Snack Attack 238
Uncooked Fruit Cake 143
Vanilla Wafer Pound Cake 145
DESSERTS, MISCELLANEOUS
(also see Candy & Snacks, and Chocolate)
Apple Dumplings 149
Apple Turnovers 167
Applesauce Salad 188
Bananas Foster 150
Bread and Butter Pudding 168
Broccoli-Raisin Salad 188
Burnt Cream 169
Butterscotch Muffins 207
Candy Bar Dessert 150
Cape Dutch Brandy Pudding 172
Caramel Custard 171
Caramel Sauce 163
Caramel Walnut Tart 164
Cherry Delight 151
Chocolate Kahlúa Cheesecake 103
Chocolate Mint Frozen Dessert 152
Chocolate Shirley 105
Chocolate Yums 152
Christmas Salad 151
Creamsicle Salad 190
Death By Chocolate 153
Easy Chocolate Mousse 153
Easy Fruit Salad 154
Frozen Fruit Cups 190
Frozen Strawberry Salad 113

Grand Mama's Banana Pudding 116
Homemade Chocolate Frosty 155
Homemade Eggless Ice Cream 155
Homemade Vanilla Ice Cream 154
Hot Fudge Sauce 163
Hot Lemon Sauce Pudding 178
Ice Cream Sandwich Dessert 155
Jon's Chocolate Dessert 154
Lemon Tart 165
Linda's Surprise 119
Malva Pudding 161
Mexican Chocolate Bread Pudding 156
Mini Cheesecakes 122
Mother's Egg Custard 179
Mrs. Katye's Pecan Tarts 180
Orange Pineapple Salad 190
Peach Crisp 158
Pecan Pie Muffins 225
Pecan Pie Tarts 182
Pecan Tarts 183
Piña Colada Wedges 157
Pumpkin Cream Cheese Rollup 159
Raspberry Almond Tarts 164
Red and White Delight 160
Sawdust Salad 157
South African Milk Tart 158
Strawberry Angel Food Dessert 161
Strawberry Soufflé 160
Summer Delight 163
Telephone Pudding 162
Tiramisu 162

DESSERTS, CAKES
14 Layer Cake 113
Apple Cake with Caramel Sauce 91
Apple Nut Cake 92
Apple Sour Cream Streusel Tart 93
Aunt Edith's Fruit Cake 93
Banana Nut Cake 94
Best Pound Cake 95
Black Walnut Cake 95
Blackberry Wine Cake 94
Brazil Nut Date Cake 96
Buttermilk Cake 96
Butternut Pound Cake 97
Cappuccino Cake 97
Caramel Pound Cake 99
CC's Cherry Chocolate Cake 149
Cherry Berry Cake 106
Cherry Cheese Cake 100
Chocolate Cake 102, 116
Chocolate Chip Cake 102
Chocolate Coconut Cake 100
Chocolate Cookie Cake 126
Chocolate Delight Cake 101
Chocolate Sheet Cake 104
Christmas Cake 104
Christmas Rum Cake 106

Cola Cake 107
Cornmeal Pound Cake 108
Cracker Cake 110
Cream Cake 107
Cream Cheese Pound Cake 108, 109
Cream Cheese Sheet Cake 110
Crunchy Upside Down Cake 109
Earthquake Cake 111
Fig or Preserve Cake 112
Fresh Coconut Sheet Cake 111
German Chocolate Cake 112
Glazed Buttermilk Pecan Lemon Cake
    with Tangy Lemon Icing 114
Gooey Cake 114
Irene's Cake 117
Joe Bailey Cake 118
Just Cake 117
Just Delicious Cake 119
Lemonade Cake 120
Love Cake 120
Martian Pound Cake 121
Milk Chocolate Bar Cake 122
Mint Chocolate Chip Cake 123
Miracle Fruit Cake 123
Miss Daisy's Five Flavor Pound Cake
    with Glaze 124
Mrs. Roxie Sawyner's Pound Cake 124
Orange Pound Cake 125
Orange Slice Cake 125
Original Pound Cake 126
Payday Cake 127
Peach and Raspberry Meringue Cake 128
Peanut Butter Pound Cake 130
Pecan Cake 127
Pecan Mango Coconut Cake 129
Pecan Pie Cake 129
Piña Colada Cake 130
Pineapple Cranberry Upside-Down Cake 131
Poppy Seed Cake 132
Potato Cake 132
Punch Bowl Cake 133
Red Velvet Cake 134, 135
Salad Dressing Cake 131
Senator Fred Thompson's Mother's
    Fresh Coconut Cake 136
Shock Cake 137
Shortcake 137
Skillet Coffee Cake 136
Sour Cream and Peach Pound Cake 138
Sour Cream Coffee Cake 138
Sweet and Sour Cake 139
Swiss Chocolate Cake 140
Swiss Chocolate Sheet Cake 139
Texas Sheet Cake 141
Three Musketeer Cake 142
Tiger Cake 141
Triple Chocolate Mess
    for the Crockpot 140

Turtle Cake 142
Uncooked Fruit Cake 143
Upside Down Chocolate Cake 143
Upside Down German
   Chocolate Cake 144
Vanilla Wafer Pound Cake 145
Wet Caramel Cake 144
White Chocolate Layer Cake 145
Wonderful Carrot Cake 148
Yummy Cake 147

DESSERTS, CAKES
Frostings & Icings
   Brandy Caramel Sauce 204
   Brown Sugar Frosting 205
   Buttermilk Frosting 146
   Caramel Frosting 99
   Caramel Icing 146
   Caramel Sauce 163
   Chocolate Frosting 146
   Chocolate Icing 105
   Cream Cheese Filling 159
   Frosting 95, 101, 104, 121, 130,
               135, 136, 139, 140
   Glaze 120, 124, 132, 141
   Hot Fudge Sauce 163
   Icing 102, 107, 118, 134,
            137, 141, 142, 143, 148
   Mocha Frosting 119
   Orange Glaze 125
   Orange Mallow Cream 131
   Raspberry Almond Filling 164
   Tangy Lemon Icing 114

DESSERTS, COOKIES & BARS
   Brown Sugar Pecan Cookies 205
   Brownies with Caramel Sauce 204
   Cake Mix Cookies 207
   CC's White Chocolate
      Chunk Cookies 206
   Chewy Oatmeal Cookies 208
   Chocolate Chews 207
   Chocolate Chip Cookies 195, 208
   Chocolate Coconut Bars 209
   Chocolate Oatmeal Bars 209
   Chocolate Oatmeal Cookies 210
   Cinnamon Buttons 210
   Cracker Cookies 206
   Cream Cheese Cookies 210
   Creamy Cashew Brownies 211
   Crystal's Cookies 211
   Date Bars 212
   Della's Butter Cookies 213
   Double Chocolate Bars 213
   Double Chocolate Cookies 195
   Dream Bars 214
   Extra Good Cookies 215
   Freckles 216
   Fudge Brownies 214
   Gene's Tea Cakes 216

Gingersnaps 217
Graham Cracker Bars 215
Lemon Squares 218
LJ's Chocolate Peanut Butter
   Oatmeal Cookies 217
Lollipop Cookies 219
Mackie Nell's 100 Cookies 220
Mexican Wedding Cookies 219
Mint Sugar Cookies 220
Mother's Brownies 221
Oatmeal Chess Bars 222
Oatmeal Cookies 222
Orange Blossoms 223
Overnight Cookies 224
Peachy Potato Cookies 223
Peanut Butter Bars 224
Peanut Butter Oat Bars 225
Pecan Tassies 226
Potato Chip Cookies 226, 227
Pumpkin Squares 228
Russian Tea Cakes 229
Sandies 231
Sinful Squares 229
Skinny Hermits 230
Sour Cream Cookies 231
Tea Cakes 230
Toffee Bars 232
Unbaked Chocolate
   Oatmeal Cookies 205
Vienna Bars 233
Walnut Bars 232
Walnut Whoppers 233

DESSERTS, PIES
Apple Cobbler Pie 165
Apple Pie 167
Aunt Dutchie's Chocolate Pie 166
Banana Split Pie 168
Black Walnut Pie 169
Buttermilk Pie 170
Caramel Coconut Cream Cheese Pies . . . 171
Caramel Pie 172
Chess Pie 179
Chocolate Chess Pie 170
Chocolate Chess Pies 174
Chocolate Pie 173
Coconut Caramel Pie 173
Cracker Pie 185
Divinity Nut Pie 147
Easy Custard Pie 175
Easy Lemon Chess Pie 174
Easy Pecan Pie 174
Egg Custard Pie 175
Egg Nog Pie 176
Fresh Peach Pie 175
Grandmother White's Key Lime Pie 176
Key Lime Pie 176
Lemon Ice Box Pie 118
Lemon Rub Pie 177

INDEX

Marie's Apple Pie 177
Millionaire Pie 179
Millionaire's Pie 178
Mother's Chocolate Pie 181
Mother's Egg Custard 179
Mother's Old-Fashioned Coconut Pie 180
Old-Fashioned Chess Pie 181
Old-Fashioned Chocolate Pie 182
Peanut Butter Pie 182
Pecan Pie 183
Perfect Pie Crust 183
Piña Colada Pie 184
Pineapple Cloud Pie 185
Pineapple Delight Pie 184
South Florida Key Lime Pie 177
Strawberry Custard Pie 186
Sweet Potato Pie 186, 187
Turtle Pie 187
Two-Minute Pie 188
Wolfe's Dairy Bar Chocolate Pie 189
Wolfe's Dairy Bar Coconut Pie 189
Dilly Vegetable Dip 72
DIPS & SPREADS *(also see Appetizers)*
Adrienne's Delight 36
Alligator Eyes 37
Another Mexican Dip 78
Apple Brickle Dip 68
Bacon and Cheddar Dip 67
Barbecued Chicken Dip 67
Black Bean Dip 39
BLT Dip 68
Brenda's Vegetable Dip 68
Bumpy Road Dip 69
Cheese Ball 41
Cheese Ham Log 42
Cheese Wafers 43
Chili Cheese Dip 70
Chili Dip 70
Chutney Shrimp Dip 71
Country Caviar 43
Crab Dip 70
Crab Dip with Crackers 71
Cranberry-Horseradish Sauce
   and Cream Cheese 44
Date Cheese Ball 44
Dilly Vegetable Dip 72
Dream Fruit Dip 72
El-Brenda's Dunk 73
Encrusted Brie 45
Four Cheese Pâté 46
French Bread Spread 76
Fresh Vegetable Mexican Dip 73
Fruit Dip 72, 73
Ham Ball 48
Hawaiian Cheese Ball 42
Hawaiian Fruit Dip 75
Hot Dip 76
Jiffy Fruit Dip 75

Layered Mexican Dip 75
Layered Tamale Dip 77
Linda's Cheese Ball 42
Margarita Dip 74
Mediterranean Dip 76
Mexican Dip 77
Olive Cheese Ball 51
Onion Dip 78
Onion Soufflé 51
Pacesetter Picante Dip 78
Pepper Cheese Ball 53
Ranch Dipping Sauce 79
Russian Dip 79
Shrimp Dip 55, 79, 81
Shrimp Spread 81
Smoked Salmon Spread 82
Southwestern Shrimp Dip 82
Spinach and Artichoke Dip 80
Spinach Artichoke Dip 56
Spinach Dip 80, 81
Sunset Dip 82
Surprise Spread 58
Taco Dip 83
Tamale Dip 83
Tangy Grecian Spread 83
Texas Caviar 57
Tropical Salsa 59
Vegetable Dip 84
Veggie Dip 84
Veggie Veggie Dip 84
White Cheese Dip 85
Divinity 197
Divinity Nut Pie 147
Dwanna Pusser 25

E

Earthquake Cake 111
Easy Cherry Tart 151
Easy Chocolate Mousse 153
Easy Custard Pie 175
Easy Fruit Salad 154
Easy Lemon Chess Pie 174
Easy Pecan Pie 174
Egg Custard Pie 175
Egg Nog Pie 176
EGGS
Baked French Toast 61
Caviar Pie 40
Death By Chocolate 153
Easy Chocolate Mousse 153
French Toast 61
Irish Cream Liqueur 24
Mama Rock's Boiled Custard 15
Vanilla Wafer Pound Cake 145
Warm Welcome Appetizer 60
Encrusted Brie 45
English Toffee 196, 200

F

Festive Bruschetta with a
 Three Tomato Salsa 63
FIGS
 Fig or Preserve Cake 112
 Mexican Chocolate Bread Pudding 156
FISH
 Grilled Salmon Summer Rolls with
  Spicy Citrus Dipping Sauce 47
 Smoked Salmon Spread 82
Four Cheese Pâté 46
Freckles 216
French Bread Spread 76
French Toast 61
Frozen Fruit Cups 190
Frozen Margaritas 21
Frozen Russian 22
Frozen Strawberry Salad 113
FRUIT, CANDIED
 Aunt Edith's Fruit Cake 93
 Miracle Fruit Cake 123
 Uncooked Fruit Cake 143
Fruit Dip 72, 73
Fruit Juice Pops 235
Fruit Kabobs with Margarita Dip 74

G

German Chocolate Cake 112
Gingersnaps 217
Glazed Buttermilk Pecan Lemon Cake
 with Tangy Lemon Icing 114
Graham Cracker Bars 215
GRAINS & CEREALS
 Candy Bar Dessert 150
 Chewy Oatmeal Cookies 208
 Chocolate Chip Cookies 195
 Chocolate Oatmeal Bars 209
 Chocolate Oatmeal Cookies 210
 Cornflake Crunch 236
 Crystal's Cookies 211
 Date Bars 212
 Date Bourbon Crispies 197
 Double Chocolate Bars 213
 Freckles 216
 LJ's Chocolate Peanut Butter
  Oatmeal Cookies 217
 Mackie Nell's 100 Cookies 220
 Oatmeal Cookies 222
 Party Mix 85
 Payday Cake 127
 Peach Crisp 158
 Peanut Butter Oat Bars 225
 Peanut Butter Treats 202
 Quick Candy Bars 204
 Skinny Hermits 230
 Snack Attack 238

Sweet Nothings 238
Unbaked Chocolate Oatmeal Cookies 205
GRAPEFRUIT
 Carpet Tax 20
 Monkey Wrench 24
 Pink Pussycat 25
 Ruby Martini 26
GRAPES
 Grand Pete's Summer Tea 12
 Grape Party Salad 191
 Mock Champagne 14
GRILLING RECIPES
 Grilled Salmon Summer Rolls with
  Spicy Citrus Dipping Sauce 47

H

Ham Ball 48
Ham Rollups 48
Ham-Pickle Rollup 48
Hanky Panky Party Pizzas 49
Happy Undertaker 32
Hawaiian Cheese Ball 42
Hawaiian Fruit Dip 75
Hawaiian Grab Bag 74
Hedgehogs 218
Holiday Cocoa 12
Holiday Orange Vodka Truffles 200
Homemade Amaretto 12
Homemade Chocolate Frosty 155
Homemade Eggless Ice Cream 155
Homemade Kahlúa 13
Homemade Toffee Bars 199
Homemade Vanilla Ice Cream 154
HOMINY
 Country Caviar 43
 Texas Caviar 57
Hot Buttered Rum 23
Hot Buttered Rum Mix 23
Hot Dip 76
Hot Fudge Sauce 163
Hot Lemon Sauce Pudding 178
Hot Spiced Fruit 191
Hot Spiced Tea 13

I

Ice Cream Sandwich Dessert 155
Instant Russian Tea 13
Irish Cream Liqueur 24
Island Bubbly 23
Italian Flat Bread 64

J

Jalapeño Cheese Bread 65
Jiffy Fruit Dip 75
Jigglers 235
Just Cake 117
Just Delicious Cake 119

INDEX

K

Key Lime Pie 176
Key Lime Shake 14
KIWI, White Sangría 18

L

Layered Mexican Dip 75
Layered Tamale Dip 77
Lemon Chess Pie, Easy 174
Lemon Ice Box Pie 118
Lemon Rub Pie 177
Lemon Sauce Pudding, Hot 178
Lemon Squares 218
Lemon Strawberry Salad 192
Lemon Tart 165
Lemonade Cake 120
Lollipop Cookies 219
Love Cake 120
Luscious Lips 27

M

Mahogany Chicken Wings 49
Make-Ahead Lemonade Mix 14
Malva Pudding 161
Mama Rock's Boiled Custard 15
MANGO
  Mucho Good Fruit Compote 191
  Pecan Mango Coconut Cake 129
  Tropical Salsa 59
Margarita Dip 74
Marshmallow Rolls 62
Martian Pound Cake 121
Martimmy 32
Mediterranean Dip 76
MEXICAN
  Another Mexican Dip 78
  Chili Cheese Dip 70
  Chili Dip 70
  Fresh Vegetable Mexican Dip 73
  Frozen Margaritas 21
  Layered Mexican Dip 75
  Layered Tamale Dip 77
  Mexican Chocolate Bread Pudding 156
  Mexican Corn Bread Salad 65
  Mexican Dip 77
  Mexican Wedding Cookies 219
  Southwestern Shrimp Dip 82
  Taco Appetizer Platter 58
  Taco Dip 83
  Tamale Dip 83
  Tortilla Rollups 59
  Watermelon Margaritas 31
  White Sangría 18
MICROWAVE DISHES
  Another Mexican Dip 78
  Cheese Fudge 202

Coconut Bonbons 196
Easy Chocolate Mousse 153
Microwave Candy 199
Microwave Peanut Brittle 201
Party Mix 85
Peanut Butter Snowballs 202
South African Milk Tart 158
Sunset Dip 82
Mother's Brownies 221
Mother's Chocolate Pie 181
Mother's Egg Custard 179
Mother's Old-Fashioned Coconut Pie 180
MUSHROOMS
  Buried Treasures 69
  Hawaiian Grab Bag 74
  Mushroom Turnovers 50
  Stuffed Mushrooms 57

N

NUTS
  Adrienne's Delight 36
  Almond Ham Rollups 36
  Anniversary Chicken Salad 38
  Apple Cobbler Pie 165
  Apple Crisp 166
  Apple Nut Cake 92
  Apple Sour Cream Streusel Tart 93
  Aunt Edith's Fruit Cake 93
  Banana Nut Bread 62
  Banana Nut Cake 94
  Banana Split Pie 168
  Black Walnut Cake 95
  Black Walnut Pie 169
  Blackberry Wine Cake 94
  Brazil Nut Date Cake 96
  Brown Sugar Pecan Cookies 205
  Brownies with Caramel Sauce 204
  Buttermilk Fudge 199
  Cape Dutch Brandy Pudding 172
  Caramel Coconut Cream Cheese Pies 171
  Caramel Icing 146
  Caramel Walnut Tart 164
  CC's White Chocolate Chunk Cookies 206
  Cheese Ball 41
  Cheese Fudge 202
  Cheese Ham Log 42
  Cheese Wafers 43
  Cherry Berry Cake 106
  Cherry Delight 151
  Chewy Oatmeal Cookies 208
  Chocolate Balls 198
  Chocolate Candy 198
  Chocolate Chess Pie 170
  Chocolate Chews 207
  Chocolate Chip Cake 102
  Chocolate Chip Cookies 195, 208
  Chocolate Chip Truffles 237

Chocolate Coconut Bars 209
Chocolate Oatmeal Bars 209
Chocolate Shirley 105
Chow Mein Candy Clusters 196
Christmas Cake 104
Chutney Shrimp Dip 71
Cocktail Pecans 85
Coconut Caramel Pie 173
Cracker Cake 110
Cracker Cookies 206
Cracker Pie 185
Cream Cake 107
Cream Cheese Cookies 210
Creamy Cashew Brownies 211
Crunchy Upside Down Cake 109
Crystal's Cookies 211
Date Bars 212
Date Bourbon Crispies 197
Date Cheese Ball 44
Divinity 197
Divinity Nut Pie 147
Double Chocolate Bars 213
Double Chocolate Cookies 195
Dream Bars 214
Earthquake Cake 111
Easy Pecan Pie 174
English Toffee 196, 200
Extra Good Cookies 215
Fig or Preserve Cake 112
Freckles 216
Frozen Fruit Cups 190
Fudge Brownies 214
German Chocolate Cake 112
Glazed Buttermilk Pecan Lemon Cake
  with Tangy Lemon Icing 114
Gooey Cake 114
Graham Cracker Bars 215
Grape Party Salad 191
Ham Rollups 48
Hawaiian Cheese Ball 42
Hedgehogs 218
Homemade Toffee Bars 199
Ice Cream Sandwich Dessert 155
Just Delicious Cake 119
Lemon Strawberry Salad 192
Linda's Cheese Ball 42
Mexican Wedding Cookies 219
Microwave Candy 199
Microwave Peanut Brittle 201
Millionaire Pie 179
Millionaire's Pie 178
Miracle Fruit Cake 123
Mother's Brownies 221
Mrs. Katye's Pecan Tarts 180
Nana Bars 221
Nuts and Corn 236
Oatmeal Chess Bars 222
Olive Cheese Ball 51

Onion Walnut Muffins 66
Orange Slice Cake 125
Overnight Cookies 224
Party Mix 85
Party Pecans 235
Payday Cake 127
Peach Crisp 158
Peachy Potato Cookies 223
Peanut Brittle 201
Pecan Cake 127
Pecan Mango Coconut Cake 129
Pecan Pie 183
Pecan Pie Cake 129
Pecan Pie Muffins 225
Pecan Pie Tarts 182
Pecan Tarts 183
Pecan Tassies 226
Penuche 203
Pineapple Cloud Pie 185
Potato Cake 132
Potato Chip Cookies 227
Pumpkin Cream Cheese Rollup 159
Punch Bowl Cake 133
Raspberry Almond Tarts 164
Red and White Delight 160
Rocky Road Clusters 228
Rum Balls 203
Russian Tea Cakes 229
Sandies 231
Scalloped Sweet Potatoes and Apples . 57
Sinful Squares 229
Skinny Hermits 230
Snack Attack 238
Snowflake Pecans 237
Sour Cream Coffee Cake 138
Sour Cream Cookies 231
Strawberry Nut Salad 194
Strawberry Soufflé 160
Summer Delight 163
Sweet and Sour Cake 139
Texas Sheet Cake 141
Three Musketeer Cake 142
Tiger Cake 141
Toffee Bars 232
Tropical Salsa 59
Turtle Cake 142
Turtle Pie 187
Two-Minute Pie 188
Uncooked Fruit Cake 143
Upside Down Chocolate Cake 143
Upside Down German Chocolate Cake ... 144
Vienna Bars 233
Walnut Bars 232
Walnut Whoppers 233
Wonderful Carrot Cake 148

INDEX

O

Oatmeal Chess Bars .222
Oatmeal Cookies .222

OLIVES
Alligator Eyes 37
Buried Treasures 69
Fresh Vegetable Mexican Dip 73
Hawaiian Grab Bag 74
Layered Mexican Dip 75
Layered Tamale Dip 77
Mediterranean Dip 76
Olive Cheese Ball .51
Olive Cheese Balls 51
Taco Dip 83
Tangy Grecian Spread 83

ONIONS
Onion Dip 78
Onion Soufflé 51
Onion Walnut Muffins 66

ORANGES OR ORANGE JUICE
Afternoon Delight .8
Apple Dumplings 149
Beach Bubble 19
Brunch Juice 9
Christmas Eve Punch 10
Cool Splash 9
Creamsicle Salad 190
Easy Fruit Salad 154
Fantastic T 22
Four Fruit Cooler 11
Frosty Fruit Cooler 11
Happy Undertaker 32
Hot Spiced Tea 13
Irene's Cake 117
Mama Rock's Boiled Custard 15
Martimmy 32
Orange Blossoms 223
Orange Cream Fruit Salad 192
Orange Pineapple Salad 190
Orange Pound Cake 125
Orange Slice Cake 125
Salad Dressing Cake 131
Silver Monkey 26
Slush Punch 17
Southern Lemonade 16
Uncooked Fruit Cake 143
Wassail 18
White Sangría 18

P

Pacesetter Picante Dip 78
Party Lemonade 16
Party Mix 85
Party Pecans 235
Party Pizzas 52
Party Popcorn 236

Party Punch 16

PASSION FRUIT
Mucho Good Fruit Compote 191
Payday Cake 127

PEACHES
Easy Fruit Salad 154
Fresh Peach Pie .175
Hot Spiced Fruit 191
Mucho Good Fruit Compote 191
Orange Cream Fruit Salad 192
Peach and Raspberry Meringue Cake 128
Peach Crisp 158
Peaches and Cream 24
Snack Attack 238
Peachy Potato Cookies 223
Peanut Brittle 201
Peanut Butter Bars .224
Peanut Butter Oat Bars 225
Peanut Butter Pie 182
Peanut Butter Pound Cake 130
Peanut Butter Snowballs 202
Peanut Butter Treats 202

PEARS
Hot Spiced Fruit 191

PECANS (see Nuts)

Penuche 203
Perfect Pie Crust 183
Piña Colada Cake 130
Piña Colada Pie 184
Piña Colada Wedges 157, 193

PINEAPPLE
Afternoon Delight 8
Banana Split Pie 168
Beach Bubble 19
Bride's Pink Punch 8
Cheese Ball 41
Cherry Delight .151
Christmas Eve Punch 10
Christmas Salad 151
Dreamcicle Orange Punch 11
Dwanna Pusser .25
Easy Fruit Salad 154
Fantastic T 22
Flirtini 29
Four Fruit Cooler 11
Frosty Fruit Cooler 11
Frozen Fruit Cups 190
Frozen Strawberry Salad 113
Fruit Dip 73
Hawaiian Cheese Ball 42
Hawaiian Fruit Dip 75
Hot Spiced Fruit 191
Hot Spiced Tea 13
Island Bubbly 23
Just Delicious Cake 119
Lemon Strawberry Salad 192
Linda's Surprise 119

Millionaire Pie 179
Miracle Fruit Cake 123
Orange Cream Fruit Salad 192
Orange Pineapple Salad 190
Party Punch 16
Pecan Cake 127
Piña Colada Pie 184
Piña Colada Wedges 157, 193
Pineapple Cloud Pie 185
Pineapple Cranberry Upside-Down Cake . 131
Pineapple Delight 193
Pineapple Delight Pie 184
Pink Pussycat 25
Punch Bowl Cake 133
Raspberrytini 32
Sawdust Salad 157
Sea Breeze Cocktail 31
Slush Punch 17
Southern Breeze 30
Strawberry Nut Salad 194
Summer Delight 163
Sweet and Sour Cake 139
Tropical Salsa 59
Two-Minute Pie 188
Wonderful Carrot Cake 148

PIZZA
Hanky Panky Party Pizzas 49
Party Pizzas 52
Pizza Burgers 54
Smoky Barbecue Chicken Pizza 54
Vegetable Pizza 60
Poppy Seed Cake 132

PORK
Bacon
Bacon and Cheddar Dip 67
Bacon Filled Cherry Tomatoes 39
Bacon Wrapped Water Chestnuts 39
BLT Dip 68
Broccoli-Raisin Salad 188
Rumaki 53
Ham
Almond Ham Rollups 36
Cheese Ham Log 42
Ham Rollups 48
Ham-Pickle Rollup 48
Sausage
Chili Cheese Dip 70
Hanky Panky Party Pizzas 49
Party Pizzas 52
Sausage Balls 53
Sausage Crescents 55
Stuffed Mushrooms 57
Potato Cake 132
Potato Chip Cookies 226, 227

POULTRY
Anniversary Chicken Salad 38
Barbecued Chicken Dip 67

Mahogany Chicken Wings 49
Smoky Barbecue Chicken Pizza 54

PUMPKIN
Pumpkin Cream Cheese Rollup 159
Pumpkin Squares 228
Sinful Squares 229
Punch Bowl Cake 133

Q

Quiches, Miniature 50
Quick Candy Bars 204

R

RAISINS
Adrienne's Delight 36
Apple Cobbler Pie 165
Apple Nut Cake 92
Aunt Edith's Fruit Cake 93
Broccoli-Raisin Salad 188
Chutney Shrimp Dip 71
Miracle Fruit Cake 123
Rocky Road Clusters 228
Skinny Hermits 230
Snack Attack 238
Uncooked Fruit Cake 143
Wonderful Carrot Cake 148
Ranch Dipping Sauce 79

RASPBERRIES
Peach and Raspberry
Meringue Cake 128
Raspberry Almond Filling 164
Raspberrytini 32
White Sangría 18
Rice, Mexican Dip 77
Rolls 66
Rum Balls 203
Rumaki 53
Russian Dip 79
Russian Tea Cakes 229

S

Salad Dressing Cake 131
SALADS
Anniversary Chicken Salad 38
Brenda's Cucumber Salad 41
College Carrots 43
Grape Party Salad 191
Mexican Corn Bread Salad 65
SALADS, FRUIT
Hot Spiced Fruit 191
Lemon Strawberry Salad 192
Mucho Good Fruit Compote 191
Orange Cream Fruit Salad 192
Piña Colada Wedges 193
Pineapple Delight 193
Strawberry Nut Salad 194

Sally Lunn 67
Sandies 231
SAUCES & SEASONINGS
   Caramel Sauce 91
   Spicy Citrus Dipping Sauce 47
Sausage Balls 53
Sausage Crescents 55
SEAFOOD
   Crabmeat
     Crab Dip 70
     Crab Dip with Crackers 71
     Snappetizer 55
   Shrimp
     Buried Treasures 69
     Chutney Shrimp Dip 71
     Hawaiian Grab Bag 74
     Miniature Quiches 50
     Shrimp Dip 55, 79, 81
     Shrimp Spread 81
     Southwestern Shrimp Dip 82
     Surprise Spread 58
Senator Fred Thompson's Mother's
   Fresh Coconut Cake 136
Sour Cream and Peach Pound Cake 138
Sour Cream Coffee Cake 138
Sour Cream Cookies 231
South African Milk Tart 158
South Florida Key Lime Pie 177
Southern Breeze 30
Southern Lemonade 16
Southwestern Shrimp Dip 82
SPINACH
   Spinach and Artichoke Dip 80
   Spinach Artichoke Dip 56
   Spinach Balls 56
   Spinach Dip 80, 81
   Veggie Dip 84
STRAWBERRIES
   Banana Split Pie 168
   Cherry Berry Cake 106
   Easy Fruit Salad 154
   Frozen Strawberry Salad 113
   P K's Sting 25
   Red and White Delight 160
   Strawberry Angel Food Dessert 161
   Strawberry Custard Pie 186
   Strawberry Nut Salad 194
   Strawberry Soufflé 160
   The Art of Champagne 7
   White Sangría 18
SWEET POTATOES
   Scalloped Sweet Potatoes and Apples 57
   Sweet Potato Pie 186, 187

T

Taco Appetizer Platter 58
Taco Dip 83

Tamale Dip 83
Texas Caviar 57
Texas Sheet Cake 141
Tiramisu 162
TOMATOES
   Ann's Tomato Tart 37
   Bacon Filled Cherry Tomatoes 39
   BLT Dip 68
   Buried Treasures 69
   Country Caviar 43
   Crab Dip 70
   Festive Bruschetta with a
     Three Tomato Salsa 63
   Fresh Vegetable Mexican Dip 73
   Hawaiian Grab Bag 74
   Layered Mexican Dip 75
   Layered Tamale Dip 77
   Mediterranean Dip 76
   Mexican Corn Bread Salad 65
   Taco Appetizer Platter 58
   Taco Dip 83
   Texas Caviar 57
Tortilla Rollups 59
Tropical Salsa 59
Tropical Tea 15

U

Unbaked Chocolate Oatmeal Cookies 205
Uncooked Fruit Cake 143

V

Vanilla Coffee 30
Vanilla Wafer Pound Cake 145
Vegetable Dip 84
Vegetable Pizza 60
Veggie Dip 84
Veggie Veggie Dip 84
Vienna Bars 233

W

Walnut Bars 232
Walnut Whoppers 233
Wassail 18
Watermelon Margaritas 31
White Sangría 18
Wolfe's Dairy Bar Chocolate Pie 189
Wolfe's Dairy Bar Coconut Pie 189

Y

Yummy Cake 147

Charlotte Wolfe

P.O. Box 520
Savannah, TN 38372

Please send _____ copy(ies)   @ $19.95 each _____

          Postage and handling   @ $ 5.00 each _____

          Tennessee residents add 9.5% sales tax   @ $ 1.89 each _____

          TOTAL _____

Name _____

Address _____

City _____ State _____ Zip _____

Make checks payable to Charlotte Wolfe

— —

Charlotte Wolfe

P.O. Box 520
Savannah, TN 38372

Please send _____ copy(ies)   @ $19.95 each _____

          Postage and handling   @ $ 5.00 each _____

          Tennessee residents add 9.5% sales tax   @ $ 1.89 each _____

          TOTAL _____

Name _____

Address _____

City _____ State _____ Zip _____

Make checks payable to Charlotte Wolfe

— —

Charlotte Wolfe

P.O. Box 520
Savannah, TN 38372

Please send _____ copy(ies)   @ $19.95 each _____

          Postage and handling   @ $ 5.00 each _____

          Tennessee residents add 9.5% sales tax   @ $ 1.89 each _____

          TOTAL _____

Name _____

Address _____

City _____ State _____ Zip _____

Make checks payable to Charlotte Wolfe